Québec City

3rd Edition
Stéphane G.-Marceau
François Rémillard

Travel better, enjoy more
ULYSSES
Travel Guides

Authors Stéphane G.-Marceau François Rémillard *Collaboration* Isabel Gosselin Alain Rondeau Maxime Soucy Christopher Woodward Nathalie Boucher **Publisher** Pascale Couture **Editor** Caroline Béliveau **Copy Editing** Cindy Garayt Jacqueline Grekin Wayne Hiltz *Editing Assistance* Bonnie Barnett	**Translation** Janet Logan **Page Layout** *Typesetting* Élyse Leconte Anne Joyce *Visuals* Alexandra Gilbert Raphaël Corbeil **Cartographers** André Duchesne Patrick Thivierge Yanick Landreville **Computer Graphics** Stéphanie Routhier **Artistic Director** Patrick Farei (Atoll)	**Illustrations** Myriam Gagné Lorette Pierson **Photography** *Cover Page* Stéphan Poulin/Super Stock *Inside Pages* Y. Tessier/Reflexion P.Quittemelle/ Megapress S. Schanz/Megapress T. Philiptchenko/ Megapress R. Edgar/Magapress Louise Leblanc/ Commision de la capitale nationale Perry Mastrovito/ Reflexion

OFFICES
CANADA: Ulysses Travel Guides, 4176 Rue St-Denis, Montréal, Québec, H2W 2M5, ☎ (514) 843-9447 or 1-877-542-7247, ≠(514) 843-9448, info@ulysses.ca, www.ulyssesguides.com

EUROPE: Les Guides de Voyage Ulysse SARL, BP 159, 75523 Paris Cedex 11, France, ☎ 01 43 38 89 50, ≠01 43 38 89 52, voyage@ulysse.ca, www.ulyssesguides.com

U.S.A.: Ulysses Travel Guides, 305 Madison Avenue, Suite 1166, New York, NY 10165, ☎ 1-877-542-7247, info@ulysses.ca, www.ulyssesguides.com

DISTRIBUTORS
CANADA: Ulysses Books & Maps, 4176 Saint-Denis, Montréal, Québec, H2W 2M5, ☎ (514) 843-9882, ext.2232, 800-748-9171, Fax: 514-843-9448, info@ulysses.ca, www.ulyssesguides.com

GREAT BRITAIN AND IRELAND: World Leisure Marketing, Unit 11, Newmarket Court, Newmartket Drive, Derby DE24 8NW, ☎ 1 332 57 37 37, Fax: 1 332 57 33 99 office@wlmsales.co.uk

SCANDINAVIA: Scanvik, Esplanaden 8B, 1263 Copenhagen K, DK, ☎ (45) 33.12.77.66, Fax: (45) 33.91.28.82

SPAIN: Altaïr, Balmes 69, E-08007 Barcelona, ☎ 454 29 66, Fax: 451 25 59, altair@globalcom.es

SWITZERLAND: OLF, P.O. Box 1061, CH-1701 Fribourg, ☎ (026) 467.51.11, Fax: (026) 467.54.66

U.S.A.: The Globe Pequot Press, 246 Goose Lane, Guilford, CT 06437 - 0480, ☎1-800-243-0495, Fax: 800-820-2329, sales@globe-pequot.com

Other countries, contact Ulysses Books & Maps, 4176 Rue Saint-Denis, Montréal, Québec, H2W 2M5, ☎ (514) 843-9882, ext.2232, 800-748-9171, Fax: 514-843-9448, info@ulysses.ca, www.ulyssesguides.com

No part of this publication may be reproduced in any form or by any means, including photocopying, without the written permission of the publisher.
Canadian Cataloguing in Publication Data (see page 7)
© ISBN2-89464-277-6 June 2000, Ulysses Travel Guides. All rights reserved Printed in Canada

"Dans la ville où je suis né,
le passé porte le présent
comme un enfant sur les épaules..."

*"In the town where I was born,
the past carries the present
like a child on it shoulders..."*

Robert Lepage
Le Confessionnal

Table of Contents

Portrait **13**
    History 14
    Politics 21
    Economy 24
    Culture 26
    Architecture 28

Practical Information **31**
    Entrance Formalities . 31
    Embassies and
      Consulates 32
    Tourist Information .. 35
    Getting Here 37
    Airport 38
    Finding Your Way
      Around 39
    Guided Tours 46
    Money and Banking . 48
    Currency 50
    Insurance 50
    Health 51
    Time Difference 51
    Business Hours and
      Holidays 51
    Climate and Clothing 52
    Taxes and Tipping .. 56
    Wine, Beer and
      Alcohol 58
    Advice for Smokers .. 59
    Senior Citizens 59
    Gay and Lesbian Life 59
    Travellers with
      Disabilities 59
    Children 60
    Pets 60
    Miscellaneous 60

Outdoors **63**
    Parks 64
    Outdoor Activities ... 66

Exploring **75**
    Tour A: Vieux-
      Québec 78
    Tour B: Petit-Champlain
      to Vieux-Port 104

Exploring (ctd...)
    Tour C: Grande
      Allée 120
    Tour D: Saint-Jean-
      Baptiste 132
    Tour E: chemin
      Sainte-Foy 136
    Tour F: Saint-Roch . 142
    Tour H: Saint-
      Sauveur 154
    Tour K: Côte-de-Beaupré
      and Île d'Orléans .. 167

Accommodations **179**
    Tour A: Vieux-
      Québec 182
    Tour B: Petit-Champlain
      to Vieux-Port ... 187
    Tour C: Grande Allée
      and Avenue Cartier 190
    Tour D: Saint-Jean-
      Baptiste 192
    Tour E: Chemin Sainte-
      Foy 193
    Tour F: Saint-Roch . 195
    Tour J: Heading
      North 195
    Tour K: Côte-de-Beaupré
      and Île d'Orléans . 196

Restaurants **201**
    Tour A: Vieux-
      Québec 208
    Tour B: Petit-Champlain
      to Vieux-Port 217
    Tour C: Grande Allée
      and Avenue Cartier 223
    Tour D: Saint-Jean-
      Baptiste 230
    Tour E: Chemin Sainte-
      Foy 233
    Tour F: Saint-Roch . 234
    Tour G: Limoilou .. 235
    Tour I: Sillery to Cap-
      Rouge 235
    Tour K: Côte-de-Beaupré
      and Île d'Orléans . 237

Entertainment **241**
    Bars and Nightclubs   241
    Cultural Events 249
    Spectator Sports ... 251
    Festivals and Cultural
        Events 251

Shopping **255**
    Antiques 256
    Art Galleries 256
    Bookstores 256
    CDs and Cassettes .. 257
    Clothing 257

Shopping (ctd...)
    Craft Shops and Artisans'
        Studios 259
    Decorative Objects . 262
    Food 262
    Miscellaneous 264
    Newspapers and
        Tobacco 265
    Outdoor Clothing and
        Equipment 265
    Stationery 266
    Sweets 266

Symbols

🚢	Ulysses's Favourite
☎	Telephone Number
≈	Fax Number
≡	Air Conditioning
⊘	Fan
≈	Pool
ℜ	Restaurant
⊛	Whirlpool
ℝ	Refrigerator
K	Kitchenette
△	Sauna
⊙	Exercise Room
tv	Colour Television
pb	Private Bathroom
sb	Shared Bathroom
½ b	Half Board (Lodging + 2 Meals)
bkfst incl.	Breakfast Included
🐕	Pets allowed
♿	Wheelchair access
P	Parking
ℑ	Fireplace
✚	Health Centre
ℜ	Restaurant

ATTRACTION CLASSIFICATION

★	Interesting
★★	Worth a visit
★★★	Not to be missed

The prices listed in this guide are for the admission of one adult.

HOTEL CLASSIFICATION

The prices in the guide are for one room, double occupancy in high season.

RESTAURANT CLASSIFICATION

$	$10 or less
$$	$10 to $20
$$$	$20 to $30
$$$$	$30 and more

The prices in the guide are for a meal for one person, not including drinks and tip.

All prices in this guide are in Canadian dollars.

Write to Us

The information contained in this guide was correct at press time. However, mistakes can slip in, omissions are always possible, places can disappear, etc. The authors and publisher hereby disclaim any liability for loss or damage resulting from omissions or errors.

We value your comments, corrections and suggestions, as they allow us to keep each guide up to date. The best contributions will be rewarded with a free book from Ulysses Travel Guides. All you have to do is write us at the following address and indicate which title you would be interested in receiving (see the list at the end of guide).

Ulysses Travel Guides
4176 Rue Saint-Denis
Montréal, Québec
Canada H2W 2M5
www.ulyssesguides.com
E-mail: text@ulysses.ca

Acknowledgements

We acknowledge the financial support of the Government of Canada through the Book Publishing Industry Development Program (BPIDP) for our publishing activities.

We would also like to thank SODEC (Québec) for its financial support.

Cataloguing

Canadian Cataloguing in Publication Data

Canadian Cataloguing in Publication Data
Guimont-Marceau, Stéphane, 1969
    Québec City
    (Ulysses travel guide)
    Translation of: Ville de Québec
    Includes index.
    ISBN 2-89464-277-6

1. Québec (Québec) - Guidebooks. I. Titre. II. Series.
FC2946.18R4513 2000   917.14'471044   C00-940801-0
F1054.5.Q3R4513 2000

List of Maps

Area Around Québec City	11
Accommodations	
Tour A: Vieux-Québec	183
Attractions	175
Tour A: Vieux-Québec	79
Tour B: Petit-Champlain to Vieux-Port	105
Tour C: Grande-Allée	121
Tour D: Saint-Jean-Baptiste	133
Tour E: Chemin Sainte-Foy	137
Tour F: Saint-Roch	143
Tour G: Limoilou	149
Tour H: Saint-Sauveur	155
Québec	10
Restaurants	201
Tour A: Vieux-Québec	209
Tour B: Petit-Champlain to Vieux-Port	219
Tour C: Grande Allée	225
Tour C: Avenue Cartier	227
Suggested Tours	77
Table of Distances	41
Where is Québec?	9

Map Symbols

Symbol	Meaning	Symbol	Meaning
✈	Airport	H	Hospital
✪	Capital	?	Tourist Information (seasonal service)
🚋	Funicular	?	Tourist Information (permanent service)
🚆	Train Station	⛴	Car Ferry
🚌	Bus Station		

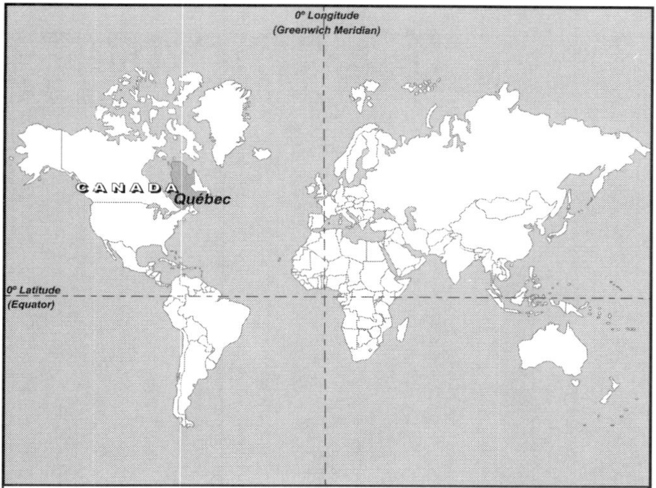

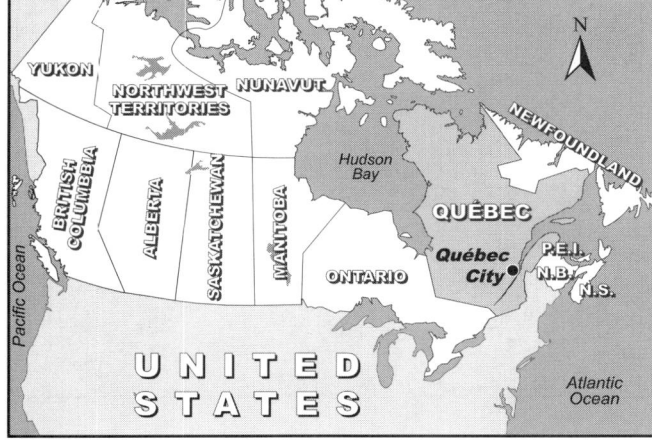

Where is Québec City?

 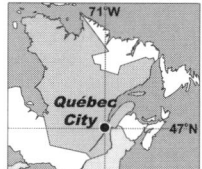

QUÉBEC	QUÉBEC CITY
Capital: Québec City	Population: 167,000 inhab.
Population: 7,500,000 inhab.	Population of the Communauté
Area: 1,550,000km²	Urbaine de Québec: 504,000 inhab.
Currency: Canadian dollar	Area: 94km²

©ULYSSES

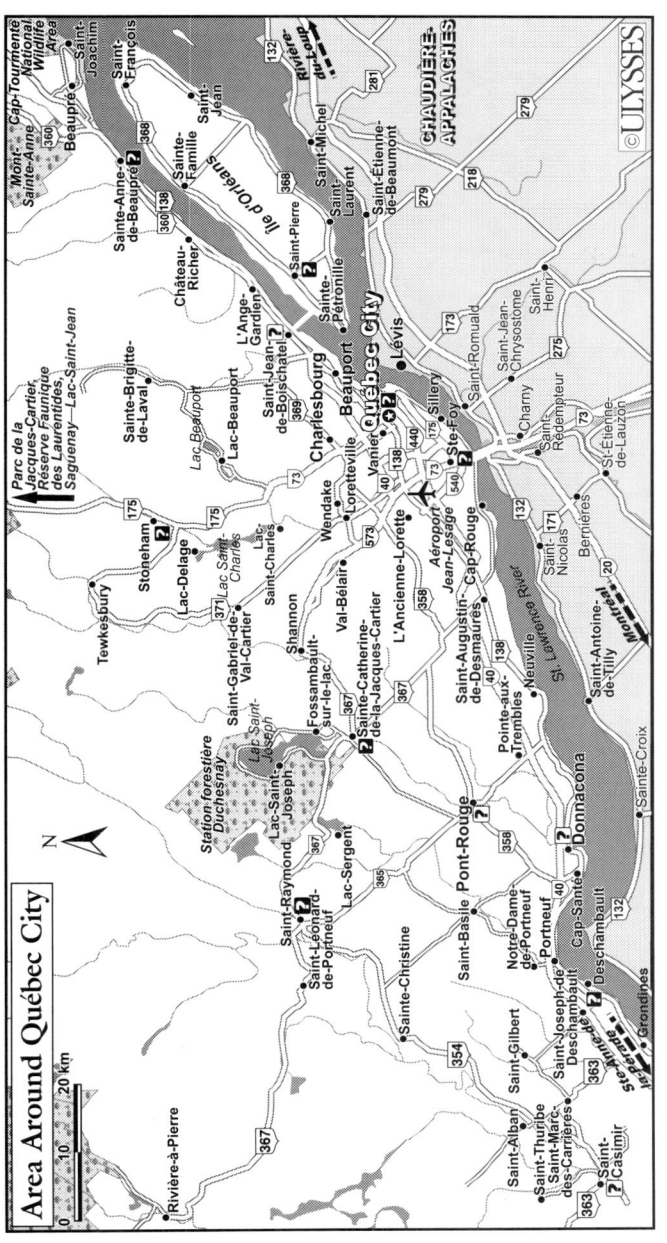

Portrait

Québec City is an exceptional town. Not only is it rich in history and architecture, it is also magnificently set.

Compared to other cities in the world, Québec City is not old; however, it is one of the oldest cities in North America and the oldest in Canada. The Haute-Ville (upper town) sits on a promontory, Cap Diamant, which is more than 98m high and juts out over the St. Lawrence River. Jacques Cartier called this rocky outcrop "Cap aux Diamants," believing he had discovered diamonds here. But he quickly learned that these precious stones were only common iron pyrites. Nevertheless, Cap Diamant became the future site of Québec City when Champlain established a fur trading post and fortified buildings, creating the settlement known as "Abitation."

The choice of this site played a strategic role in New France's defence system. Here the river is only 1km wide, and it is this narrowing of the St. Lawrence that gave Québec City its name "Kebec," an Algonquin word meaning "place where the river narrows." Perched on top of Cap Diamant and the site of major fortifications from very early on, the city is now dubbed the "Gibraltar of North America."

This fortification did not succeed, however, in driving back the English troops, who would finally take over the city during the Battle of the Plains of Abraham. Yet, the French colony managed to retain its cultural identity after the conquer. Well protected inside its walls, Québec City's heart continued to beat, making it the centre French Canadian culture in North America.

In 1985, in order to preserve and promote Québec City and its cultural treasures, UNESCO declared the city's historic area – the only walled city in North America, – the first World Heritage Site in North America.

This "Vieille Capitale," often simply called "Québec" by the Québécois, is the soul of French speaking America. Thousands of tourists visit it every year and marvel at the city's many charms, its European atmosphere and its inhabitants' *joie de vivre* and hospitality. The architecture and narrow cobblestone streets give the city its character. A romantic place that always fascinates, Québec City has been a source of inspiration to artists for more than three centuries. It is a delight to both the eye and the soul. This little gem is one of those irresistible cities, and whether you visit in the summer, winter, spring or autumn, you cannot help but succumb to its charm.

History

The first Europeans to reach the coast of North America were the Vikings who explored the region in the 10th century. They were followed by whalers and fishers in search of cod.

However, beginning in 1534, Jacques Cartier made three journeys that marked a turning point in this segment of North American history and were the first official contacts between France and the New World. Cartier's mission for the king of France, François I, was to discover a passage to the East and find the gold and other riches that France so badly needed at the time. After Cartier's failure to fulfill his mission, France abandoned these new lands, considering them unimportant.

A few centuries later, the considerable profit to be made in the fur trade rekindled French interest in New France. In 1608, Samuel de Champlain chose the site where Québec City is now located to set up the first permanent trading post. Champlain was surprised not to see the Aboriginal people that Cartier had described following his journeys. During this time, the sedentary Iroquois, who farmed and hunted, had moved south and were replaced by the nomadic Algonquins who lived by hunting and gathering. The Algonquins became France's main allies. Contrary to the Iroquois, they did not have a very developed sense of ownership and did not resist the French when they settled in their territory. The Algonquins agreed to take part in the fur trade with the French.

To understand Québec City's place in history is to appreciate all the advantages of its location. From the top of Cap Diamant, the city has an important strategic position overlooking the only waterway leading to the North American interior. When Samuel de Champlain established the first permanent outpost to trade furs and built a fort around the few existing buildings here, it was primarily because of Cap Diamant's strategic advantages. Here, the river narrows considerably and it is easy to stop passing ships. Champlain had a wooden fortress built here, which he called "Abitation." It enclosed the trading post and the homes of various fur traders. The first winter spent at Abitation was particularly difficult: some 20 of Champlain's men died of scurvy or malnutrition. However, this first prolonged stay in New France marked the beginning of a permanent French presence in North America.

During these first years and up until 1618, there was no desire to colonize. In order to flourish, the fur industry did not need farmers cutting down forests to grow wheat in New France. The development of the fur trade and the colonization of New France were, in fact, contradictory pursuits. In order to develop this new country's other riches, the Compagnie des Cents-Associés was created. The company received exclusive rights to the furs traded on condition that it sent 4,000 colonists to New France over a period of 15 years.

From this moment, Québec City began to develop. But despite the presence of significant tributaries nearby—water being the only efficient means of communication at this time—it was never able to profit as much from the fur trade as Montréal or Trois-Rivières did. Throughout the 17th century, merchants, farmers and craftspeople came to settle in Québec City and its surrounding region. The city's economy diversified, partly because of its port (which became one of the busiest in the world), its shipbuilding yard and its lumber, which was exported mainly to France. The fur trade, however, remained the leading area of economic activity up until the beginning of the 19th century.

During the 17th century, Québec City became one of the most important centres of commerce in the New World. It was the apex of the economic triangle formed by Acadia, New France and Louisiana and would become the seat of French power in America. Also, since religious institutions and political powers looked for protection inside the walls of the Haute-Ville, Québec City quickly became the political, administrative and military centre of New France.

Many colonists settled in the town. The Basse-Ville (lower town) developed rapidly, expanding to the point where it was necessary to fill in parts of the St. Lawrence River to gain more land. At this time, the risk of fire was great because of the proximity of the buildings in the Basse-Ville and the use of wood as the main construction material. In August 1682, flames devastated Québec's Basse-Ville, and the city was later rebuilt according to new imposed standards requiring stone instead of wood for building construction. Unfortunately, a number of inhabitants did not have the money to abide by these new requirements and were forced to build outside the city walls, creating the first suburbs. Most of the stone houses in Vieux-Québec today date from this period.

The economic and strategic importance of Québec City made it a choice target very early on and the capital of New France had to defend itself against a covetous England. These conflicts between France and England had repercussions in the North American colony. Declarations of war and peace treaties were, in fact, the result of European politics and did not correspond to the preoccupations of the colony. Consequently, the citadel fell in 1629 when it was attacked by British forces led by the Kirke brothers, but it was quickly returned to France in 1632.

During the 18th century, the French-English rivalry increased as their colonies developed. The ever increasing pressure of British forces in New France finally resulted in the infamous Battle of the Plains of Abraham, part of the Seven Years' War. Arriving near Québec City in July 1759, General Wolfe's troops captured the town on September 13 of the same year, before reinforcements could arrive from France. During the night, the English climbed Cap Diamant to the west of the fortified walls and in the morning, to the great surprise of the French, they were on the Plains of Abraham. The battle began and ended a short time later with the defeat of the Marquis de Montcalm's troops at the hands of General Wolfe; neither general survived.

The Treaty of Paris, signed February 10, 1763, sealed the French defeat by officially giving New France to the British, marking the end of the French colony in Canada. Under the British Regime, Québec City was transformed. For French Canadians, the Conquest meant that they were now under British rule and ties between the colony and France were cut off, leaving Québec an orphan. Significant changes took place as the English took the situation in hand and replaced the francophones in political and administrative positions. Many of New France's well-to-do inhabitants decided to return to France at the suggestion of the British government. However, most of the inhabitants and small merchants could not afford the journey and had no other choice but to remain in the British colony. The summit of Cap Diamant was also where the English set up their government, which now had the task of managing a considerable portion of North America.

Like the rest of the colony, Québec City was able to resist British assimilation thanks to the Catholic Church and very limited anglophone immigration until the arrival of the Empire Loyalists from the United States. Sheltered behind its walls, Québec City remained almost completely francophone for a long time. However, the situation changed rapidly when the American War of Independence came to an end and the Empire Loyalists, faithful to the British Crown, left the United States to settle on British soil. Many of these new arrivals chose Québec City and Montréal, radically changing the look of the capital, which then saw its anglophone population grow considerably.

In addition to this emigration of Empire Loyalists, many immigrants arrived from the British Isles to settle in Québec City and work in factories or as stevedores in the port. Among them were a significant number of Irish immigrants who had an important common trait with the local population: the Catholic religion. Anglophones represented approximately 40% of the population in the Québec City region, which at that time was seeing significant economic growth. This great anglophone immigration, however, was balanced by the mass arrival of francophones from rural Québec.

This period of prosperity was primarily the result of Napoleon's maritime embargo against England, which then suffered from a great lack of raw materials. This demand made Québec City an important trade link between the colony, the West Indies and England. Québec City's port, with its various shipyards set up by the French Regime, continued to develop until the invention of iron hulls and the digging of the channel in the St. Lawrence, enabling heavy-tonnage ships to reach Montréal, thus eliminating any advantages for Québec City. From then on, Québec City's importance began to decline in favour of Montréal, thanks in part to its an excellent railway system that further established it as the centre of industrial and economic power in Québec and Canada.

Although Québec City lost its economic importance at the beginning of the 20th century and was now limited to light industry such as footwear, among others, it continued to play a significant role in politics and administration as the capital of the province of Québec. This state of affairs continued until the Révolution Tranquille (Quiet Revolution) in the 1960s. This "revolution" in Québec marked the end of a long period

A Brief Summary of Québec's History

More than 12,000 years ago: Nomads from Northern Asia cross the Bering Strait and gradually populate the Americas. With the melting of the glaciers, some of them settle on the peninsula now known as Québec: these are the ancestors of aboriginal nations of Québec.

1534: Jacques Cartier, a navigator from Saint-Malo in Brittany, France, makes the first of three explorations of the Gulf St. Lawrence and the St. Lawrence River. These were the first official French contacts with this territory.

1608: Samuel de Champlain and his men found Québec City, marking the beginning of a permanent French presence in North America.

1663: New France officially becomes a French province. Colonization continues.

1759: Québec City falls to British forces. Four years later, the king of France officially relinquishes all of New France, which now has a population of about 60,000 colonists of French origin.

1837-1838: The British army suppresses the Patriotes rebellion.

1840: Following the Durham Report, the Union Act seeks to create an English majority and eventually assimilate French Canadians.

1867: This year marks the birth of Canadian Confederation. Four provinces, including Québec, sign the agreement. Six others eventually follow suit.

1914-1918: Canada participates in World War I. Anglophones and francophones disagree about the level of participation of the country. Canada comes out of the conflict very divided.

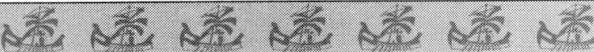

1929-1939: The economic crash hits Québec hard. In 1933, unemployment reaches 27%.

1939-1945: Canada participates in World War II. Once again, anglophones and francophones are divided on the issue of conscription.

1944-1959: Premier Maurice Duplessis leads Québec with a strong hand. This period is known as the *"grande noirceur,"* or "great darkness."

1960: The Liberal Party is elected, marking the beginning of the *Révolution Tranquille*, or Quiet Revolution.

October 1970: A small terrorist group, the Front de Libération du Québec (FLQ), kidnaps a British diplomat and a Québec cabinet minister, igniting a serious political crisis.

November 1976: The Parti Québécois, a party favouring independence for Québec, wins the provincial election.

May 1980: A majority of the Québec population votes against holding negotiations aimed at Québec independence.

1982: The Canadian Constitution is repatriated without Québec's consent.

June 1990: The failure of the Meech Lake Accord on the Canadian Constitution is poorly accepted in Québec. Following this, opinion polls show that a majority of Quebecers are in favour of Québec sovereignty.

October 22, 1992: The federal government and the provinces organize a referendum on new constitutional offers. Considered unacceptable, these are rejected by a majority of Quebecers and Canadians.

October 30, 1995: The Parti Québécois government holds a referendum on the sovereignty of Québec: 49.4% of Quebecers vote "yes" to a sovereignty project and 50.6% vote "no."

spent under the yoke of religion and tradition, and set the province astir. Morals and institutions were modernized; political habits changed. The province of Québec saw the size of its government increase remarkably and Québec City, at the centre of this wave of change, was transformed as well.

At the same time, the nationalist movement made its appearance in Québec as the province's francophones expressed their desire to end the anglophone minority's control over the development of Québec society. During this period, Québec City's anglophone population began to decline, making up only 1 or 2 % of the region's total population.

The reduction of the State and the decentralization of power in favour of Montréal and the regions affected employment stability in the area. Although unemployment in Québec City is fairly low, the city now relies mostly on its great industrial and technological potential. In fact, Québec City and its surrounding region have a market of more than 650,000 consumers. Tourism is also an important source of revenue; various tourist attractions such as Vieux-Québec, Mont-Sainte-Anne and Montmorency Falls account for 12 to 13% of employment in the greater Québec City region. But one of the most promising areas of economic development remains the advanced technology sector that includes biotechnology, computers, optics and telecommunications.

Politics

Political life in Québec City is deeply marked, monopolized even, by the duality between two levels of government: the federal government and the provincial government. To gain a better understanding of the political situation in Québec, one must first comprehend its historical context. Québec City is the cradle of French Canadian culture in North America. The Canadian Confederation, created in 1867, had important consequences for all francophones in Québec, one of the most significant being the position of minority held by the French Canadian population whose culture differs from the anglophone majority in Canada. The government set up in 1867 was a copy of the British model, giving legislative power to a Parliament elected by universal vote. The new constitution introduced a two-tiered regime composed of the federal government and the provincial government. In Québec City the parliament is called the National Assembly while in Ottawa this role belongs to the House of Commons. As a result of this new division of power, the minority position of francophones in Canada was confirmed. In Québec, however, their authority increased thanks to the creation of a provincial State, which would manage the major areas francophones have always tried to preserve, such as education, culture and French civil law.

Québec has always been in favour of provincial autonomy as opposed to a centralized federal government. From the first years of the Constitution, politicians like Honoré Mercier pushed for more autonomy for the provinces. Among other things, he claimed that only in Québec were the rights of French Canadians efficiently respected. However, when he became premier, he praised the French Catholic character of Québec without questioning federalism. From then on, the influence of Québec's political leaders and the ethnic and linguistic tensions between francophones and anglophones gave Québec an increasingly active role in the struggle for provincial autonomy.

In the last 30 years, the relationship between the federal government and the province has taken a different turn. In fact federal-provincial exchanges have been intense and rather tumultuous since the Quiet Revolution. The 1960s even saw the creation of an extremist group, the Front de Libération du Québec (FLQ), that demanded Québec independence. The group's political activities resulted in the 1970 October Crisis, during which Québec was subjected to the War Measures Act and the Canadian army was brought in.

The various Québec governments that have since followed have all been considered protagonists for a distinct language and culture and have all claimed a special status as well as increased power for Québec. The Québec government believes it understands the needs of the Québécois population better than the federal government and demands the right to greater autonomy, power and resources.

The event that would radically change the political scene was the election of the Parti Québécois in 1976. This party succeeded very quickly in uniting the sovereigntists forces, particularly because of the personality and charisma of its founder, René Lévesque. This political party, whose raison d'être was Québec sovereignty, proposed the 1980 referendum on the question of statehood and asked the Québec people for permission to negotiate sovereignty-association with the rest of Canada. The Québécois voted 60% against sovereignty-association. The same party, with Jacques Parizeau as leader, (Lucien Bouchard has been the premier since 1996), would again ask Québécois to express their opinion on the same question on October 31, 1995. This time the results were much closer – 50.6% of the population voted against the Québec government's independence project while 49.4% declared they were in favour. In the eyes of many, the issue was once again postponed but it remains present today in most political speeches.

The attitude of Québec's political leaders regarding relations between the State and the economy changed radically when Jean Lesage's Liberal Party came to power in the 1960s. This redefinition of the State's role in the economy disrupted the social, political and economic life of the province, particularly in Québec City. The number of employees in the public administration sector grew from 15,000 to 45,000 between the 1960s and the 1980s. This new direction, mapped out by the Quiet Revolution, was generally maintained throughout the 1960s, 1970s and even the 1980s. Québec's political leaders were inspired by their liberal European counterparts, supporting the Keynesian principles of a welfare state, making it a major participant in the economy and a partner in private enterprise. The presence of a large public administration provides the Vieille Capitale region and its inhabitants with steady, well-paid jobs.

The government's new economic role increased the presence and importance of francophones within the Québec economy. This phenomenon was due particularly to growth in the public and semi-public sectors and the State's contribution to the private sector. Th e rise of francophones was felt in all sectors of the economy but mostly in the areas of finance and public administration. However, this kind of State intervention on the part of Québec City or Ottawa has its drawbacks. Since the beginning of the 1980s, the Canadian and Québec governments, increasingly restricted by tight budgetary constraints, have found it more and more difficult to apply their interventionist politics and have incurred high budget deficits each year.

To remedy this situation, radical and difficult decisions have to be taken. In order to reduce the deficit, power must be decentralized and reductions made in the public service wage bill by cutting jobs and salary increases. But there is a problem: the Québec City region's economy is strongly oriented towards the service industries, which employ about 85% of the population. This decline is compensated, however, by growth in other sectors such as finance, insurance and real estate, showing that the dynamism and ingenuity of the region can adjust quickly and successfully to an unfavourable situation.

Economy

The historic and romantic aspects of Québec City are so often emphasized that it is easy to forget that this city is the province's second most important economic centre. Situated on the banks of the St. Lawrence River, greater Québec City has more than 600,000 inhabitants with 175,000 in the city alone. Its economy is strongly oriented towards the service industries and public administration, which employ about 85% of the population. A significant increase in employment has also taken place in areas such as tourism, finance and business, at the expense of manufacturing.

The colossus that the Québec public administration represented was a result of the Quiet Revolution. Supporters of the principles of a welfare state wanted to make the Québec State a major player in the economy and a partner in private enterprise. Subsequently, the welfare state had the objective of modernizing and improving the role of French Canadians in the Québec economy. Between the 1960s and the 1980s, the number of jobs in this sector tripled and francophone control of the economy grew from 47% to 60%. This increase in the region's public sector also had important repercussions on the region's economy since, on average, one job in the public service brings on the creation of another job in the private sector.

During the 1980s, and more particularly in the 1990s, the government attempted to reverse the situation. The welfare state and its numerous expenditures put Canada so much in debt that it is became one of the most indebted of the industrialized nations. The solution seems quite simple: cut expenses. This means that the public service has to limit its spending as much as possible by slashing employment and subsidies, then by privatizing and decentralizing the administration.

Even though Québec City has one of the lowest unemployment rates in the province, the general transformations that the province's economy has gone through have affected Québec City and its region's employment stability. The reduction and decentralization of the Québec government has therefore forced Québec City to turn to other directions.

To cope with government decentralization in favour of Montréal and the regions and to compensate for job losses, Québec City has had to diversify its economy. Provided with rich energy resources, a port with water deep enough to stay open all year and a solid road and railway network, Québec City is an ideal link between the major agricultural and economic centres of North America. During the past few years, the region has made a great effort to attract new industries, several of which have been set up in greater Québec City, in particular on the south shore of the St. Lawrence. One example of this is the Ultramar refinery, built in 1979. Other companies that flourish in the Québec City area: include Groupe MIL-Davies, which employs 500 to 2,000 workers in the construction and repair of ships and oilrigs; Alcan, an aluminum producer; and Louis Garneau, manufacturer of outdoor clothing and accessories now being exported to the United States and Europe. Québec City is also interested in cultivating the economic potential of advanced technology. However, despite the number of new jobs these large companies have generated, Québec City's population has been less than enthusiastic. The primary reason for this is the fear of pollution often associated with heavy industry, as well as the fear that unplanned development of industries will spoil Québec City's appearance.

Université Laval (Laval University) also plays an important role in the region's economic development by providing a qualified work force. It features a research and development department whose primary task is promoting and managing the transfer of technology from the university to various companies in the area. The creation of a technological park, an initiative of Université Laval and the Groupe d'Action Pour l'Avancement Technologique et Industriel de la Région de Québec (the group working for technological and industrial advancement in the Québec City Region) is a good example of the influence this institution has on the region's economic vitality.

The economic situation in Québec City is therefore far from hopeless: this great capital has the necessary potential to revitalize its economy with its specialized work force and the possibilities for research and development offered by the university and leading industries. In addition, Québec City is the seat of the provincial government and despite the reductions imposed on the public service, it will continue to be a driving force in the region.

Tourism also occupies an important place in the region's economy, generating approximately the same number of jobs as the manufacturing sector. Activities related to the hotel and restaurant business represent roughly 24,000 jobs to which can be added about 9,000 jobs linked to services and recreation. Tourism is thus an important ever growing economic sector in the region. Cruise ships coming from Europe and the United States make Québec City an increasingly popular stopover. With Mont-Sainte-Anne close by, Montmorency Falls just a few minutes from downtown, a carnival in the winter and numerous festivals in the summer, tourism is booming in any season.

Culture

For over 200 years, Québec City has enjoted a very impressive and varied cultural life. Numerous artists such as Cornelius Krieghoff, Maurice Cullen, James Wilson Morrice, Clarence Gagnon, Adrien Hébert, Jean-Paul Lemieux, Jean-Guy Desrosiers and others have been influenced by this city and at the same time have enriched the city's image. During the 19th century, Québec City was the setting of many novels. Although the most popular genre at the time was European-style adventure stories, Québec literature was usually limited to glorifying the past and idealizing country life, and was clearly behind the times when compared to Western literature in general. In the beginning, the use of Québec City as a setting was hardly recognizable but has become increasingly evident over the years. As novels have been published, from *Les Anciens Canadiens* by Philippe Aubert de Gaspé to Roger Lemelin's well known *Au Pied de la Pente Douce* (1944) and *Les Plouffe* (1948), Québec City's image has transformed from that of a vague, undefined place to a very lively, bustling French Canadian city. Even though it was once conquered by the British and is not as commercially significant as other cities, Québec remains the intellectual capital of French Canada and a symbol of resistance for French Canadians.

Several artists have chosen to settle in Québec City or its surroundings. For example, Félix Leclerc (1914-1988), composer, poet and performer, was the first Québec singer to gain success in Europe, opening the way for many other Québec artists. Leclerc liked to spend his free time on Île d'Orléans, a place that was close to his heart and that is prominently featured in his work.

Roger Lemelin (1919-1994), a successful writer who described the colourful poor neighbourhoods of Québec City in his novels *Au Pied de la Pente Douce*, *Les Plouffe* and *Le Crime d'Ovide Plouffe* (1982), was born in Québec City. These last two works became very popular and were adapted for radio and television, then for the movies. In 1974, Lemelin was elected as a foreign member to France's Académie Goncourt.

Québec City is also the birthplace of Robert Lepage. Born in the Haute-Ville on December 12, 1957, this Québec director and producer has had remarkable international success. Not unlike Félix Leclere, it took his huge popularity in Europe to make Québec recognize the immense talent of its protégé. This talent is particularly visible in his plays *Les Plaques Tectoniques*, *La Trilogie des Dragons* and *Les Aiguilles et l'Opium* as well as his films *Le Confessionnal* and *Le Polygraphe*. *Le Confessionnal* takes place in Québec City and draws a parallel with the movie *I Confess* filmed here by Alfred Hitchcock in the 1950s. Lepage's film presents magnificent images of Québec City. Opera, theatre, cinema, rock concerts... Robert Lepage is involved in everything. He has chosen Québec City as the setting of his latest project, Ex Machina. Installed in the Vieux-Port (see p 116), Ex Machina allows creators to explore the vast possibilities their art has to offer, whether it is in film, theatre or any other form.

Architecture

Québec City is first and foremost the only walled city on the North American continent. The city was fortified for security reasons and its position on top of Cap Diamant was also strategic. Champlain had Fort Saint-Louis built at the beginning of the 17th century. Originally, the walls served to face British threats and ward off Aboriginal attacks. Very early on, major fortification work transformed Québec City into a veritable stronghold: the construction of the Batterie Royale in 1691, the Dauphine redoubt in 1712, and in 1720, the walls that more or less correspond to the ramparts we see today. The buildings inside the walls and the Vieux-Québec give the city its Old French Regime look.

Québec City has one of the richest architectural heritages in North America. As the cradle of New France, it is especially evocative of Europe in its architecture and atmosphere. But the architecture had to be adapted, particularly because of the harsh winters and lack of specialized workers and materials. The buildings here are simple and efficient without extravagance. A typical house of this period was rectangular in shape with a two-sided sloping roof covered with cedar shingles. To combat the cold Québec City winters, this type of habitation was fitted with only a few windows and one or two fireplaces. The interior was quite rustic since the main preoccupation was to keep warm at all times.

Although this type of dwelling was found mainly in the countryside, the same kind of architecture could also be seen in the city itself. As well as having to think about the cold, the city's inhabitants had to be careful about fires. Because of the proximity of the buildings and the wood used in their construction, fire could spread very quickly. Following the great fire of 1682 which almost completely destroyed the Basse-Ville, the Intendents of New France issued two edicts in 1721 and in 1727 regulating construction in order to reduce the risk of fire inside the city walls. From then on, the use of wood and the construction of mansard roofs – their structure was complex and compact, presenting a great danger for fire – were both prohibited. All buildings had to be constructed of stone and equipped with firebreaking walls. In addition, the floors that separated a house's various storeys had to be covered with terra cotta tiles. All of these changes

Architecture 29

then allowed the realignment of Basse-Ville streets and the creation of Place Royale.

In neighbourhoods like Petit-Champlain you will find stone houses dating from this era, such as the Louis-Jolliet House (16 Rue du Petit-Champlain) or the Demers House (28 Boulevard Champlain). The decision to forbid the use of wood also resulted in the creation of the first suburbs outside city walls since the poorer settlers were forced to move out of town, unable to meet the costly requirements.

Following the British victory on the Plains of Abraham, New France became part of the British Empire and the face of Québec City gradually changed as the anglophone population increased. For instance, on Grande Allée, a previously simple tree-lined country road, large domains appeared where the English built Second Empire and, later on, Victorian mansions. Today these buildings have been transformed into bars or restaurants with terraces overlooking Grande Allée.

Place-Royale

Practical Information

Information in this chapter will help you to better plan your trip, not only well in advance, but once you've arrived in Québec City.

Important details on entrance formalities and other procedures, as well as general information, have been compiled for visitors from other countries. We will also explain how to use this guide. All this said, we wish you a great trip to Québec City!

The area code for Québec City and region is 418.

Entrance Formalities

Passports

A valid passport is usually sufficient for most visitors planning to stay in Canada less than three months; visas are not required. A three-month extension is possible, but a return ticket and proof of sufficient funds to cover this extension may be required.

Caution: some countries do not have an agreement with Canada concerning health and accident insurance, so it is advisable to have the appropriate coverage. For more information, see the section entitled "Health" (p 51)

Extended Visits

Visitors must submit a request to extend their visit **in writing** and **before** the expiration of their visa (the date is usually written in your passport) to an Immigration Canada office. To make a request, you must have a valid passport, a return ticket, proof of sufficient funds to cover the stay, as well as the $65 non-refundable filing-fee. In some cases (work, study), however, the request must be made **before** arriving in Canada.

Embassies and Consulates

Abroad

AUSTRALIA
Canadian Consulate General
Level 5, Quay West, 111 Harrington Road, Sydney, N.S.W. Australia 2000
☎ *(612) 364-3000*
≠ *(612) 364-3098*

BELGIUM
Canadian Embassy
2 Avenue de Tervueren 1040 Brussels (Métro Mérode)
☎ *(02) 735.06.40*
≠ *(02) 735.06.09*

DENMARK
Canadian Embassy
Kr. Bernikowsgade 1, DK=1105 Copenhagen K
☎ *33.48.32.00*
≠ *33.48.32.20*

FINLAND
Canadian Embassy
Pohjos Esplanadi 25 B 00100 Helsinki
☎ *(9) 171-141*
≠ *(9) 601-060*

GERMANY
Canadian Consulate General
Internationales Handelzentrum, Friedrichstrasse 95, 23rd Floor
10117 Berlin
☎ *(30) 261.11.61*
≠ *(30) 262.92.06*

GREAT BRITAIN
Canadian High Commission
Macdonald House,
One Grosvenor Square, London W1X 0AB
☎ *(171) 258-6600*
≠ *(171) 258-6384*

ITALY
Canadian Embassy
Via G.B. de Rossi 27, 00161 Rome
☎ *(6) 44.59.81*
≠ *(6) 44.59.87*

NETHERLANDS
Canadian Embassy
Parkstraat 25, 2514JD The Hague
☎ *(70) 361-4111*
≠ *(70) 365-6283*

Embassies and Consulates

NORWAY
Canadian Embassy
Wergelandsv. 7, 1244 Oslo
☎ *(47) 46.69.55*
⇌ *(47) 69.34.67*

SPAIN
Canadian Embassy
Edificio Goya, Calle Nuñez de
Balboa 35, 28001 Madrid
☎ *(1) 431.43.00*
⇌ *(1) 431.23.67*

SWEDEN
Canadian Embassy
Tegelbacken 4, 7th floor, Stockholm
☎ *(8) 613-9900*
⇌ *(8) 24.24.91*

SWITZERLAND
Canadian Embassy
Kirchenfeldstrasse 88, 3000 Berne 6
☎ *(31) 352.63.81*
⇌ *(31) 352.73.15*

UNITED STATES
Canadian Embassy
501 Pennsylvania Ave. N.W.
Washington DC, 20001
☎ *(202) 682-1740*
⇌ *(202) 682-7726*

Canadian Consulate General
1175 Peachtree St.
1700-100 Colony Sq.,
Atlanta, Georgia 30361
☎ *(404) 532-2000*
⇌ *(404) 532-2050*

Canadian Consulate General
Three Copley Pl., Suite 400
Boston Massachusetts, 02116
☎ *(617) 262-3760*
⇌ *(617) 262-3415*

Canadian Consulate General
Two Prudential Plaza,
180 N. Stetson Ave., Suite 2400,
Chicago Illinois 60601
☎ *(312) 616-1860*
⇌ *(312) 616-1877*

Canadian Consulate General
St. Paul Pl., Suite 1700,
750 N. St. Paul St., Dallas, Texas,
75201
☎ *(214) 922-9806*
⇌ *(214) 922-9815*

Canadian Consulate General
600 Renaissance Center, Suite 1100
Detroit, Michigan, 48234-1798
☎ *(313) 567-2085*
⇌ *(313) 567-2164*

Canadian Consulate General
550 South Hope St., 9th Floor
Los Angeles, California, 90071
☎ *(213) 347-2700*
⇌ *(213) 620-8827*

Canadian Consulate General
Suite 900, 701 Fourth Ave. S
Minneapolis, Minnesota 55415-1899
☎ *(612) 333-4641*
⇌ *(612) 332-4061*

Canadian Consulate General
1251 Avenue of the Americas,
New York, NY, 10020-1175
☎ *(212) 596-1600*
⇌ *(212) 596-1793*

Canadian Consulate General
One Marine Midland Center
Suite 3000, Buffalo, NY, 14203-2884
☎ *(716) 852-1247*
⇌ *(716) 852-4340*

Canadian Consulate General
412 Plaza 600, Sixth and Stewart Sts.,
Seattle, WA 98101-1286
☎*(206) 442-1777*
(206) 443-1782

In Montréal

AUSTRALIA
Australian High Commission
(*no office in Montréal*)
50 O'Connor St.
Ottawa, Ontario K1N 5R2
☎*(613) 236-0841*
(613) 236-4376

DENMARK
Consulate General of Denmark
1 Place-Ville-Marie, 35th Floor
H3B 4M4
☎*(514) 871-8977*

FINLAND
Consulate General of Finland
800 Square Victoria, Suite 3400
H4Z 1E9
☎*(514) 397-7600*

GERMANY
Consulate General of Germany
1250 Boulevard René-Lévesque Ouest,
Suite 4315, H3B 4X1
☎*(514) 931-2277*

GREAT BRITAIN
British Consulate General
1000 de la Gauchetière Ouest
Suite 901, H3B 3A7
☎*(514) 866-5863*

ITALY
Consulate General of Italy
3489 Rue Drummond, H3G 1Z6
☎*(514) 849-8351*
(514) 499-9471

NETHERLANDS
Consulate General of the Netherlands
1002 Rue Sherbrooke Ouest
Suite 2201, H3A 3L6
☎*(514) 849-4247*
(514) 849-8260

NORWAY
Consulate General of Norway
1155 Boul. René-Lévesque Ouest Suite
3900, H3B 3V2
☎*(514) 874-9087*

SPAIN
Consulate General of Spain
1 Westmount Square, H3Z 2P9
☎*(514) 935-5235*
(514) 935-4655

SWEDEN
Consulate General of Sweden
8400 Boul. Décarie, H4P 2N2
☎*(514) 345-2727*

SWITZERLAND
Consulate General of Switzerland
1572 Avenue Dr Penfield, H3G 1C4
☎*(514) 932-7181*
(514) 932-9028

UNITED STATES
American Consulate General
Place Félix-Martin,
1155 Rue Saint-Alexandre, H3B 3Z1
☎*(514) 398-9695*

In Québec City

UNITED STATES
Consulate General
2 Place Terrasse Dufferin, G1R 4T9
☎*(418) 692-2095*

GREAT BRITAIN
(see Montréal; no office in Québec City)
☎ *866-5863*

Tourist Information

Tourist information is available from Tourisme Québec, the Délégations Générales du Québec abroad, Québec City tourist offices and the various offices of the Office du Tourisme et des Congrès de la Communauté Urbaine de Québec. A tourist information service is also available from people on mopeds in Vieux-Québec during the summer. The mopeds are painted green and have a question mark on them.

Tourisme Québec
P.O. Box 979, Montréal, H3C 2W3
☎ *(514) 873-2015*
☎ *800-363-7777*
www.bonjourquebec.com

Canada and abroad

BELGIUM
Délégation Générale du Québec
46 Avenue des Arts, 7e étage
1040 Bruxelles
(Métro Art-Loi)
☎ *(02) 512.00.36*
⇝ *(02) 514.26.41*

Comission Canadienne du Tourisme
Rue Américaine, 27, 1060 Bruxelles
☎ *(02) 538-5792*
⇝ *(02) 539-2433*

CANADA
Bureau du Québec
20 Queen St., West, Suite 1504 Box 13, Toronto, Ontario, M5H 3S3
☎ *(416) 977-6060*
⇝ *(416) 596-1407*

GERMANY
Destination Québec
c/o MEKS, GmbH, Vautierstrasse 92
D-40235 Düsseldorf, Germany
☎ *(211) 914-26-0*
⇝ *(211) 914-26-14*

GREAT BRITAIN
Destination Québec
c/o Aurora Marketing, Suite 154
4th Floor, 35-37 Grosvenor Gardens
House, Grosvenor Gardens, Victoria
London, SW1W 0BS
☎ *(171) 233-8011*
⇝ *(171) 233-7203*

SWITZERLAND
Welcome to Canada!
22, Freihofstrasse, 8700 Küsnacht
☎ *(1) 910 90 01*
⇝ *(1) 910 38 24*

UNITED STATES
Tour & Travel
140W, 69th St., New York, NY 10023-5107
☎ *(718) 579-8401*

In Québec City

Maison du Tourisme de Québec
12 Rue Sainte-Anne, Québec G1R 3X2
☎ *694-1602 or 800-665-1528*

Business hours:
The office is open from 8:30am to 7:30pm every day in the summer from mid-June until Labour Day. The rest of the year the hours are from 9am to 5pm. They give detailed information and supply road maps, travel brochures, and lodging guides for all of Québec's tourist regions.

Centre d'Information de l'Office du Tourisme et des Congrès de la Communauté Urbaine de Québec
835 Avenue Wildfrid Laurier, Québec G1R 2L3
☎ *649-2608*
www.quebecregion.com

Business hours:
It is open from the end of June to mid-Oct every day from 8:30am to 7pm; mid-Oct to end of Apr, Mon to Sat 9am to 5:30pm, Fri 9 am to 6pm, Sun 10am to 4pm; May 1 to June 23, Mon to Sun 9am to 5:30pm, Fri 9am to 6pm.

Sainte-Foy

Centre d'Information de l'Office du Tourisme et des Congrès de la Communauté Urbaine de Québec
3300 Avenue des Hôtels, G1R 2L3
☎ *649-2608*
≠ *522-0830*
www.quebecregion.com

Business hours:
From the end of June to mid-Oct, it is open every day from 8:30am to 7pm; mid-Oct to end Apr, Mon to Sat 9am to 5pm, Fri 9am to 6 pm, Sun 9:30am to 4:30pm; beginning of May to end of Jun, every day 9am to 5:30pm, Fri 9am to 6pm.

Beauport

Bureau touristique du Parc de la Chute-Montmorency
4300 Boulevard Sainte-Anne (Route 138)

Business hours:
Open every day from the end of Jun to mid-Oct from 9am to 5pm.

Sainte-Anne-de Beaupré

Bureau d'Information Touristique de la Côte-de-Beaupré
9310 Boulevard Sainte-Anne
☎ *827-5281*

Business hours:
End of Jun to beginning of Sep and Christmas to begin-

ning of Mar every day 9am to 9pm, rest of the year every day from 9am to 8pm.

Île d'Orléans

Bureau touristique de l'île d'Orléans
490 Côte du Pont, Saint-Pierre
☎ *828-9411*

Business hours:
A friendly face will welcome you from Jun to Aug every day from 9am to 7pm and the rest of the year Mon to Fri from 9am to 5pm.

On the Internet

Here are some Web sites that will help you find out about Québec City online.

Tourisme Québec
www.bonjourquebec.com

Office du Tourisme et des Congrès de la Communauté Urbaine de Québec
www.quebecregion.com

Québec City
www.ville.quebec.qc.com

Cultural information
www.quebecplus.ca
www.iciquebec.ca
www.telegraph.com

Getting Here

If you are leaving from Montréal take the Jean-Lesage Autoroute (20 Est) as far as the Pierre-Laporte Bridge, cross the bridge and take Boulevard Laurier which will successively change its name to Chemin Saint-Louis and Grande Allée. This road leads you directly to the Haute-Ville. You can also arrive by Félix Leclerc Autoroute (40 Est) which will you take as far as Sainte-Foy and from there signs for Boulevard Charest will lead you to the centre of Basse-Ville. To get to the Haute-Ville just take Rue Dorchester and then Côte d'Abraham.

Arriving from Ottawa on Autoroute 417, take Félix Leclere Autoroute (40 Est) to Sainte-Foy and then follow the signs for Boulevard Charest Est. You will arrive in the Basse-Ville. From Toronto, take the Jean-Lesage Autoroute (20 Est) until the exit for the Pierre-Laporte Bridge. Cross the bridge and follow the signs for Boulevard Laurier which will eventually become Grande Allée.

From the United States, take Highway 55 then Autoroute 20 Est. You will enter Québec City by the Pierre-Laporte Bridge and then take Boulevard Laurier.

When arriving in Québec City by car, the most common route is via Grande Allée. After passing through a typical North American-style suburb, you come to a rather British-looking part of town with tree-lined streets. Next come the provincial capital's government buildings and finally the imposing medieval-looking gates and behind them the historic streets of the old city, Vieux-Québec.

Airport

Jean-Lesage Airport (Québec City)

Aéroport International Jean-Lesage is the only airport in the vicinity of Québec City. Despite its small size, it does have international flights to the United States and France and serves Québec and the other Canadian provinces.

510 Rue Principale, Sainte-Foy
G2E 5W1
☎*640-2600*

Location

Situated in L'Ancienne-Lorette, the airport is about 20km northwest of Québec City. To get downtown, head south on Route de l'Aéroport to Autoroute 40 Est and then take Boulevard Charest Est. The trip takes about 20min.

Information

For information about airport services (arrivals, departures, etc.) call ☎640-2600, 24hrs a day for a recorded message. Call the same number and choose option "0" to speak to an agent Monday to Friday from 8am to 4:30pm. There is no toll-free line for general information. Here are the telephone numbers of several airline companies that you might want to call:

Air Canada:
☎*692-0770 or 800-361-8620*

Air Transat:
☎*877-872-8728*

Inter Canadien:
☎*692-1031 or 800-363-7530*

Airport Shuttle

La Québécoise
☎*570-5379*
This bus company travels between the airport and several hotels in downtown Québec City. The cost is $6 for Sainte-Foy and $9 for Québec City per adult (half-price for children).

Car Rentals

Various car rental agencies, such as Budget, Thrifty,

Hertz and National, are located at the airport. (see p 42)

Foreign Exchange

The **Thomas Cook** (☎877-5768) foreign exchange office is open every day from 8am to 9pm.

Finding Your Way Around

By Car

Québec City has a very good public transportation system and plenty of taxis so it is not necessary to use your car; it is even preferable to visit on foot. Most of the tourist attractions are relatively close together and all the tours we suggest are within walking distance. However, for the surrounding areas (Île d'Orléans for example), a car or bicycle is needed to cover the distance.

It is easy to get around by car in Québec City. In Vieux-Québec, parking lots are numerous but expensive. You can park on the street but read the signs limiting parking times carefully and do not forget to feed the parking meters regularly. Inspectors check the streets often and fines are expensive. The signs to leave town are clearly marked.

Things to Consider

Driver's License: As a general rule, foreign driver's licenses are valid for six months from the arrival date in Canada.

Winter Driving: Although roads are generally in good condition, the dangers brought on by drastic climatic conditions must be taken into consideration.

Highway Code: Turning right on a red light is **forbidden** in Québec. Priority to the right is the law here; however, it is not always observed, so pay attention. Red signs marked "Arrêt" or "Stop" must always be respected. Come to a complete stop even if there is no apparent danger.

Traffic lights are often located on the opposite side of the intersection, so make sure to stop on the stop line.

When a school bus (usually yellow) has stopped and has its signals flashing, you must come to a complete stop, no matter what direction you are travelling in. Failing to stop at the flashing signals is considered a serious offense and carries a heavy penalty.

Wearing seatbelts in the front and back seats is compulsory at all times.

Pay attention to reserved bus lanes! They are marked by a large white diamond and signs clearly indicating the hours you cannot drive in these lanes, except when making a right turn.

There are no tolls on Québec highways (*autoroutes*), and the speed limit on them is 100km/h. The speed limit on secondary highways is 90km/h, and 50km/h in urban areas.

Gas Stations: Gasoline prices are less expensive than in Europe. Some gas stations (especially in the downtown areas) might ask for payment in advance as a security measure, especially after 11pm.

Accidents and Emergencies

In case of serious accident, fire or other emergency, dial ***911*** or ***0***.

If you run into trouble on the highway, pull onto the shoulder of the road and turn the hazard lights on. If it is a rental car, contact the rental company as soon as possible. Always file an accident report. If a disagreement arises over who was at fault in an accident, ask for police help.

If you are planning a long car trip, it is a good idea to become a member of the Canadian Automobile Association, or CAA, which can offer help throughout Canada. If you are a member in your home country of an equivalent association (U.S.A.: American Automobile Association; Great Britain: Automobile Association; Australia: Australian Automobile Association), you have the right to some free services. For further information, contact your association or the CAA in Québec City ☎***624-0708***

Car Rentals

Generally a package including airfare, hotel and car or just hotel and car is less expensive than renting a car once you get here. Many travel agencies have agreements with the major car-rental companies (Avis, Budget, Hertz, etc.) and offer good values; contracts often include added bonuses (reduced ticket prices for shows, etc.). Package deals are usually a good deal. However, if you cannot get a package, it is cheaper to rent your car here than it is from abroad. However, here are the addresses of the main car rental companies:

Table of Distances (km)
Via the shortest route

	Baie-Comeau	Boston (Mass.)	Charlottetown (PE)	Chibougamau	Chicoutimi	Gaspé	Halifax (NS)	Hull/Ottawa	Montréal	New York (NY)	Niagara Falls (ON)	Québec City	Rouyn-Noranda	Sherbrooke	Toronto (ON)	
Baie-Comeau		1040	724	679	316	337	807	869	676	1239	1334	422	1304	662	1224	545
Boston (Mass.)	1081		1152	849	1247	1165	701	512	352	767	648	1136	426	906	566	
Charlottetown (PE)	1347	992		867	265	1404	1194	1421	1836	984	1833	1187	1746	1089		
Chibougamau	363	1039	1430		725	700	1308	1298	515	493	724	1124	574			
Chicoutimi	649	1076	662	464		1045	1126	211	831	451	1000	338				
Gaspé	952	1124	930	1550	1590		700	1559	915	1476	808					
Halifax (NS)	1488	1290	1508	1919	1056	1916	1271	1828	1173							
Hull/Ottawa	207	814	543	451	536	347	399	331								
Montréal	608	670	253	638	147	546	142									
New York (NY)	685	834	1246	657	823	750										
Niagara Falls (ON)	925	858	827	141	814											
Québec City	877	240	802	130												
Rouyn-Noranda	782	606	747													
Sherbrooke	693	158														
Toronto (ON)	688															
Trois-Rivières																

Example : The distance between Québec City and Montréal is 253km.

©ULYSSES

42 Pratical Information

Budget
Jean-Lesage Airport
☎*872-9885*

Vieux-Québec
29 Côte du Palais
☎*692-3660*

Sainte-Foy
2481 Chemin Sainte-Foy
☎*651-6518*

Discount
Sainte-Foy
Centre Innovation
2360 Chemin Sainte-Foy
☎*652-7289*

Hertz
Jean-Lesage Airport
☎*871-1571*

Québec
580 Grande Allée
☎*647-4949*

Vieux-Québec
44 côte du Palais
☎*694-1224*

National
Jean-Lesage Airport
☎*871-1224*

Québec
Rue St-Paul
☎*694-1727*
≠*694-1872*

Via Route
2605 Boulevard Hamel Ouest
☎*682-2660*

When renting a car, find out if:
The contract includes unlimited kilometres and if the insurance offered provides full coverage (accident, property damage, hospital costs for you and passengers, theft).

Don't forget:
To rent a car in Québec, you must be at least 21 years of age and have had a driver's license for **at least** one year. If you are between 21 and 25, certain companies will ask for a $500 deposit, and in some cases they will also charge an extra sum for each day you rent the car. These conditions do not apply for those over 25 years of age.

A credit card is extremely useful for the deposit to avoid tying up large sums of money.

Most rental cars have an automatic transmission; however, you can request a car with a manual shift.

Child-safety seats cost extra.

By Public Transportation

When visiting Québec City, we strongly advise you to use public transportation. Run by the Société de Transport de la Communauté Urbaine de Québec (STCUQ), it has a network of bus routes covering the entire city. There is no subway in Québec City; however, a

Métrobus service has recently been established which leaves Beauport or Charlesbourg and goes as far as Sainte-Foy and vice versa. The buses go through Vieux-Québec, along Rue Saint-Jean, Avenue Cartier, across the university campus, stop opposite the large Sainte-Foy shopping centres and near the Sainte-Foy bus terminal. Métrobuses are no. 800 or 801 and are fast because they run on reserved lanes (see p 40) and they stop less often than other buses. Métrobuses also run often, about every 10min.

You will find the public transportation guide in the telephone book. This map of the bus routes also contains the main landmarks to help you get around.

For unlimited use of public transportation, a monthly bus pass costs $54 (on sale at the beginning of each month). You can also buy tickets costing $1.75 each or pay a fare of $2.25 in exact change for each trip. Children, students and senior citizens have reduced rates. Children 5 years of age travel free of charge. Tickets can be bought at most pharmacies or corner stores. These places also have folders describing the individual bus routes. **Take note, bus drivers do not sell tickets and do not give change**.

When you want to change buses, you must ask the driver for a transfer.

Most bus routes operate between 6am and 12:30am except for Saturday night when they run later. Also, on Saturday and Sunday nights, additional "late-night" buses, numbers 800, 801, 7, 11 and 25, leave Place d'Youville at 3am.

For more information about public transportation:
☎*627-2511*

By Taxi

A taxi from the airport to downtown costs about $25.

Taxi Co-op
☎*525-5191*

Taxi Quebec
☎*525-8123*

Taxi Co-op Sillery - Sainte-Foy
☎*653-7777*

From mid-November to the end of March, there is a taxi shuttle service for people interested in the outdoors but who want to stay in the city. **L'Hiver Express** *($18 return per person from downtown; $23 return from Ste-Foy;* ☎*525-5191)* stops in front of the main hotels in Québec City and Sainte-Foy every morning. These taxis will take you to the region's tourist attractions such as

Mont Saint-Anne and pick you up at the end of the afternoon.

By Bus

The Québec City bus terminal is located in the Gare du Palais. Buses leave for Montréal every hour from 6am to 11pm. There is also a shuttle-bus service that goes directly to Montréal's Dorval or Mirabel airports.

Terminus d'Autocars de Québec
320 Rue Abraham-Martin
☎*525-3000*

There is the same bus service in Sainte-Foy because buses coming from Montréal stop in Sainte-Foy before continuing to the Gare du Palais.

Terminus d'autocars Sainte-Foy
3001Chemin des Quatre-Bourgeois
☎*650-0087*

By Train

Trains from Montréal arrive at the Gare du Palais in the Basse-Ville and those coming from the east stop at Lévis on the other side of the river where the ferry crosses.

Gare du Palais
450 Rue de la Gare-du-Palais
☎*800-835-3037*

Gare de Charny
2326 Rue de la Gare Est

Gare de Sainte-Foy
3255 Chemin de la Gare
☎*800-835-3037*
www.viarail.com

Hitchhiking

During the summer, "free" hitchhiking is common and is easier outside large centres. Hitchhiking is prohibited on major highways and expressways.

"Organized" hitchhiking, or ridesharing, with Allo-Stop, works very well in all seasons. This reputed company pairs drivers who want to share their car for a small payment with passengers needing a ride. A membership card is required and costs $6 for a passenger and $7 for a driver per year. The driver receives part (approximately 60%) of the fees paid by the passengers. Destinations include virtually everywhere in the province of Québec. For example, a one-way trip between Quebec and Montreal costs $15.

Children under 5 years of age cannot travel with Allo-Stop because of a regulation requiring the use of child-safety seats. Not all drivers accept smokers, and not all passengers want to be exposed to smoke, so check on this ahead of time.

For registration and information:

Allo-Stop Québec
665 Rue Saint-Jean, Québec, G1R 1P7
and
2360 ch. Ste Foy, G1V-4H2
☎ *(418) 522-0056*

By Ferry

Even if you have no reason to go to Lévis on the south shore of the St. Lawrence River, you should take the ferry trip just for the view. The ferry dock is across from Place Royale; you should have no trouble finding it. The return trip from Lévis gives you a magnificent view of Québec City. A one-way trip costs $1.75 for an adult and $4.75 ($3 for the car, $1.75 for the driver) for a car. The timetable varies from one season to the next so it is better to check directly for the times.

Ferry Québec-Lévis

Société des Traversiers du Québec
10 Rue des Traversiers
☎ *644-3704*

By Bicycle

One of the best ways to get around in the summer is on a bicycle. Bicycle paths and shared road spaces have been laid out to give cyclists access to certain parts of the City. To help you get around, there is a brochure as well as a map showing the bicycle paths and shared road spaces in the city and surrounding area. Travel bookshops sell guides and maps of the bicycle paths in Québec City and region.

Cars are not always attentive and cyclists must be careful. Cyclists must follow the rules of the road and although not obligatory in Québec, we strongly recommend you wear a helmet.

Promo-Vélo can provide you with information on the different types of tours in the region.

Promo-Vélo
P.O. Box 700 Succ. Haute-Ville
Québec, G1R 4S9
☎*522-0087*

Bicycle rentals

Some bicycle shops have a rental service. These shops are listed in the chapter on outdoor activities (p 63) For other addresses consult the yellow pages under "Bicyclettes-Location" or "Bicycle Rental." Insurance is a good idea. Some places include theft insurance in the rental fee, but be sure to check this when you rent the bicycle.

Guided Tours

Several tourist agencies organize tours that give visitors the opportunity to discover the city in various ways. A walking tour provides a more intimate perspective of a neighbourhood than a tour bus. Cruises also provide a unique perspective of the city – its outline from the water. Although there are many options, a few should be mentioned as they are particularly worthwhile.

On Foot

Located in the tourist information office on Rue Sainte-Anne, **CD Tour** *($10, $15 for two people; 12 Rue Sainte-Anne,* ☎*990-8687)* rents out portable audio-tours for various parts of the city, including Vieux-Québec, the Colline Parlementaire, Parc-de-l'Artillerie and the Plaines d'Abraham and surroundings, such as the Aquarium de Québec or the Parc de la Chute Montmorency. These tours are recorded on laser disc, enabling visitors to stop where and when they please. In the lively recordings, historic figures are brought back to life to tell visitors about the major events that shaped Québec City.

Another option is to take a "Québec, Fortified City" walking tour, offered by the **Centre d'Initiation aux Fortifications de Québec** *($10; 90 min; end of Jun to beginning of Sep 9am to 5pm, rest of the year 10am to 5pm;* ☎*648-7016)* (see p 80). These start at the kiosk on Terrasse Dufferin.

The **Société Historique de Québec** *($12; $10 group; 72 Côte de la Montagne,* ☎*692-0556 or 692-0614)*, on Côte de la Montagne, offers guided tours of Vieux-Québec. There are a number of

Guided Tours

themes from which to choose. such as "L'Invasion Américaine de 1775-1776 (The American Invasion 1775-1776)" and "Les Lieux Anciens du Pouvoir (Former Alaces of Power)." These visits last from 2 and 3hrs and will allow you to discover many aspects of Quebec City.

Les Tours Adlard *($14; duration: 2hrs 15min; end of Jun to mid-Sep every day 8:30am to 7:30pm, rest of the year 9am to 5pm; 12 Rue Ste-Anne, ☎692-2358, ≠692-0838)* offers tours that relive history while recounting short anecdotes about how the city has evolved. They also organize bus and trolley bus tours in the city and surrounding region.

By Bus

Les Tours Adlard (see above)

Les Tours du Vieux-Québec
☎*664-0460 or 800-267-TOUR*
Guided tours of the city and its surroundings are given in the comfort of a small air-conditioned bus. Visits to the area around Québec City include Côte-de-Beaupré, Sainte-Anne-de-Beaupré and Île d'Orléans. Tours last about 2 hrs, cost $20.95 per person. They are given all year long.

Visites Touristiques Autocars Dupont
(member of Orléans Express)
☎*649-9226*
This company gives classical tours of the city and excursions to the surrounding area in a luxury bus, an air-conditioned minibus or a trolley bus. The city tour lasts 2hrs and is $20.95. Children 5 years and under are free. These tours are given throughout the year.

By Calèche (Horse-Drawn Carriage)

Calèches du Vieux-Québec
☎*683-9222*
You can visit Vieux-Québec by *calèche carriage* all year long. This original way of discovering the city adds to its charm. *Calèches* can be found almost anywhere in the old town. A ride costs $60 for about 35min.

By Boat

The **Croisières AML** *(Rue Dalhousie, ☎692-1159 or 800-563-4643, ≠692-0845; www.croisieresaml.com)* and the **Croisières de la Famille Dufour** *(☎827-5711 or 800-463-5250, ≠827-1115)* both have cruises on the St. Lawrence where you can discover Québec City from another point of view (see the ch on "Outdoor Activities," p 63).

Money and Banking

There are several banks and *caisses populaires* in Vieux-Québec that exchange foreign currency. In most cases these institutions charge a commission. The *bureau de change* may not charge a fee but their rates are less competitive. You must compare rates and ask about fees. Most banks will exchange U.S. dollars.

Caisse Populaire Desjardins du Vieux-Québec
19 Rue Desjardins
☎*694-1774*

Échange de Devises Montréal
12 Rue Sainte-Anne
☎*694-1014*
46, rue Petit-Champlain
☎*694-0011*

Transchange International
Promenades du Vieux-Québec
43 Rue de Buade
☎*694-6906*

Traveller's Cheques

Traveller's cheques are usually accepted in most department stores and hotels but it is more convenient to change them at the above mentioned places. In Québec City you can buy traveller's cheques in Canadian or U.S. dollars at most banks.

Credit Cards

Most major credit cards are accepted at stores, restaurants and hotels. While the main advantage of credit cards is that they allow visitors to avoid carrying a large sums of money, using a credit card makes leaving a deposit for car rental much easier. Also, some cards, gold cards for example, automatically insure you when you rent a car. In addition, the exchange rate with a credit card is generally better. The most commonly accepted credit cards are Visa, MasterCard, and American Express.

By using a credit card credit card you can avoid service charges when exchanging money. By overpaying your credit card (to avoid interest charges) you can then withdraw against it. You can thus avoid carrying large amounts of money or traveller's cheques. Withdrawals can be made directly from an automatic teller using the personal identification number for your card.

Banks

Most banks offer a standard service to tourists. Visitors who chose to stay for a long period should note that non-residents cannot

Exchange Rates

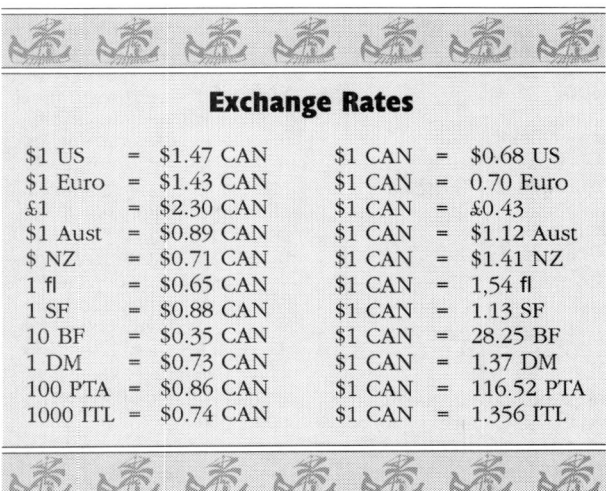

$1 US	=	$1.47 CAN	$1 CAN	=	$0.68 US
$1 Euro	=	$1.43 CAN	$1 CAN	=	0.70 Euro
£1	=	$2.30 CAN	$1 CAN	=	£0.43
$1 Aust	=	$0.89 CAN	$1 CAN	=	$1.12 Aust
$ NZ	=	$0.71 CAN	$1 CAN	=	$1.41 NZ
1 fl	=	$0.65 CAN	$1 CAN	=	1,54 fl
1 SF	=	$0.88 CAN	$1 CAN	=	1.13 SF
10 BF	=	$0.35 CAN	$1 CAN	=	28.25 BF
1 DM	=	$0.73 CAN	$1 CAN	=	1.37 DM
100 PTA	=	$0.86 CAN	$1 CAN	=	116.52 PTA
1000 ITL	=	$0.74 CAN	$1 CAN	=	1.356 ITL

open bank accounts. In this case, the best way to have ready money is to use traveller's cheques. Withdrawing money from foreign accounts can be expensive because of the commission. People who have residence status, permanent or not (landed-immigrants, students) can open a bank account. A passport and proof of residence status are required.

Money can be withdrawn from any automatic banking machine with the Interac and Cirrus systems. Most automatic tellers are open 24hrs and many will now accept European bank cards so you can withdraw money directly from your account (check that you have access before you leave). You can also get money from a credit card but this is considered a loan and interest rates are high. Another possibility is to buy money-orders on which you do not have to pay a commission but this takes longer.

Banks are open Monday to Friday from 10am to 3pm. Most of them are also open Thursday and Friday evenings to either 6pm or 8pm. Some are even open on Saturday morning.

Caisse Populaire Desjardins du Vieux-Québec
19 Rue Desjardins
☎ *694-1774*

Banque Royale
700 Place d'Youville
☎ *692-6800 or 800-769-2599*

Banque Nationale
1199 Rue Saint-Jean
☎ *647-6273*

Currency

The monetary unit in Québec is the Canadian dollar ($), which is divided into cents (¢). One dollar=100 cents.

Bills come in 5-, 10-, 20-, 50-, 100-, 500- and 1000-dollar denominations, and coins come in 1-, 5-, 10-, 25-cent pieces and in 1- and 2-dollar coins.

Insurance

Cancellation

Your travel agent will usually offer you cancellation insurance when you buy your airline ticket or vacation package. This insurance allows you to be reimbursed for the ticket or package deal if your trip must be cancelled due to serious illness or death.

Theft

Most residential insurance policies protect some of your goods from theft, even if the theft occurs in a foreign country. To make a claim, you must fill out a police report. It may not be necessary to take out further insurance, depending on the amount covered by your current home policy. As policies vary considerably, you are advised to check with your insurance company.

Health

This is the most useful kind of insurance for travellers and should be purchased before your departure. Your insurance plan should be as complete as possible because health-care costs add up quickly. When buying insurance, make sure it covers all types of medical costs, such as hospitalization, nursing services and doctor's fees. Make sure your limit is high enough, as these expenses can be costly. A repatriation clause is also vital in case the required care is not available on site. Furthermore, since you may have to pay immediately, check your policy to see what provisions it includes for such situations. To avoid any problems during your vacation, always keep proof of your insurance policy on you.

Health

Vaccinations are not necessary for people coming from Europe, the United States and Australia. On the other hand, it is strongly suggested, particularly for medium or long-term stays, that visitors take out health and accident insurance. There are different types, so it is best to shop around. Bring along all medication, especially prescription drugs. Unless otherwise stated, the water is drinkable throughout Québec.

In case of an emergency dial ☎*911*.

Time Difference

Québec is 6hrs behind continental Europe and 3hrs ahead of the North American west coast. The entire province of Québec (save for the Îles-de-la-Madeleine, which are an hour ahead) operates on Eastern Standard Time. Keep in mind that there are several time zones across Canada. Daylight Savings Time (+1hr) starts the first Sunday in April and finishes the last Sunday in October (-1hr)

Business Hours and Holidays

Stores

The law respecting business hours allows stores to be open the following hours:

- Monday to Wednesday from 8am to 9pm; most stores open at 9:30am and close at 5:30pm

- Thursday and Friday from 8am to 9pm; most open at 9:30am

- Saturday from 8am to 5pm; most open at 9:30am

- Sunday from 8am to 5pm; most open at noon. Not all stores open on Sundays.

Dépanneurs (convenience stores that sell food) are found throughout Québec and are open later, sometimes 24hrs a day.

Holidays

January 1st and 2nd

Easter Monday

3rd Monday in May
(*Fête de Dollard and Victoria Day*)

June 24
(*Saint-Jean-Baptiste Day, Québec's national holiday*)

July 1st
(*Canada Day*)

1st Monday in September (*Labour Day*)

2nd Monday in October
(*Thanksgiving*)

November 11
(*Remembrance Day; only banks and federal government services are closed*)

December 25 and 26
(*Christmas*)

Climate and Clothing

Québec's seasonal extremes set the province apart from much of the world. Temperatures can rise above 30°C in summer and drop to -25°C in winter. Visiting Québec during the two "main" seasons (summer and winter) is like having visited two totally different countries, with the seasons influencing not only the scenery, but the lifestyles and behaviour of the province's residents. Because of the extremes in Québec City weather, you should carefully choose clothing appropriate to the season of your visit

Winter

"Mon pays ce n'est pas un pays, c'est l'hiver..."

("My country is not a country, it is winter")

– Gilles Vigneault

Mid-November to the end of March is the best time for skiing, snowmobiling, skating, snowshoeing and other winter sports. In general, there are five or six large snowstorms each winter. Howling wind often makes the temperatures bitterly cold, causing "drifting snow" (very fine snow that is blown by the wind). One bright spot is that though the weather may be freezing cold Quebec still gets more hours of sunshine than most of Europe.

With sweaters, gloves a scarf,, a hat (called "a tuque"), you will be ready to confront winter. Well... almost! Remember, don't ignore the cold. Here are a few tips:

Wear a coat, preferably a long one with a hood. Otherwise do not hesitate to buy yourself a hat or earmuffs to protect your "sound receivers."

If you are fond of your shoes, buy a pair of galoshes, (they are quite harmless). They are a kind of rubber overshoe that is very practical for avoiding the corrosive salts used to melt the ice. They are easy to find and do not cost very much.

Visitors usually find the stores and other public places are overheated. The trick is to remove your scarf and open your coat the moment you enter one of these places.

If you feel a sudden chill while window-shopping, do not hesitate to go into a store to get warm. This way you will avoid catching a cold.

If you are going to ski, do not forget your sunglasses.

Spring

Spring is short, lasting roughly from the end of March to the end of May, and heralded by the arrival of "slush," a mixture of melted snow and mud, and the break up of ice in the St. Lawrence River. As the snow disappears, long-buried plants and grass, yellowed by frost and mud, come to life again. Nature's welcomed reawakening is spectacular. One of the signs that announce spring is the return of the snow geese flying in long *V* formations. Their calls mingle with those of the Québécois shouting, "It's spring!"

Heavy sweaters, woolen clothes and scarves are recommended for the in-between seasons of Spring and autumn. Do not forget your umbrella and raincoat.

Summer

Summer in Québec blossoms from the end of May to the end of August and may surprise some who think of Québec as a land of snow and igloos. The heat can be quite extreme and often seems much hotter because of the accompanying humidity. The vegetation becomes lush, and don't be surprised to see some rather exotic-looking red and green peppers growing in window boxes. City streets are decorated with flowers, and restaurant terraces are always full.

Bring T-shirts, light shirts and trousers, shorts and sunglasses; a sweater will also be useful in the evening.

Autumn

The autumn colours can last from September to November. Maple trees form one of the most beautiful living pictures on the North American continent. Leaves are transformed into a kaleidoscope of colours from bright green to scarlet red, to golden yellow. Temperatures will stay warm for a while, but eventually the days and especially the nights will become quite cold.

Like in Spring, heavy sweaters, wool clothing and scarves are recommended for autumn as are a raincoat and umbrella.

Indian Summer

This relatively short period (only a few days) during the late fall is like summer's triumphant return! Referred to as "Indian Summer", it is in fact the result of warm air currents from the Gulf of Mexico. It is called Indian Summer because it represented the last hunt before winter. Aboriginals took advantage of the warm weather to stock up on provisions before the cold weather arrived.

Security

Quebec City is not a violent place. The quality of life here is quite outstanding and you should feel perfectly safe.

If you take normal precautions you should not be overly worried about personal security. However, in case of an emergency dial ***911***.

Telecommunications

You do not need to dial the area code for the Quebec City region (418) if you make a local call. For long-distance calls, dial 1 followed by the area code you are calling then the telephone number. Telephone numbers preceded by 800 or 888 mean you can call without incurring long-distance charges if you are dialing from Canada and often even from the United States. To reach the telephone operator, dial 0.

Considerably less expensive than in Europe, public phones are scattered throughout the city, easy to use and some even accept credit cards. Local calls cost $0.25 for unlimited time. For long distance calls, equip yourselves with quarters ($0.25 coins), or purchase a $10, $15 or $20 Smart Card ("La Puce"), on sale at newsstands in convenience stores, or at Bell Téléboutiques. For example, a call from Montréal to Québec City will cost $2.50 for the first 3min and $0.38 for every additional minute. Calling from a private residence will cost even less. Paying by credit card or with the prepaid "HELLO!" card is also possible, but be advised that they are considerably more expensive.

When calling abroad you can use a local operator and pay local phone rates. First dial **011** then the international country code and then the phone number:

AUSTRALIA *61*
BELGIUM *32*
GERMANY *49*
IRELAND *353*
ITALY *39*
NETHERLANDS *31*
NEW ZEALAND *64*
SPAIN *34*
SWITZERLAND *41*
UNITED KINGDOM *44*

To call Great Britian, dial ***011*** + ***44*** + the area code (London ***171*** or ***181***) + the number you are trying to reach. The same goes for Australia, New Zealand and most European countries.

Another way to call abroad is by using the direct access numbers below to contact an operator in your home country.

UNITED STATES
AT&T
☎*(800) CALL-ATT*
MCI
☎*(800) 888-8000*

British Telecom Direct
☎*(800) 408-6420*
☎*363-4144*

Australia Telstra Direct
☎*(800) 663-0683*

New Zealand Telecom Direct
☎*(800) 663-0684*

Post Offices

Major post offices are open from 8am to 5:45pm. However, smaller outlets can be found all over the city, either in shopping centres, in *"depanneurs"*, and even pharmacies. The Tabagie Saint-Jean-Baptiste (620 Rue St-Jean) and the Pharmacie Jean Coutu (corner of Avenue Cartier and Boulevard René-Lévesque), for example offices are open much later than the others.

Bureau de Poste Principal
300 Rue Saint-Paul
☎*694-6176*

Station B
58 Rue Dalhousie
☎*694-6190*

Succursale Haute-Ville
3 Rue de Buade
☎*694-6102*

Taxes and Tipping

Taxes

The ticket price on items usually **does not include tax**. There are two taxes, the GST (federal Goods and Services Tax, TPS in French) of 7% and the PST (provincial sales tax, TVQ in French) at 7.5% on goods and on services. They are cumulative, therefore you must add 14.59% in taxes to the price of most items and to restaurant and hotel prices. There is an additional $2/night tax on hotel rooms.

There are some exceptions to this taxation system, such as books, which are only taxed 7% and food (except for ready-made meals), which is not taxed at all.

Tax Refunds for Non-Residents

Non-residents can be refunded for taxes paid on their purchases made while in Québec. To obtain a refund, it is important to keep your receipts. A separate form for each tax (federal and provincial) must be filled out to obtain a refund. Conditions for refunds are different for the GST and the PST. For further information, call ☎*800-668-4748* (GST) and ☎*(514) 873-4692* (PST).

Tipping

Tipping applies to all table services, in restaurants or other places where customers are served at their tables (fast-food service is therefore not included in this category). Tipping is also compulsory in bars, nightclubs and taxis.

Depending on the quality of the service, patrons must leave approximately 15% of the bill before tax. Unlike in Europe, the tip is not included in the bill, and clients must calculate the amount themselves and give it to the server. "Service charges" and "tip" have the same meaning in North America; do not forget to leave it.

Quebec Cuisine

Although many restaurant dishes are similar to those served in the rest of Canada or the United States, some of them are prepared in a typically Québécois way. These unique dishes should definitely be tasted:

La soupe aux pois
pea soup

La tourtière
meat pie

Le pâté chinois
(also known as shepherd's pie) layered pie consisting of ground beef, potatoes, and corn

Les cretons
a type of pâté of ground pork cooked with onions in fat

Le jambon au sirop d'érable
ham with maple syrup

Les fèves au lard
baked beans

Le ragoût de pattes de cochon
pigs'-feet stew

Le cipaille
layered pie with different types of meat

La tarte aux pacanes
pecan pie

La tarte au sucre
sugar pie

La tarte aux bleuets
blueberry pie

Le sucre à la crème
rich maple-syrup fudge

In the country, you may also have the opportunity to enjoy some exceptional regional specialties like venison, hare, beaver, Atlantic salmon, Arctic char and Abitibi caviar.

The Corporation de la Cuisine Régionale au Québec has been promoting Québec regional cuisine since the 1993. In the spring of 1999, in collaboration with Les Éditions Ulysse, they published *La Cuisine Régionale au Québec*, a French-language guide to restaurants and producers who have helped promote this cuisine throughout Québec.

Wine, Beer and Alcohol

In Québec, the provincial government is responsible for regulating alcohol, sold in liquor stores known as Société des Alcool du Québec (SAQ). If you wish to purchase wine, imported beer or hard liquor, you must go to a branch of the SAQ. Some, known as "Sélection," offer a more varied and specialized selection of wines and spirits. SAQ outlets can be found throughout the city, but their opening hours are fairly limited, with the exception of so-called "Express" branches, open later but offering a more limited choice. As a general rule, their opening hours are the same as those of stores. Convenience and grocery stores have authorization to sell Canadian beer and a few wines, but the choice is slim and the quality of wines mediocre.

You must be at least 18 years old to purchase alcohol, the sale of which is not permitted after 11pm.

A few SAQ addresses:
1059 Avenue Cartier
☎ *643-4334*

888 Rue Saint-Jean, almost at the corner of Avenue Dufferin
☎ *643-4337*

S.A.Q. Sélection
400 Boul. Jean-Lesage, near the Gare du Palais
☎ *643-4339*

Beer

Two huge breweries share the largest part of the beer market in Québec: Labatt and Molson-O'Keefe. They each produce different types of beer, mostly light ales, with varying levels of alcohol. In bars, restaurants, and nightclubs, draft beer is cheaper than bottled beer.

Besides these large breweries, some interesting independent micro-breweries have developed in the past few years. The variety and taste of these beers make them quite popular in Québec. However, because they are micro brews, they are not available everywhere. Here are a few of the micro-brewery beers: Unibroue (Maudite, Blanche de Chambly and Fin du Monde), McAuslan (Griffon, St-Ambroise), Le Cheval Blanc (Cap Tourmente, Berlue), Les Brasseurs du Nord (Boréale) and GMT (Belle Gueule).

Advice for Smokers

Smoking is considered a problem that must be eliminated. It is prohibited to smoke:

- in most shopping centres;
- on buses;
- in government offices.

Smoking sections in most public places (restaurants, cafés) must be closed off. Cigarettes are still sold in most places though (bars, grocery and convenience stores, and newspaper and magazine shops). You must be 18 years old to buy cigarettes.

Senior Citizens

Older people who would like to meet people their age can do so through the organization listed below. It provides information about activities and local clubs throughout Québec:

Fédération de l'Âge d'Or du Québec
4545 Avenue Pierre-de-Coubertin C.P. 1000, Succursale M, Montréal H1V 3R2
☎ *(514) 252-3017*
≈ *(514) 252-3154*

Reduced transportation fares and entertainment tickets are often made available to seniors. Do not hesitate to ask.

Gay and Lesbian Life

Québec City provides some services for the gay community, which is concentrated mainly in Faubourg Saint-Jean-Baptiste.

There is a telephone service called **Gai Écoute** (*☎888-505-1010*). And several support groups have been set up to meet the community's various needs of as well. For information about these groups, call CLSC Haute-Ville (*☎641-0784*).

Two free magazines *Magaizine* and *Fugues* are published monthly and are available in bars. They include information on the gay community's favourite meeting places.

Travellers with Disabilities

The Keroul Association, which specializes in tourism for people with disabilities, publishes a free guide called *Accès Tourisme*, which lists places accessible to disabled people throughout the province. These places are classed by tourist region. The booklet is available for $10 ($15 money order to send abroad). In most of Quebec's 10 regions, the associations organize leisure and sports activities as well. For the addresses of these associations, contact the Association Québécoise de Loisir pour Personnes Handicapées.

KEROUL
4545 Avenue Pierre-de-Coubertin
C.P. 1000 Succursale M
Montreal H1V 3R2
☎ *(514) 252-3104*

Association Régionale de Loisir pour Personnes Handicapées/Québec–Chaudière-Appalaches
525 Boulevard Hamel Est, suite A-22
Québec, G1M 2S8
☎ *529-6134*
≠ *529-8184*

Children

Children in Québec are treated like royalty. Facilities are available almost everywhere you go, whether it be transportation or leisure activities. Generally, children under 5 years of age travel for free, and those under 12 are eligible for fare reductions. The same rules apply for various leisure activities and shows. Find out before you purchase tickets. High chairs and children's menus are available in most restaurants, while a few of the larger stores provide a babysitting service while parents shop.

Pets

As a rule, animals are not allowed in most public places. If you decide to travel with your dog, you will not be able to take a bus. It is also impossible to go shopping with a dog in most places (even shopping centres) and certain covered markets. However, some hotels accept pets; those that do are indicated with a 🐕 in their description. Animals however, are not permitted in food stores, restaurants or buses.

Miscellaneous

Barbers and Hairstylists: like in restaurants, it is usual to tip 10% to 15% of the bill before taxes.

Cinemas: There are no ushers, so there is no tipping.

Drugs: Recreational drugs are against the law and not tolerated (even "soft" drugs). Anyone caught with drugs in their possession risks severe consequences.

Weights and Measures

Although the metric system has been in use in Canada for more than 10 years, some people continue to use Imperial system in casual conversation. Here are some equivalents :

Weights
1 pound (lb) = 454 grams (g)
1 kilogram (kg) = 2.2 pounds (lbs)

Linear Measures
1 inch = 2.54 centimetres (cm)
1 foot (ft) = 30 centimetres (cm)
1 mille = 1.6 kilometres (km)
1 kilometre (km) = 0.63 miles
1 metre (m) = 39.37 inches

Land Measures
1 acre = 0.4 hectare (ha)
1 hectare (ha) = 2.471 acres

Volume Measures
1 U.S. gallon (gal) = 3.79 litres
1 U.S. gallon (gal) = 0.83 imperial gallons

Temperature
To convert °F into °C : subtract 32, divide by 9, multiply by 5.
To convert °C into °F : multiply by 9, divide by 5, add 32.

Économusées: this new form of educational, working museum is now found almost everywhere in Québec.

The *économusées* are intended to present Québec's traditional arts and crafts. They are located in forges, flour mills, sculpture studios and other places where you can watch people at their craft.

Electricity: Voltage is 110 volts throughout Canada, the same as in the United States. Electricity plugs have two parallel, flat pins. Adaptors are available here.

Laundromats: Laundromats and dry cleaners are found almost everywhere in urban areas. In most cases, detergent is sold on site. Although change machines are sometimes provided, it is best to bring plenty of quarters (25-cent coins) with you.

Museums: Most museums charge admission; however, permanent exhibits at some museums are free on Wednesday evenings from 6pm to 9pm, while reductions are offered for temporary exhibits. Reduced prices are available for seniors, children, and students. Call the museum for further details.

Newspapers: International newspapers are readily available here. Québec City's major newspapers are *Le Soleil* and *Le Journal de Québec*.

Pharmacies: In addition to traditional pharmacies, there are huge chain stores (medical- and beauty- product supermarkets). Do not be surprised to find chocolates and detergent next to cough drops and headache medication.

Public Washrooms: Most shopping centres have public toilets. But if you cannot find one do not hesitate to go into a bar, restaurant or snack bar.

Religion: Almost all religions are represented. Unlike English Canada, the majority of the Québec population is Catholic, although most Quebecers are not practising.

Weather: For road conditions, call ☎*643-6830*; for weather forecasts, call ☎*648-7766*.

Outdoors

Québec City is certainly a choice destination for outdoor enthusiasts.

The greater Québec City region has many rich and varied natural attractions, as well as numerous beautiful parks that are scattered throughout the area and even in the city itself.

Québec City's most beautiful gardens are grouped together by an association called **Les Jardins du Québec** *(82 Grande Allée Ouest, G1R 2G6, ☎647-4347)*. These gardens are a treasures to be preserved and certainly to be explored. They are open to the public, whether they want to learn more about horticulture and botany or simply stroll around and enjoy their beauty. There are five of these gardens in Québec City, namely the Parc des Champs-de-Bataille (see p 130), Jardin Roger-Van den Hende (see p 141),

Domaine Maizerets (see p 151 or below), Maison Henry-Stuart (see p 128) and Bois-de-Coulonge (see p 159).

If you feel so inclined during your stay, you will certainly get the chance to participate in several outdoor activities. To find the right equipment, you can consult our list of stores in the Shopping chapter, p 255. Here is a general overview of the many possibilities offered to you.

Parks

Tour C: Grande Allée

The Parc des Champs de Bataille (see p 130), better known as the Plains of Abraham, is Québec City's undisputed park of parks. This immense green space covers about 100ha and stretches all the way to Cap Diamant, which slopes down to the river. It is a magnificent place for local residents to enjoy all sorts of outdoor activities. Strollers and picnickers abound during the summer, but there is enough space for everyone to enjoy a little peace and quiet.

Tour G: Limoilou

With its big trees and lawns, **Domaine Maizerets** *(free admission; 2000 Boulevard Montmorency, ☎691-2385)* is the perfect place for a leisurely stroll. Gardening buffs will love the arboretum and the landscaping; the Domaine also belongs to the Jardins du Québec organization. A number of historic buildings can also be found here, including the château that houses a small exhibition on the history of the estate. All sorts of outdoor activities can be enjoyed here in both summer and winter. Outdoor concerts, plays and conferences on ornithology and other subjects are held at the Domaine Maizerets year-round.

Parc Cartier-Brébeuf (see p 152) is a small park on the banks of Rivière Saint-Charles. It has recently been redesigned to make it a more pleasant sight for people to enjoy. Cement walls used to contain the river but it is now free of this yoke, at least in this area, and is adorned with aquatic plants. Flowers and decorative trees also embellish the park.

Tour J: Heading North

Throughout the year, hordes of visitors come to **Parc de la Jacques-Cartier** ★★★ *(Free admission, Highway 175 N., Km 74, ☎848-3169 or 644-8844)*, located in the Réserve Faunique des Laurentides,

40km north of Quebec. The area is called Vallée de la Jacques-Cartier, after the river of the same name that runs through it, winding between steep hills. As a result of the microclimate caused by the river being hemmed in on both sides, the site is suitable for a number of outdoor activities. The vegetation and wildlife are abundant and diverse. The winding and well-laid-out paths sometimes lead to interesting surprises, like a moose and its offspring foraging for food in a marsh. Before heading out to discover all the riches the site has to offer, you can get information at the nature centre's reception area. Campsites (see p 196), chalets and equipment are all available for rent.

At the park, specialists organize **Safaris d'Observation de l'Orignal** (moose observation safaris) from mid-September to mid-October as well as **Écoute des Appels Nocturnes des Loups**, nocturnal wolf-call listening sessions (☎/≈-848-5099) from the beginning of July until mid-October, in order to familiarize people with these animals. The cost is $15 for adults; each of these activities lasts at least 3hrs and involves a walk through the forest.

Tour K: Côte-de-Beaupré and Île d'Orléans

The **Cap-Tourmente National Wildlife Area** ★★★ *($5; 570 Chemin du Cap-Tourmente, Saint-Joachim, Apr to Oct ☎827-4591, Nov to Apr ☎827-3776)* is located on pastoral, fertile land. Each spring and autumn its sandbars are visited by countless snow geese that stop to gather strength for their long migration. The reserve also has bird-watching facilities and naturalists on hand to answser your questions about the 250 species of birds and 45 species of mammals you might encounter on the hiking and walking trails that cross the park.

Station **Mont-Sainte-Anne** ★★ *(2000 Boulevard Beaupre, P.O. Box 400, Beaupre, ☎827-4561, www.mont.sainte.anne.com)* covers 77km² and includes the 800m-high

Moose

Mont Sainte-Anne, one of the most beautiful downhill-ski sites in Québec. There are a few hotels close to the ski hill and the park. Various other activities are also offered, since the park has 200km of mountain-bike and cross-country ski trails. Sports equipment can be rented on site.

Outdoor Activities

Hiking

Tour J: Heading North

The trails in **Parc de la Jacques-Cartier** ★★★ *(free admission; end of May to mid-Oct; Highway 175 N., ☎848-3169)* are among the favorites for hiking in this region. Peaceful or abrupt, they will allow you to discover the hidden corners of the forest, as well as superb views on the valley and the river.

Tour K: Côte-de-Beaupré and Île d'Orléans

At **Cap Tourmente** *(Saint-Joachim, ☎827-4591 or 827-3776)* you can, if your legs are willing, climb the trail that leads to a magnificent view of the river and its surroundings. You can also use the wooden sidewalks (adapted for people with disabilities) for an equally enjoyable walk.

Station Mont-Sainte-Anne *(Hwy. 360, Beaupré, ☎827-4579 or 827-4561)* has several hiking trails.

Cycling

The Communauté Urbaine de Québec is developing its cycling infrastructure. A new bicycle path called **Corridor des Cheminots** *(☎649-2636)* means cyclists and other sports enthusiasts can travel 22km through various municipalities to Val-Bélair, not far from the beginning of the Jacques-Cartier/Portneuf path.

It should also be mentioned that some bicycle paths have existed for a number of years, such as the one that leads to Beauport or the one that runs along the Rivière Saint-Charles. Many paths are marked out on the road or are shared routes, which makes Québec City and its neighbouring communities enjoyable places to discover on a bicycle.

The Association Promo-Vélo has a great deal of information on various kinds of tours in the region.

Promo-Vélo
C.P. 700, Succ. Haute-Ville
Québec, G1R 4S9
☎*522-0087*

Bicycle Rentals

You can rent mountain bikes at Station Mont-Sainte-Anne and in Parc de la Jacques-Cartier (see above).

Cyclo Services
$18 / day
84 Rue Dalhousie
☎*692-4052*
Cyclo Services also organizes excursions in the city and surrounding area.

Vélo Passe-Sport Plein air
$24 / day
77A Rue sainte-Anne
☎*692-3643*
This organization also organizes excursions in the city and surrounding area.

Vélotek
$25 / day (plus a deposit equivalent to the value of the bicycle)
463 Rue Saint-Jean
☎*648-6022*
Closed Sun to Mon in winter; Spring, summer, autumn, closed Sun.

Bicycle Repairs

Bicycles Falardeau
174 Rue Richelieu
☎*522-8685*
You can also get judicious advice on bicycle touring in the area from the owner, who is a seasoned cyclist.

Boutique Le Pédalier
91 Maurice-Bastien, Wendake
☎*842-2734*

Mont-Vélo
1968 Avenue St-Michel, corner of Avenue Maguire, Sillery
☎*683-9979*
They specialize in the sales and repair of mountain bikes. For the keen enthusiast.

Vélotek
463 Rue Saint-Jean
☎*648-6022*
They also rent bicycles (see above)

Le Vélomane
957 Avenue Royale, Beauport
☎*663-3930*

Tour K: Côte-de-Beaupré and Île d'Orléans

A bicycle path runs from the Vieux-Port of Québec City to the Parc de la Chute Montmorency, passing through Beauport on the way. Also, roads such as Chemin du Roy, on the Côte de Beaupré and Île d'Orléans *(bike rental at the Le Vieux-Presbytère guesthouse, see p 199)*, are meant to be shared by motorists and cyclists. Caution is always in order, but these trips are definitely worth the effort.

Station Mont-Sainte-Anne *($10 for cablecar; Beaupré, ☎827-4561)* has 200km of trails to offer mountain-bike enthusiasts! Climb to the top of the mountain or rush down the slopes after having been carried up with your bicycle in the cable car. There are more than 20 trails with most evocative names such as *La Grisante* (the exhilarating one) or *La Vietnam*. This is a well-known place; World Cup Mountain Bike races are held here every year (see p 252).

Tour J: Heading North

In 1997, a brand new bicycle path was inaugurated in the Quebec region. Following the route of old railway lines, the **Piste Jacques-Cartier** Portneuf *(100 Rue St-Jacques, C.P. 238, St-Raymond, G0A 4G0, ☎337-7525, ≈337-8017)* crosses through the Réserve Faunique Portneuf and the Station Forestière Duchesnay (where you can park your car and rent bicycles, and borders some lakes. Including the most recent additions, it is 63 km long, stretching from Rivière-à-Pierre to Shanon. Its magical setting and safe passage have already attracted many cyclists. In winter, the path is used for snowmobiling.

In **Parc de la Jacques-Cartier** *(free admission; Rte. 175 Nord, ☎848-3169)* (see p 64), the trails are for both hikers and mountain-biking enthusiasts. Bike rental is available.

Cruises

Croisières AML *($22-24; tickets sold at Quai Chouinard, ☎692-1159 or 800-563-4643, www.croisieresaml.com)* offers cruises all summer, with a great view of Québec City and its surroundings from another angle. One of the ships owned by this company is the **M/V Louis-Jolliet** *(departures 11:30am, 2pm, 4pm, 8pm)* sailing from Québec City, its port of registry. Day cruises last 1hr 30min and go as far as the Montmorency Falls. At night, you can go up to Ile d'Orleans and enjoy dinner in one of the ship's two dining rooms. These evening cruises last a few hours and feature musicians and dancing.

Croisières de la Famille Dufour *($85 to $140;* ☎*827-8836, 827-8206 or 800-463-5250)* take passengers to the lovely region of Charlevoix, to Pointe-au-Pic, to Île-aux-Coudres and even to the heart of the breathtaking Saguenay fjord aboard a big, modern catamaran.

In-line Skating

In-line-skaing enthusiasts should take note that the Communauté Urbaine de Québec is not particularly welcoming to this sport. In fact, several cities in the region such as Québec City, Charlesbourg, Sainte-Foy, Sillery and Beauport have strictly forbidden skaters access to their bicycle paths. Without the right to skate on the streets, in-line skaters have no other choice than to skate on reserved paths. Fortunately, a few of these paths do exist. Also, the intermunicipal bicycle paths are not subject to these rules. The new Corridor des Cheminots, for example, is open to in-line skaters.

On the **Plains of Abraham**, in front of the Musée du Québec, there is a big, paved rink for in-line skating. Scores of children and adults wearing protective helmets can be seen blading around the track on fine summer days. Equipment rentals are available at a small stand by the rink. This is the only spot on The Plains of Abraham where skating is allowed.

Jogging

Again, the place to go is the **Plains of Abraham**. The big, flat track in front of the Musée du Québec is a good place for a run, though people also go jogging on the paved streets and trails.

Fruit-picking

Tour K: Côte-de-Beaupré and Île d'Orléans

From strawberries to raspberries to corn, pears and apples all summer long, the harvests follow one another, changing the look of the surrounding countryside. On **Île d'Orléans**, farmers open their doors to anyone, parents and children alike, who wishes to spend a day playing in an orchard or a field. Learn the secrets of picking and enjoy the fruit of your labour!

Rafting

Rafting

Tour D: Jacques-Cartier

In spring and summer the Rivière Jacques-Cartier gives adventurers a good run for their money. Two long-standing companies offer well-supervised rafting expeditions with all the necessary equipment. At **Village Aventure** *(1860 Boulevard Valcartier, St-Gabriel-de-Valcartier, ☎844-2200 or 888-384-5524, www.valcartier.com)*, they promise lots of excitement on an 8km ride. With **Excursions Jacques-Cartier** *(978 Av. Jacques-Cartier, Tewkesbury, ☎848-7238, ≠848-5687)*, you can also experience some very exciting runs.

Bird-watching

Tour K: Côte-de-Beaupré and Île d'Orléans

One of the best places in the region for bird-watching is definitely the **Cap Tourmente National Wildlife Area** *(570 Chemin du Cap-Tourmente, Apr to late Oct every day 8:30am to 5pm, except last weekends of Oct 7:30am to 6pm, late Oct to Apr every day 8am to 4pm, early Nov to early Jan closed weekends; Saint-Joachim, ☎827-4591 or 827-3776)*. During spring and autumn, the thousands of migrating snow geese that overtake the area are a fascinating sight to behold. Any questions you might have after seeing these creatures up close and in such great numbers

Snow Goose

can be answered here. The reserve is also home to many other avian species. They are drawn here throughout the year by a number of bird houses and feeders.

Golf

Tour J: Heading North

The **Royal Charlesbourg** *($30 weekdays; $35 weekends; 2180 Chemin de la Grande-Ligne, Charlesbourg, ☎841-3000)* is an 18-hole golf course far from the hustle and bustle of the city.

Tour K: Côte-de-Beaupré and Île d'Orléans

There are two 18-hole courses at the **Mont-Sainte-Anne** *(C.P. 653, Beaupré, G0A 1E0, ☎827-3778, ≠826-0162)* at the foot of the mountain: the Beaupré *(45 weekdays; $55 weekends, ☎8227-4653)* and the Saint-Ferréol *($27.50 weekdays; $32.50 weekends)*.

Ice Skating

Tour A: Vieux-Québec

Each winter, an ice rink is laid out on **Terrasse Dufferin**, enabling skaters to swirl about at the foot of the Château Frontenac with a view of the icy river. You can put on your gear at the kiosk *(mid-Dec to mid-Mar, every day 11am to 11pm, ☎692-2955)*, which also rents out skates *($2; late Dec to mid-Mar, Mon to Fri 1pm to 4pm, Sat and Sun 10am to 4pm, some nights 6pm to 9pm)*.

Tour D: Saint-Jean-Baptiste

On beautiful winter days, Place d'Youville is turned into a magical place, with skaters, snow, frost-covered Porte-Saint-Jean, the illuminated Capitole and Christmas decorations suspended from lampposts. In the centre of the square is a skating rink with music and even if you don't feel like joining in the ice waltz, you can still enjoy the sights. The skating rink opens early in the season, around the end of October, and shuts down in late spring so that Québécois can skate for as long as possible! There are restrooms for skaters *(every day, noon to 10pm; ☎691-4685)*.

Tour G: Limoilou

A lovely skating rink winds beneath the trees of **Domaine Maizerets** *(free admission; 2000 Boulevard Montmorency, ☎691-2385 see p 151)*. There's a small chalet nearby where you can take off your skates and warm up next to a wood stove. Skate rentals *($2; mid-Dec to mid-Mar, Mon to Fri 1pm to 4pm, Sat and Sun 10am to 4pm)*.

Once it has iced over, **Rivière Saint-Charles** is turned into a natural skating rink that, wether permitting, winds several kilometres between the neighbourhoods of Limoilou and Saint-Roch, in Basse-Ville. The **Marina Saint-Roch** *(Mon to Fri noon to 9pm, Sat and Sun 10am to 9pm; 691-7188)* offers skaters a heated place to rest.

Cross-country Skiing

Tour C: Grande Allée

The snow-covered **Plains of Abraham** provide an enchanting setting for cross-country skiing. Trails criss-cross the park from one end to the other, threading their way through the trees or leading across a headland with views of the icy river. All this right in the heart of the city!

Tour G: Limoilou

Some extremely pleasant cross-country-ski trails can also be found at **Domaine Maizerets** *(free admission; 2000 Boulevard Montmorency, ☎691-2385 see p 151)*. At the starting point, there is a little chalet heated with a wood-burning stove. Equipment rentals *($2; mid-Dec to mid-Mar, Mon to Fri 1pm to 4pm, Sat and Sun 10am to 4pm)* are available.

Tour J: Heading North

In winter, **the Station Écotouristique Duchesnay** *($7; Ste-Catherine-de-la-Jacques-Cartier, G0A 3M0, ☎875-2511)* is very popular among skiers in the area. In this great forest, there are 125km of well-kept trails and many little crested tits and other bird species that don't mind the cold!

Nestled in the heart of the Réserve Faunique des Laurentides, **Camp Mercier** *($8; mid-Nov to late Apr, every day 8:30am to 4pm; Rte. 175 North, Réserve Faunique des Laurentides, ☎848-2422 or*

800-665-6527) is criss-crossed with 192km of well-maintained trails in an extremely tranquil landscape. Given its ideal location, you can ski here from fall to spring. Long routes (up to 68km) with heated huts offer some interesting opportunities. There are also cottages for rent that can accommodate from two to 14 people.

Tour K: Côte-de-Beaupré and Île d'Orléans

Mont-Sainte-Anne *($13.05; Mon to Fri 9am to 4pm, Sat and Sun 8:30am to 4pm; Rte. 360, C.P. 400, Beaupré, G0A 1E0, ☎827-4561, www.mont-sainte-anne.com)* has 250km of well-maintained cross-country ski trails with some heated huts set up along the way. Ski equipment can be rented *($15/day)*.

Once it has iced over, **Rivière Saint-Charles** is turned into a natural skating rink that, wether permitting, winds several kilometres between the neighbourhoods of Limoilou and Saint-Roch, in Basse-Ville.

The **Marina Saint-Roch** *(Mon to Fri noon to 9pm, Sat and Sun 10am to 9pm; 691-7188)* offers skaters a heated place to rest.

Downhill Skiing

Tour J: Heading North

Le Relais *($25 / day, 1084 Boulevard du Lac, ☎849-1851)* has 24 downhill skiing trails, all of which are lit for night skiing.

The **Station Touristique Stoneham** *($39; Stoneham, ☎848-2411, 800-463-6888)* welcomes visitors year-round. In the winter there are 25 runs, 16 of which are lighted. For cross-countrys skiers there are 30km of maintained trails, which in the summer are at the disposal of hikers, mountain-bikers and horse-back riders.

Tour K: Côte-de-Beaupré and Île d'Orléans

Mont-Sainte-Anne *($45/day; Mon 9am to 4pm, Tue to Fri 9am to 10pm, Sat 8:30am to*

10pm, Sun 8:30pm to 4pm; Route 360, C.P. 400, Beaupré, G0A 1E0, ☎827-4561, ≠827-3121, www.mont-sainte-anne.com) is one of the biggest ski resorts in Québec. Among the 51 runs, some reach 625m in height and 14 are lit for night skiing. It's also a delight for snowboarders. Instead of buying a regular ticket, you can buy a pass worth a certain number of points, valid for two years, and each time you take the lift, points are deducted. Equipment rentals are also available *(skiing $21/day, snowboarding $33/day)*.

Tobogganing and Waterslides

Tour A: Vieux-Québec

During winter, a hill is created on **Terrasse Dufferin**. You can slide down it comfortably seated on a toboggan. First purchase your tickets at the little stand in the middle of the terrace *($1/ride; late Dec to mid-Mar, every day 11am to 11pm; 692-2955)*, then grab a toboggan and climb to the top of the slide. Once you get there, make sure to take a look around: the view is magnificent!

Tour C: Grande Allée

The hills of the **Plains of Abraham** are wonderful for sledding. Bundle up well and follow the kids pulling toboggans to find the best spots!

Tour J: Heading North

Winter or summer, the **Village des Sports** *($14.34; early Jun to mid-Aug, every day 10am to 7pm; early Dec to late Mar, Sun to Thu 10am to 10pm; 1860 Boulevard Valcartier, St-Gabriel-de-Valcartier, ☎844-2200 or 800-384-5524, www.valcartier.com; take Route 371 N. from Quebec City)* is the undisputed authority when it comes to slides. It is an outdoor-activity centre that offers all the facilities. In the summer, waterslides and a wave pool draw huge crowds. In winter, ice slides will help you forget the cold for a little while. There are also snow rafting and skating on a 2.5km long ice rink that snakes through the woods. There is a restaurant and a bar.

Exploring

The Communauté Urbaine de Québec comprises 13 municipalities totalling about half a million people, the majority of whom speak French.

Québec City itself has a population of about 175,000. It is difficult to pinpoint a specific downtown area in this city since some of the nearby suburbs are attracting more and more people. In fact, two or three areas, such as Vieux-Québec or Grande Allée, could claim this title. On the other hand, it is easier to locate the Haute-Ville (uppertown) and Basse-Ville (lowertown), as they are often called by the Québécois. It is not difficult to distinguish them because the former, more bourgeois, is perched high on the promontory, while the latter is spread out at the foot of the north side.

In the first eight tours of this chapter, you will discover Québec City and its nearby suburbs. The last three excursions will take you outside the city to the Basilica of Sainte-Anne-de-Beaupré and the beautiful Île d'Orléans, among other places. The city tours are designed to maximize walking and use of public transportation, since visiting the city this way will allow you to feel the life that flows through its arteries. If you prefer, you can visit the city by car, but a car will be necessary to follow the last three tours.

Under each tour there is information about the main tourist attractions and a historical and cultural overview. The attractions are classified according to a system of stars so that you can choose them to suit your schedule.

★   Interesting
★★   Worth a visit
★★★   Not to be missed

The address, opening hours and cost are featured in brackets with each attraction. The admission price given is for one adult. Keep in mind that some places offer discounts to children, students and seniors, as well as family rates. Many of these attractions are only open during the tourist season; this will be indicated in the above-mentioned brackets. However, during the off season, some will welcome you if you make an appointment, especially if you are a group.

Follow this guide and let yourself be enticed by one of the most beautiful cities in the world!

Château Frontenac

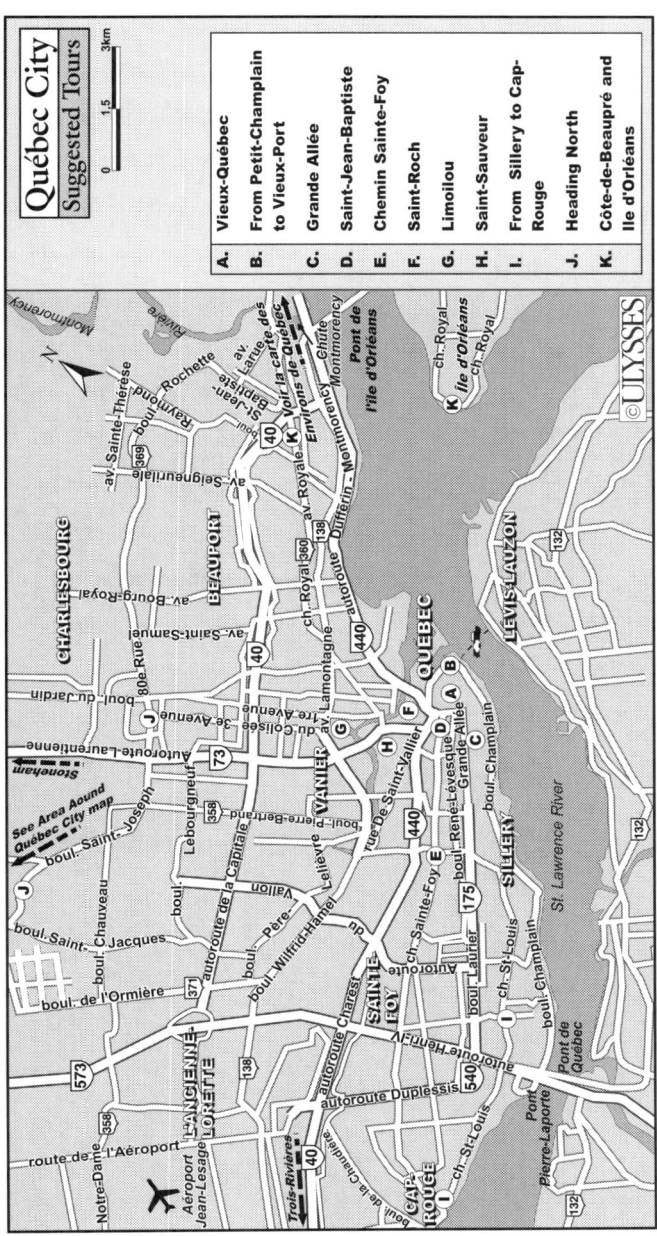

Tour A: Vieux-Québec

(two to three days)

Vieux-Québec is divided into two parts by Cap Diamant. The part that spreads out between the river and the cliff is featured in the next tour (see p 104). The section covering the plateau atop Cap Diamant is informally called Vieux-Québec. As the administrative and institutional centre, it is adorned with convents, chapels and public buildings whose construction dates back, in some cases, to the 17th century. The walls of Haute-Ville, dominated by the citadel, surround this section of Vieux-Québec and give it the characteristic look of a fortress. These same walls long contained the development of the town, yielding a densely built-up bourgeois and aristocratic milieu. With time, the picturesque urban planning of the 19th century contributed to the present-day image of Québec City through the construction of such fantastical buildings as the Château Frontenac and the creation of such public spaces as Terrasse Dufferin, in the *belle époque* spirit.

The Haute-Ville walking tour begins at Porte Saint-Louis, near the parliament buildings.

Porte Saint-Louis *(at the beginning of the street of the same name)*. This gateway is the result of Québec City merchants' pressuring the government between 1870 and 1875 to tear down the wall surrounding the city. The Governor General of Canada at the time, Lord Dufferin, was opposed to the idea and instead put forward a plan drafted by Irishman William H. Lynn to showcase the walls while improving traffic circulation. The design he submitted exhibits a Victorian romanticism in its use of grand

Porte Saint-Louis

gateways that bring to mind images of medieval castles and horsemen. The pepper-box tower of Porte Saint-Louis, built in 1878, makes for a striking first impression upon arriving in downtown Québec City.

Past Porte Saint-Louis, to the left and facing Parc de

A Vieux-Québec

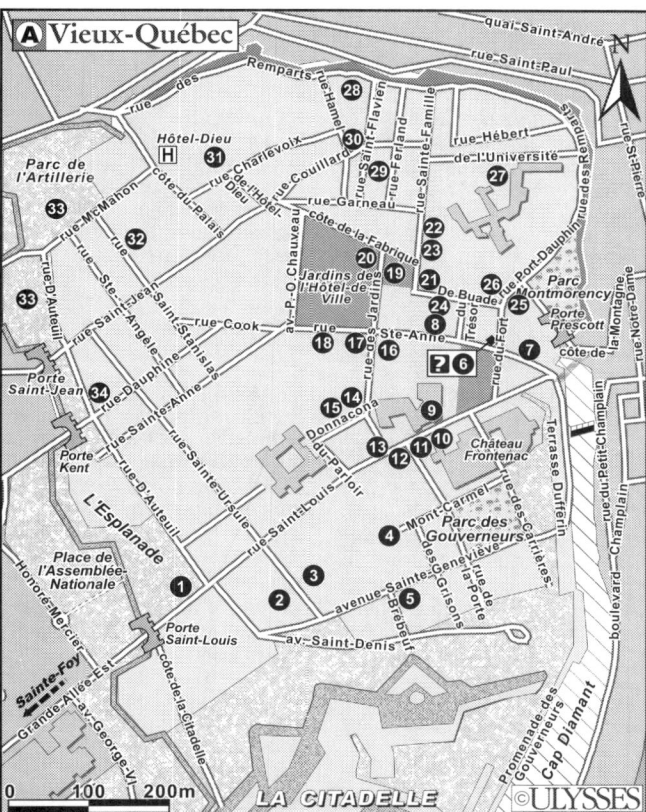

● ATTRACTIONS

1. Centre d'Initiation aux Fortifications et Poudrière de l'Esplanade
2. Chalmers-Wesley United Church
3. Sanctuaire Notre-Dame-du-Sacré-Cœur
4. Cavalier du Moulin
5. Maison Cirice-Têtu
6. Maison du Tourisme
7. Musée du Fort
8. Musée de Cire de Québec
9. Former Courthouse
10. Maison Maillou
11. Maison Kent
12. Musée d'Art Inuit Brousseau
13. Maison Jacquet
14. Monastère des Ursulines
15. Musée des Ursulines
16. Holy Trinity Anglican Cathedral
17. Hôtel Clarendon
18. Édifice Price
19. Place de l'Hôtel-de-Ville
20. Hôtel de Ville et Centre d'Interprétation de la Vie Urbaine de la Ville de Québec
21. Cathédrale Catholique Notre-Dame-de-Québec
22. Séminaire de Québec
23. Musée de l'Amérique française
24. Québec Expérience
25. Post Office and Parks Canada exhibition hall
26. Palais Archiépiscopal
27. Université Laval
28. Maison Montcalm
29. Musée Bon-Pasteur
30. Maison François-Xavier-Garneau
31. Chapelle et Musée de l'Hôtel-Dieu
32. Conservatoire d'Art Dramatique
33. Artillery Park National Historic Site
34. Église des Jésuites

l'Esplanade, are the busts of British Prime Minister Winston Churchill and U.S. President Franklin D. Roosevelt. The two statues commemorate the Québec Conferences that were held by the Allies in 1943 and 1944.

On the right, on the opposite side of the street, is the **Club de la Garnison** *(97 Rue Saint-Louis)*, reserved for army officers, as well as the road leading to the citadel. As a visit to the citadel may require 2 to 3 hrs, it is best to set aside a separate time to take a tour of the premises (see description at the end of the Haute-Ville walking tour, on p 102).

Fortifications of Québec National Historic Site ★. Québec City's first wall was built of earth and wooden posts. It was erected on the west side of the city in 1693, according to the plans of engineer Dubois Berthelot de Beaucours, to protect Québec City from the Iroquois. Work on much stronger stone fortifications began in 1745, designed by engineer Chaussegros de Léry, when England and France entered a new era of conflict. However, the wall was unfinished when the city was seized by the British in 1759. The British saw to the completion of the project at the end of the 18th century. Some work on the citadel began in 1693 however the structure as we know it today was essentially built between 1820 and 1832. Nevertheless, the citadel is largely designed along the principles advanced by Vauban in the 17th century, principles that suit the location admirably.

To learn more about these fortifications, visit the **Centre d'Initiation aux Fortifications et à la Poudrière de l'Esplanade** *($2.75; end of Jun to beginning Sep every day 9am to 5 pm, rest of the year 10am to 5pm; 648-7016)*, which displays models and maps outlining the development of Québec City's defense system. Booklets are available with a complete tour of the city's fortifications, and there are also guided tours *($10; duration: 90 min)*. Information plaques have been placed along the wall, providing another means of discovering the city's history. The walkway on top of the wall can be reached by using the stairs next to the city gates.

Continue along Rue Saint-Louis and turn right on Rue Sainte-Ursule.

Chalmers-Wesley United Church *(78 Rue Sainte-Ursule)*. Until the end of the 19th century, Québec City had a small but influential community of Scottish Presbyterians, most of whom were involved in shipping and the lumber trade. This attractive Gothic Revival church is presently used by a variety of groups, testimony to the decline in the Scottish Presbyterian community. The church was built in 1852, and designed by John Wells, an architect known for a number of famous buildings, including the Bank of Montreal headquarters. The elegant Gothic Revival spire of the church contributes to the picturesque aspect of the city. The church's organ was restored in 1985. Concerts are presented at the church every Sunday afternoon from the beginning of July until the middle of August. Donations are appreciated.

The **Sanctuaire Notre-Dame-du-Sacré-Coeur** *(free admission; open every day 7am to 8pm; 71 Rue Sainte-Ursule, ☎692-3787)* faces Chalmers-Wesley United Church. The sanctuary was originally built for the Sacré Cœur missionaries. This place of worship, erected in 1910 and drafted by François-Xavier Berlinguet, is now open to everyone. The sanctuary has a Gothic Revival facade. Its two rather narrow steeples seem dwarfed by the size of the building. The interior of the structure, with its stained glass windows and murals, is more attractive.

Return to Avenue Sainte-Geneviève and then turn left.

A short detour down Rue Mont-Carmel (to the left) brings you to one of the remnants of Québec City's earliest fortifications, located in an out-of-the-way spot behind a row of houses. The **Cavalier du Moulin** was built in 1693 by engineer Dubois Bertholot de Beaucours. It is a redoubt set within the city walls from which it would be possible to destroy them in the event of a successful enemy invasion. The fortification is named for the windmill, or *moulin*, that used to sit on top of it.

Maison Cirice-Têtu ★ *(25 Avenue Sainte-Geneviève)*. Besides the city's major historical landmarks, Québec's appeal lies with its smaller, less imposing buildings, each of which has its own separate history. It is enjoyable to simply wander the narrow streets of the old city, taking in the subtleties of architecture so atypical of North America. The Cirice-Têtu house was built in 1852. It was designed by Charles Baillargé, a member of a celebrated family of architects who, beginning in the 18th century, left an important mark on the architecture of Québec City and its surroundings. The Greek Revival facade of the house, a masterpiece of the genre, is tastefully decorated with palmettes and the discreet use of laurel. The main floor has huge bay windows that open onto a single expansive living room in the London style. From the time of its construction, the house incorporated all the modern amenities: central heating, hot running water and multiple bathrooms.

The charming square known as **Jardin des Gouverneurs** ★ was originally the private garden of the governor of New France. The square was laid out in 1647 for Charles Huaut de Montmagny to the west of Château Saint-Louis, the residence of the governor. A monument to opposing military leaders Wolfe and Montcalm, both of whom died on the battlefields of the Plains of Abraham, was erected during the restoration of the garden in 1827.

A walk on the wooden planks of the **Terrasse Dufferin** ★★★, overlooking the St. Lawrence, provides a different sensation than the pavement we are used to. It was built in 1879 at the request of the Governor General of the time, Lord Dufferin. The boardwalk's open-air pavilions and ornate streetlamps were designed by Charles Baillargé and were inspired by the style of French urban architecture common under Napoleon III. Terrasse Dufferin is one of Québec

Terrasse Dufferin

City's most popular sights and is the preferred meeting place for young people. The view of the river, the south shore and Île d'Orléans is magnificent. During the winter months, a huge ice slide is set up at the western end of the boardwalk.

Terrasse Dufferin is located where the Château Saint-Louis, the long-destroyed elaborate residence of the governor of New France, used to stand. Built at the very edge of the escarpment, this three-storey building had a long, private stone terrace on the river side while the main entrance, consisting of a fortified facade, opened onto Place d'Armes and featured pavilions with imperial-type roofs. The château was built in the 17th century by architect François de la Joue and was enlarged in 1719 by engineer Chausegros de Léry. Its rooms, linked one to the other, were the scene of elegant receptions given for French nobility. Plans for the future of the entire continent were drawn up in this building. Château Saint-Louis was badly damaged in the British invasion of the city at the time of the Conquest and was later remodelled according to British tastes before being destroyed by fire in 1834.

There are two monuments at the far end of Terrasse Dufferin. One is dedicated to the memory of Samuel de Champlain, the founder of Québec City and father of New France. It was designed by Parisian sculptor Paul Chevré and erected in 1898. The second monument informs visitors that Vieux-Québec was recognized as a World Heritage Site by UNESCO in 1985. Québec City is the first city in North America to be included on this list. A staircase just to the left of the Champlain monument leads to the Place-Royale quarter in Basse-Ville (Tour B).

Château Frontenac ★★★
(1 Rue des Carrières). The first half of the 19th century saw the emergence of Québec City's tourism industry when the romantic European nature of the city began to attract growing numbers of American visitors. In 1890, the Canadian Pacific Railway company, under Cornelius Van Horne, decided to create a chain of distinguished hotels across Canada. The first of these hotels was the Château Frontenac, named in honour of one of the best-known governors of New France, Louis de Buade, Comte de Frontenac (1622-1698).

The magnificent Château Frontenac, symbol of the province's capital city, is probably the most famous sight in Québec. Ironically, the hotel was designed by an American architect, Bruce Price (1845-1903), known for his New York skyscrapers. The look of the hotel, which combines certain elements of the Scottish manors and the châteaux of the Loire Valley in France, has come to be considered a national archetype style called "Château Style." Bruce Price, who also designed Montréal's Windsor train station and the famous Tuxedo Park development near New York, was inspired by the picturesque location chosen for the hotel and by the mix of French and English cultures in Canada.

The Château Frontenac was built in stages. Price's initial wing overlooked Terrasse Dufferin and was completed in 1893. Three sections were later added, the most important of these being the central tower (1923), the work of architects Edward and William Sutherland Maxwell. To fully appreciate the Château, one must go inside to explore the main hall, decorated in a style popular in 18th-century Parisian *hôtels particuliers*, and visit the Bar Maritime in the large main tower overlooking the river.

The Château Frontenac has been the site of a number of important events in history. In 1944, the Québec Conference was held here. At this historic meeting, U.S. President Franklin D. Roosevelt, British Prime Minister Winston Churchill and Canadian Prime Minister Mackenzie King met to discuss the future of post-war Europe. On the way out of the courtyard is a stone with the inscription of the Order of Malta, dated 1647, the only remaining piece of Château Saint-Louis. **Tours** *($6; May to mid-Oct every day 10am to 6pm; mid-Oct to end of Apr Sat and Sun 1pm to 5pm; ☎691-2166)* of Château Frontenac are given by guides dressed in period costume.

Until the construction of the citadel, **Place d'Armes** ★ was a military parade ground. It became a public square in 1832. In 1916, the *Monument de la Foi* (Monument of Faith) was erected in Place d'Armes to mark the tricentennial of the arrival of the Récollet religious order in Québec. Abbot Adolphe Garneau's statue rests on a base designed by David Ouellet.

At the other end of the square are the Maison du Tourisme (a tourist information centre) and two museums. The back of the Holy Trinity Anglican Cathedral (see p 88) is also visible from here.

The **Maison du Tourisme de Québec** *(12 Rue Sainte-Anne)* is located in the former Union Hotel, a white building with a copper roof. A group of wealthy Quebecers saw the need for a luxury hotel in Québec City and commissioned British architect Edward Cannon to head the project which was completed in 1803.

On either side of the Maison du Tourisme are two popular tourist attractions. Using an elaborate model of the city along with a sound and light show, the **Musée du Fort** *($6.25; Jul to mid-Sep every day 10am to 7pm; mid-Sep to end of Oct and Apr to the end of Jun every day 10am to 5pm; Feb and Mar Thu to Sun 10pm to 4pm; 10 Rue Sainte-Anne, ☎692-1759)* recreates the six sieges of Québec City, starting with the capture of the town by the Kirke brothers in 1629 and ending with the American invasion of 1775.

Musée de Cire de Québec *($3; May to Oct every day 9am to 10pm, rest of the year every day 10am to 5pm; 22 Rue Sainte-Anne, ☎692-2289)* displays wax likenesses of 75 individuals grouped in 15 settings that depict Québec City's history or recent events. You will see Lara Fabian and Roch Voisine (contemporary pop-music stars) alongside Churchill, Champlain and Wolfe.

Return to Rue St-Louis

Ancien Palais de Justice (Former Couthouse) ★ *(12 Rue Saint-Louis)*. This is the city's original courthouse, built in 1883 by Eugène-Étienne Taché, architect of the parliament buildings. The courthouse resembles the parliament in a number of ways. Its French Renaissance Revival design preceded the Château style as the "official" style of the city's major building projects. The interior of the building was renovated between 1922 and 1930; it has several large rooms with attractive woodwork. Since 1987, the Ancien Palais de Justice building has been used by Québec's Ministry of Finance.

Maison Maillou *(17 Rue Saint-Louis)* is the location of the seat of Québec's chamber of commerce. This attractive French Regime house was built in 1736 by architect Jean Maillou. It was saved from destruction after the stock market crash of 1929 led to the abandonment of plans to expand Château Frontenac.

The history of **Maison Kent** *(24 Rue Saint-Louis)*, once a residence of Queen Victoria's father, the Duke of Kent, is somewhat cloudy. There is some disagreement as to whether the house was built in the 17th or 18th century. It is clear, however, from its English sash windows and low-pitched roof, that the house underwent major renovations during the 19th century. The agreement that handed Québec over to the British in 1759 was signed in this house. Ironically, it is now occupied by the Consulate General of France.

The Galerie d'Art Inuit Brousseau is well known for the quality of its works of art and now includes a small museum to house the owner's private collection. **Musée d'Art Inuit Brousseau**★ *($6; every day 9:30am to 5:30pm; 39 Rue St-Louis, ☎694-1828)* is located in a newly-renovated building on Rue Saint-Louis. Each of the five exhibition rooms has its own theme such as history, materials used, etc. The works are well placed and it is a pleasure to visit the bright, airy and modern display rooms. The historical and cultural notes are interesting and quite complete. At the end of the tour you can watch a documentary video on the artists whose works are presented or return to the adjoining shop to purchase some for yourself.

Inuit Sculpture

Maison Jacquet ★ *(34 Rue Saint-Louis)*, a small, red-roofed building covered in white roughcast dating from 1690, is the oldest house in Haute-Ville; it is the only house in Vieux-Québec that still looks just as it did in the 17th century. The house is distinguished from those built during the following century by its high, steep roof covering a living area with a very low ceiling. The house is named for François Jacquet who once owned the land on which it stands. It was built by architect François de la Joue in 1690, for his own use. In 1815, the house was acquired by Philippe Aubert de Gaspé, author of the famous novel *Les Anciens Canadiens* (The Canadians of Old). The restaurant that now occupies the house takes its name from this book.

Turn right on Rue du Parloir and right again at Rue Donnacona.

Monastère des Ursulines ★★★ *(18 Rue Donnacona; ☎694-0413)*. In 1535, Sainte Angèle Merici founded the first Ursuline community in Brescia, Italy. After the community had established itself in France, it became a cloistered order dedicated to teaching (1620). With the help of a benefactor, Madame de la Peltrie, the Ursulines arrived in Québec City in 1639 and, in 1641, founded a monastery and convent where generations of young girls have received a good education. The Ursulines convent is the longest running girls' school in North America.

Maison Jacquet

Only the museum and chapel, a small part of the huge Ursulines complex, where several dozen nuns still live, are open to the public.

The Sainte-Ursuline chapel was rebuilt in 1901 on the site of the original 1722 chapel. Part of the magnificent interior decoration of the first chapel, created by Pierre-Nöel Levasseur between 1726 and 1736, survived and is present in the newer structure. The work includes a pulpit surmounted by a trumpeting angel and a beautiful altarpiece in the Louis XIV style. The tabernacle of the high altar is embellished with fine gilding applied by the Ursulinesé. The Sacred Heart tabernacle, a masterpiece of the genre, is attributed to Jaques Leblond, also known as Latour, and dates from around 1770. Some of the paintings decorating the church come from the collection of Father Jean-Louis Desjardins, a former chaplain of the Ursulines. In 1820, Desjardins bought several dozen paintings from an art dealer in Paris. The paintings had previously hung in Paris churches but were removed during the French Revolution. Works from this collection can still be seen in churches all over Québec. At the entrance hangs *Jésus chez Simon le Pharisien* (Jesus with Simon the Pharisee) by Philippe de Champaigne, and to the right of the nave hangs *La Parabole des Dix Vierges* (The Parable of the Ten Virgins), by Pierre de Cortone.

The chapel is the burial place of the Marquis de Montcalm, leader of the French troops at the decisive Battle of the Plains of Abraham. Like his rival, General Wolfe, Montcalm was fatally injured in the fighting. In an adjoining chapel is the tomb of blessed Mère Marie de l'Incarnation, the founder of the Ursulines monastery in Québec. An opening provides a view of the nuns' chancel, rebuilt in 1902 by David Ouellet who outfitted it with a cupola-shaped skylight. An interesting painting by an unknown artist, *La France Apportant la Foi aux Indiens de la Nouvelle-France* (France Bringing the Faith to the Indians of New France), also hangs in this section of the chapel.

The entrance to **Musée des Ursulines** *($4; May to Sep, Tue to Sat 10am to noon and 1pm to 5pm, Sun 1pm to 5pm; Oct to Apr Tue to Sun 1pm to 4:30pm 12 Rue Donnacona, ☎694-0694)* is across from the chapel. The museum outlines nearly four centuries of Ursuline history. On view are various works of art, Louis XIII furniture, impressive embroideries made of gold thread, and 18th-century altar cloths and church robes. Even the skull of Marquis de Montcalm is on display!

After the British Conquest of Québec, a small group of British administrators and military officers established themselves in Québec City. These men wanted to mark their presence through the construction of prestigious buildings with typically British designs. However, their small numbers resulted in the slow progress of this vision until the beginning of the 19th century when work began on The **Holy Trinity Anglican Cathedral ★ ★** *(31 Rue des Jardins)* by Majors Robe and Hall, two military engineers inspired by St. Martin's Church in London Fields. The Palladian-style church was completed in 1804. This significant example of non-French architecture changed the look of the city. The church was the first Anglican cathedral built outside Britain and, in its elegant simplicity, is a good example of British colonial architecture. The roof was made steeper in 1815 so that it would not be weighted down by snow.

The cathedral's interior, more sober than that of most Catholic churches, is adorned with various generous gifts from King George III, including several pieces of silverware and pews made of English oak from the forests of Windsor. The bishop's chair is said to have been carved from an elm tree under which Samuel de Champlain liked to sit. Stained-glass windows and commemorative plaques over the years. There is also a Casavant organ dating from 1909 that was restored in 1959. Its set of eight bells is one of the oldest in Canada.

*Continue along Rue des Jardins. To the right is a cobblestone section of **Rue Sainte-Anne** and on the left is the Hôtel Clarendon and the Price building.*

The **Hôtel Clarendon** *(57 Rue Sainte-Anne)* began receiving guests in 1870 in the former Desbarats print shop (1858). It is the oldest hotel still operating in Québec (see p 186) The Charles Baillargé-designed restaurant on the main floor is also the oldest restaurant in Canada (see p 215) The Victorian charm of the sombre woodwork evokes the *belle époque*. The Hôtel Clarendon was expanded in 1929 by the addition of a brick tower featuring an Art Deco entrance hall designed by Raoul Chênevert.

The design of **Édifice Price** ★ *(65 Rue Sainte-Anne)* manages to adhere to traditional North American skyscraper architecture and yet does not look out of place among the historic buildings of Haute-Ville. Architects Ross and MacDonald of Montréal gave the building a tall yet discreet silhouette when they designed it in 1929. It features a copper roof typical of Château-style architecture. The main hall of the building, a fine example of Art Deco design, is covered in polished travertine and bronze bas-reliefs depicting the various activities of the Price company, which specialized in the production of paper.

Walk back up to Rue des Jardins.

The next stop is quaint **Maison Antoine-Vanfelson** at 17 Rue des Jardins, built in 1780. A talented silversmith by the name of Laurent Amiot had a workshop here in the 19th century. The rooms on the second floor of this building feature wonderful Louis XV woodwork.

Place de l'Hôtel-de-Ville ★, a small square, was the location of the Notre-Dame market in the 18th century. A monument in honour of Cardinal Taschereau, created by André Vermare, was erected here in 1923.

The American Romanesque Revival influence seen in the **Hôtel de Ville** *(2 Rue des Jardins)* stands out in a city where French and British traditions have always dominated the construction of public buildings. The building was completed in 1895 following disagreements among the mayor and the city councillors as to a building plan. Sadly, a Jesuit college dating from 1666 was demolished to make room for the city hall. Under the pleasant gardens outside the building, where popular events are held in the summer, is an underground parking lot, a much needed addition in this city of narrow streets.

Centre d'Interprétation de la Vie Urbaine de la Ville de Québec *($2; late Jun to Labour Day, every day 10am to 5pm; rest of the year Tue to Sun 10am to 5pm; 43 Côte de la Fabrique, ☎691-4606).* This information centre on urban life in Québec City is located in the basement of city hall. It addresses questions of urban development and planning. An interesting model of the city provides an understanding of the layout of the area.

Cathédrale Catholique Notre-Dame-de-Québec ★★★ *(at the other end of Place de l'Hôtel-de-Ville).* The history of Québec City's cathedral underscores the problems faced by builders in New France and the determination of the Québécois in the face of the worst circumstances. The cathedral as it stands today is the result of numerous phases of construction and a number of tragedies that left the church in ruins on two occasions. The first church on this site was built in 1632 under the orders of Samuel de Champlain, who was buried nearby four years later. This wooden church was replaced in 1647 by Église Notre-Dame-de-la-Paix, a stone church in the shape of a Roman cross that would later serve as the model for many rural parish churches. In 1674, New France was assigned its first bishop in

Cathédrale Catholique Notre-Dame-de-Québec

residence. Monseigneur François-Xavier de Montmorency-Laval (1623-1708) decided that this small church, after renovations befitting its status as the heart of such an enormous ministry, would become the seat of the Catholic Church in Québec. A grandiose plan was commissioned from architect Claude Baillif, which, despite personal financial contributions from Louis XIV, was eventually scaled down. Only the base of the west tower survives from this period. In 1742, the bishop had the church remodelled by engineer Gaspard Chaussegros de Léry, who is responsible for its present layout, featuring an extended nave illuminated from above. The cathedral resembles many urban churches built in France during the same period.

During the siege of Québec in 1759, the cathedral was bombarded and reduced to ruins. It was not rebuilt until the status of Catholics in Québec was settled by the British crown. The oldest Catholic parish north of Mexico was finally allowed to begin the reconstruction of its church in 1770, using the 1742 plans. The work was directed by Jean Baillargé (1726-1805), a member of the well-known family of architects and craftsmen. This marked the beginning of the Baillargé family's extended, fervent involvement with the reconstruction and renovation of the church. In 1789, the decoration of the church interior was entrusted to Jean Baillargé's son François (1759-1830), who had recently returned from three years of studying architecture in Paris at the Académie Royale. He designed the chancel's beautiful gilt baldaquin with winged caryatids four years later. The high altar, the first in Québec to be de-

Baillargé or Baillairgé

Recent historical studies have prompted us to use the name Baillairgé to designate this famous family of Québec architects. However, documents signed by members of the family reveal that they themselves used both Baillargé and Baillairgé. Don't be surprised, therefore, if you see both; the reference is always to the same family.

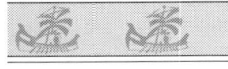

signed to look like the facade of a Basilica, was put into place in 1797. The addition of baroque pews and a plaster vault created an interesting contrast. Thus completed, the spectacular interior emphasized the use of gilding, wood and white plasterwork according to typically Québécois traditions.

In 1843, Thomas Baillargé (1791-1859), the son of François, created the present neoclassical facade and attempted to erect a steeple on the east side of the church. Work on the steeple was halted at the halfway point when it was discovered that the 17th-century foundations were not strong enough. Charles Baillargé (1826-1906), Thomas Baillargé's cousin, designed the wrought iron gate around the front square in 1858. Between 1920 and 1922, the church was carefully restored, but just a few weeks after the work was completed a fire seriously damaged the building. Raoul Chênevert and Maxime Roisin, who had already come to Québec from Paris to take on the reconstruction of the Basilica in Sainte-Anne-de-Beaupré, were put in charge of yet another restoration of the cathedral. In 1959, a mausoleum was put into place in the basement of the church. It holds the remains of Québec bishops and various governors (Frontenac, Vaudreuil, de Callière). In recent years, several masters' paintings hanging in the church have been stolen, leaving bare walls and an increased emphasis on ensuring the security of the remaining paintings, including the beautiful *Saint-Jérôme*, by Jacques-Louis David (1780), now at the Musée de l'Amérique Française.

Feux Sacrés *($7.50; early May to mid-Oct, Mon to Fri 3:30pm, 5pm, 6:30pm and 8pm; Sat-Sun 6:30pm and 8pm; Jul and Aug every day 9pm; 20 Rue Buade, ☎694-0665)*, a sound and light show, is set up inside the cathedral. It illustrates a page of Québec's history with the aid of three-dimensional effects on three screens. Shows are in French and English simultaneously.

Séminaire de Québec ★★★ *(late Jun to late Aug, contact the museum for the schedule of guided tours; 2 Côte de la Fabrique, ☎692-3981)*. During the 17th century, this religious complex was an oasis of European civilization in a rugged and hostile territory. To get an idea of how it must have appeared to students of the day, go through the old gate (decorated with the seminary's coat of arms) and into the courtyard before proceeding through the opposite entryway to the reception desk.

The seminary was founded in 1663 by Monseigneur Francois de Laval, on orders from the Séminaire des Missions Étrangères de Paris (seminary of foreign missions), with which it remained affiliated until 1763. As headquarters of the clergy throughout the colony, it was at the seminary that future priests studied, that parochial funds were administered, and that ministerial appointments were made. Louis XIV's Minister, Colbert, further required the seminary to establish a smaller school devoted to the conversion and education of native people. Following the British Conquest and the subsequent banishing of the Jesuits, the seminary became a college devoted to classical education. It also served as housing for the bishop of Québec after his palace was destroyed by the invasion. In 1852, the seminary founded the Université Laval, the first French-language university in North America. Today most of Laval's campus is located in Sainte-Foy.

The vast collection of buildings of the seminary is home to a priests' residence facing the river, a private school and the Faculty of Architecture of Université Laval, which returned to its former location in 1987.

Today's seminary is the result of rebuilding efforts following numerous fires and bombardments. Across from the old gate can be seen the wing devoted to the offices of the Procurator, complete with sundial. During the 1690 attack of Admiral Phipps, it was in the vaulted cellars of this wing that the citizens of Québec City took refuge. It also contains the private chapel of Monseigneur Briand (1785), decorated with sculpted olive branches by Pierre Emond. Forming a right angle with the chapel is the beautiful parlor wing, constructed in 1696. The use of segmented arch windows in this attractive building betrays the direct influence of French models prior to the adaptation to the climate of Québec.

The guided tours leaving from the reception centre *(2 Côte de la Fabrique)* include visits to the apartments of the seminary, the cellars, the chapel of Monseigneur Briand, and the exterior chapel built in 1890 to replace the original one from 1752 that burned down in 1888. In order to avoid any such recurrence, the interior, which is similar to that of Église de la Trinité in Paris, was covered over in tin and zinc and painted in *trompe l'oeil*, following the design of Paul Alexandre de Cardonnel and Joseph-Ferdinand Peachy. The chapel contains the most significant collection of relics in North America, including these of Saint-Augustine and Saint-Anselm, the martyrs of Tonkin, Saint Charles Borromé and Ignatius of Loyola. Some relics are both large and authentic while others are rather small and dubious. On the left is a funeral chapel housing a tomb containing the remains of Monseigneur de Laval, the first bishop of North America.

To get to Musée de l'Amérique Française, follow Rue Sainte-Famille which follows the seminary and turn right on Rue de l'Université.

Musée de l'Amérique Française ★★ *($3; package $11 with visit of Musée de la Civilisation and Centre d'Interprétation de la Place-Royale; late Jun to early Sep, every day, 10am to 5:30pm; early Sep to late Jun, Tue to Sun, 10am to 5pm; 9 Rue de l'Université, ☎692-2843)* is dedicated to the seven North American communities that were formed by French immigration. Other than the Québécois, they are the Acadians, Franco-Ontarians, francophones from the West, Metis and francophones from Louisiana and New England. It contains over 450,000 artifacts including silverware, paintings, oriental art and numismatics, as well as scientific instruments, collected for educational purposes over the course of the last three centuries by the priests of the seminary. The museum occupies five floors of what used to be the residences of the Université Laval. The first Egyptian mummy brought to America is on view, as are several items that belonged to Monseigneur de Laval. Temporary exhibitions follow, presenting figures from history as well.

On returning to Place de l'Hôtel-de-Ville, turn left on Rue Buade.

The old **Holt Renfrew** store *(43 Rue Buade)*, which opened in 1837, faces the cathedral. Originally fur sellers, which it supplied by appointment to Her Majesty the Queen, Holt's held the exclusive rights for the Canadian distribution of Dior and Saint-Laurent creations for many years. Holt's is now closed, having given way to the boutiques of the **Promenades du Vieux-Québec**.

A little further on is the entrance to **Rue du Trésor,** which also leads to Place d'Armes and Rue Sainte-Anne. Artists come here to sell paintings, drawings and silkscreens, many of which depict views of Québec City.

Rue du Trésor

This pretty little street where artists work during the summer has been called Rue du Trésor since the time of the French regime. In fact, the colonists passed through this street on the way to pay their taxes to the treasury, which was situated where the Maison Maillou now stands. Strangely enough, it now houses the Chambre de Commerce de Québec. One could say that true callings are not always lost with time!

Québec Expérience *(\$6.75; mid-May to mid-Oct, every day 10am to 10pm; mid-Oct to mid-May, Sun to Thu 10am to 5pm, Fri to Sat 10am to 10pm; 8 Rue du Trésor, 3rd floor,* *G1R 4L9,* ☎*694-4000)* is an elaborate show about the history of Québec City. This lively three-dimensional multimedia presentation takes viewers back in time to relive the great moments in the city's history through its important historical figures. A wonderful way to learn about Québec City's past, these half-hour shows are a big hit with the kids. Presented in both French and English.

The **Bureau de Poste** ★ *(3 Rue Buade),* Canada's first post office, opened in Québec City in 1837. It was for a long time housed in the old Hôtel du Chien d'Or, a solid dwelling built around 1753 for a wealthy Bordeaux merchant who ordered a bas-relief depicting a dog gnawing a bone executed above the doorway. The following inscription appeared underneath the bas-relief, which was relocated to the pediment of the present post office in 1872: "Je suis un chien qui ronge l'os, en le rongeant je prends mon repos. Un temps viendra qui n'est pas venu où je mordrai qui m'aura mordu." (I am a dog gnawing a bone, as I gnaw, I rest at home. Though it's not yet here there'll come a time when those who bit me will be paid in kind.) It is said that the message was destined for Intendant

Bigot, a man known for being a swindler, who was so outraged he had the Bordeaux merchant killed.

The dome of the post office and the facade overlooking the river were added at the beginning of the 20th century. The building was renamed **Édifice Louis-Saint-Laurent**, in honour of the former prime minister of Canada. Besides the traditional post and philatelic services a **Parks Canada Exhibition Hall** *(free admission; Mon to Fri 8am to 4:30pm, Sat and Sun 10am to 5pm; 3 Rue Buade, ☎648-4177)* was added to illustrate Canada's natural and historical heritage.

Facing the post office stands a monument to Monseigneur François de Montmorency Laval (1623-1708), the first bishop of Québec, whose diocese covered two thirds of the North American continent. Designed by Philippe Hébert and erected in 1908, the monument features an attractive staircase leading to Côte de la Montagne and from there to Basse-Ville.

The Laval Bishop's monument is located directly in front of **Palais Archiépiscopal** *(2 Rue Port-Dauphin)* or archbishopric, which was rebuilt by Thomas Baillargé in 1844. The first archbishopric stood in what is now Parc Montmorency. Designed by Claude Baillif and built between 1692 and 1700, the original palace was, by all accounts, one of the most gorgeous of its kind in New France. Drawings show an impressive building, complete with a recessed chapel whose interior was reminiscent of Paris's Val de Grace. Though the chapel was destroyed in 1759, the rest of the building was restored and then occupied by the Legislative Assembly of Lower Canada from 1792 to 1840. It was demolished in 1848 to make room for the new parliamentary buildings, which went up in flames only four years later.

Parc Montmorency ★ was laid out in 1875 after the city walls were lowered along Rue des Remparts and the Governor General of Canada, Lord Dufferin, discovered the magnificent view from the promontory. George-Etienne Cartier, prime minister of the Dominion of Canada and one of the Fathers of Confederation, is honoured with a statue here, as are Louis Hébert, Guillaume Couillard and Marie Rollet, some of the original farmers of New France. These last three disembarked in 1617 and were granted the fiefdom of Sault-au-Matelot, on the future site of the seminary, in 1623. These attractive bronzes are the work of Montréal sculptor Alfred Laliberté.

Continue along rue des Remparts.

The halls of the old **Université Laval** ★ can be seen through a gap in the wall of the ramparts. Built in 1856 in the gardens of the seminary, they were completed in 1875 with the addition of an impressive mansard roof surmounted by three silver lanterns. When the spotlights shine on them at night, it creates the atmosphere of a royal gala. Note that Université Laval is now located on a large campus in Sainte-Foy (see p 140).

Following **Rue des Remparts**, Basse-Ville (lower town) comes into view. The patrician manors of the street along the ramparts provide a picturesque backdrop for the old Latin quarter which extends behind them. The narrow streets and 18th-century houses in this neighbourhood are worth the detour.

Maison Montcalm *(45 to 51 Rue des Remparts)* was originally a very large residence constructed in 1727; it is now divided into three houses. The home of the Marquis de Montcalm at the time of the Battle of the Plains of Abraham, the building subsequently housed the officers of the British army before being subdivided and returned to private use. In the first half of the 19th century, many houses in Québec were covered in the sort of imitation stone boards that still protect the masonry of the Montcalm house. Because of this example, it was believed that the covering lent a more refined look to the houses.

Near the corner of Rue Saint-Flavien and Rue Couillard is the small Musée des Soeurs du Bon-Pasteur.

Cannon, Rue des Remparts

Musée Bon-Pasteur ★ *(free admission; all year 1pm to 5pm, closed Mon; 14 Rue Couillard, ☎694-0243)*, founded in 1993, tells the story of the Bon Pasteur (Good Shepherd) community of nuns, which has been serving the poor of Québec City since 1850. The museum is located in the Béthanie house, an eclectic brick structure built around 1887 to shelter unwed mothers and their children. The museum occupies three floors of an 1878 addition and houses furniture as well as sacred objects manufactured or collected by the nuns, as well as a video documentary recounting an adoption.

Continue on Rue Couillard.

At the corner of Rue Saint-Flavien is **Maison François-Xavier-Garneau** *(tour $5; Wed to Sun 1pm to 5pm, tours on the hour; 14 Rue St-Flavien, ☎692-2240)*. Québec City businessman Louis Garneau recently bought this neoclassical house (1862) where historian and poet François-Xavier-Garneau lived during the last years of his life. Throughout the summer, an actor dressed in period costume is on site to make the past come alive as you visit the rooms and admire the objects.

Continue on Rue Couillard. Go down Rue Hamel until Rue Charlevoix where you turn left.

The Augustinian nurses founded their first convent in Québec in Sillery. Uneasy about the Iroquois, they relocated to Québec City in 1642 and began construction of the present complex, the **Chapelle et Musée de l'Hôtel-Dieu ★★** *(32 Rue Charlevoix)*, which includes a convent, a hospital and a chapel. Rebuilt several times, today's buildings mostly date from the 20th century. The oldest remaining part is the 1756 convent, built on the vaulted foundations from 1695, hidden behind the 1800 chapel. This chapel was erected using material from various French buildings destroyed during the Seven Years' War. The stone was taken from the palace of the intendant, while its first ornaments came from the 17th-century Jesuit church. Today, only the iron balustrade of the bell tower bears witness to the original chapel. The present neoclassical facade was designed by Thomas Baillargé in 1839 after he completed the new interior in 1835. The nun's chancel can be seen to the right. Abbot Louis-Joseph Desjardins used the chapel as an auction house in 1817 and again in 1821, after he purchased the collection of a bankrupt Parisian banker who had amassed works confiscated from Paris churches during the French Revolution. *La Vision de Sainte-Thérèse d'Avila* (Saint Theresa of Avila's Vision), a work by François-Guillaume Ménageot which originally hung in the Carmel de Saint-Denis near Paris, can be seen in one of the side altars.

Musée des Augustines de l'Hôtel-Dieu *(free admission; Tue to Sat, 9:30am to noon and 1:30pm to 5pm; Sun 1:30pm to 5pm; closed Mon; 32 Rue Charlevoix, ☎692-2492)*. This museum traces the history of the Augustinian community in New France through pieces of furniture, paintings, and medical instruments. On display are the chest that contained the meagre belongings of the founders (pre-1639), as well as pieces from the Château Saint-Louis, the residence of the first governors under the French Regime, including portraits of Louis XIV and of Cardinal Richelieu. Upon request, visitors can see the chapel and the vaulted cellars. The remains of Blessed Marie-Catherine de Saint-Augustin, the founder of the community in New France, are kept in an adjoining chapel, as is a beautiful gilded reliquary in the Louis XIV style, sculpted in 1717 by Noël Levasseur.

Follow the small street opposite the chapel (Rue Collins). At the corner of Rue Saint-Jean is a pleasant view of Côte de la Fabrique, with the Hôtel de Ville on the right and Cathédrale Notre-Dame in the background on the left. Turn right on Rue Saint-Jean, a lovely commercial street in the heart of Vieux-Québec.

A short detour to the left down Rue Saint-Stanislas gives a view of the old **Methodist Church** *(42 Rue Saint-Stanislas)*, a beautiful Gothic Revival building of 1850. Today it houses the **Institut Canadien**, a centre for literature and the arts. Before the Quiet Revolution of the 1960s, this centre was the focus of many a contentious dispute with the clergy over its "audacious" choice of books. The institute is home to a theatre and a branch of the municipal library.

The neighbouring building, number 44, is the **Ancienne Prison de Québec** (the old jail) built in 1808 by François Baillargé. In 1868, it was renovated to accommodate Morrin College, affiliated with Montréal's McGill University. This venerable institution of English-speaking Québec also houses the library of the **Québec Literary and Historical Society**, a learned society founded in 1824. The building on the corner of Rue Cook and Rue Dauphine surmounted by a palladian steeple is **St. Andrew's Presbyterian Church**, completed in 1811.

Returning to Rue Saint-Jean, cross toward the Conservatoire d'Art Dramatique.

Rue Sainte-Ursule

The **Conservatoire d'Art Dramatique** *(9 Rue Saint-Stanislas)* occupies what used to be Holy Trinity Chapel, built in 1824 according to the plans of Georges Blaiklock. Its elegant, sparse, neoclassical architecture has housed the theatre school since 1970.

Turn left on Rue McMahon, and continue on to the reception and information centre of the Artillery Park.

Artillery Park National Historic Site ★★ *($3.25; hours vary according to the season; 2 Rue d'Auteuil, ☎648-4205)*, also called Lieu Historique National du Parc-de-l'Artillerie, takes up part of an enormous military emplacement running alongside the walls of the city. The reception and information centre is located in the old foundry where munitions were manufactured until 1964. On display is a fascinating model of Québec City built between 1795 and 1810 by military engineer Jean-Baptiste Duberger for strategic planning. The model has only recently been returned to Québec City, after having been sent to England in 1813. It is an unparalleled source of information on the layout of the city in the years following the British Conquest.

The walk continues with a visit to the Dauphine redoubt, a beautiful white roughcast building near Rue McMahon. In 1712, military engineer Dubois Berthelot de Beaucours drafted plans for the redoubt which was completed by Chaussegros de Léry in 1747. A redoubt is an independent fortified structure that serves as a retreat in case the troops are obliged to fall back. The redoubt was never really used for this purpose but rather as military barracks. Behind it can be seen several barracks and an old cartridge factory constructed by the British in the 19th century. The officers' barracks (1820), which has been converted into a children's centre for heritage interpretation, makes a nice end to the visit.

Walk back up Rue d'Auteuil.

The newest of Québec City's gates, **Porte Saint-Jean** actually has rather ancient origins. As of 1693 it was one of only three entrances to the city. It was reinforced by Chaussegros de Léry in 1757, and then rebuilt by the British. To satisfy merchants who were clamouring for the total destruction of the walls, a "modern" gate equipped with tandem carriage tunnels and corresponding pedestrian passageways was erected in 1867. However, this structure did not fit in with Lord Dufferin's romantic vision of the city and was thus eliminated in 1898. The present gate did not replace it until 1936.

Number 29, on the left, is an **old Anglican orphanage** built for the Society for Promoting Christian Knowledge in 1824, and was the first Gothic Revival style building in Québec City. Its architecture was portentous, as it inaugurated the romantic current that would eventually permeate the city.

The last of Québec's Jesuits died in 1800, his community having been banished by the British and then, in 1774, by the Pope himself. The community was resuscitated in 1814, however, and returned to Québec City in 1840. Since its college and church on Place de l'Hôtel-de-Ville were no longer available, they were welcomed by the Congregationists, a brotherhood founded by the Jesuit Ponert in 1657 with a view to propagating the cult of the Virgin. These latter parishioners, built the **Église des Jésuites** ★ *(Rue d'Auteuil, at the corner of Rue Dauphine).*

François Baillargé designed the plans for the church, which was completed in 1818. The facade was redone in 1930. The decoration of the interior began with the construction of the counterfeit vaulting. Its centrepiece is Pierre-Noël Levasseur's altar of 1770. Since 1925, the Jesuit church has been Québec's sanctuary for the worship of Canada's martyred saints.

Porte Kent, like Porte Saint-Louis, is the result of Lord Dufferin's romantic vision of the city. The plans for this gate, Vieux-Québec's prettiest, were drawn up in 1878 by Charles Baillargé, following the ideas of Irishman William H. Lynn.

Climb the stairway to the top of Porte Kent and walk along the wall towards Porte Saint-Louis.

On the other side of the walls is the **Hôtel du Parlement** as well as several patrician homes along the Rue d'Auteuil. Number 69, **Maison McGreevy** *(no visiting)* stands out by its sheer size. The house is the work of Thomas Fuller, the architect of the Parliament Buildings in Ottawa, as well as of New York's State Capitol. It was built in 1868 by McGreevy, a construction entrepreneur who also built Canada's first Parliament Buildings. Behind the rather commercial-looking facade of yellow Nepean sandstone is a perfectly preserved Victorian interior.

Climb down from the wall at Porte Saint-Louis. Côte de la Citadelle is on the other side of Rue Saint-Louis.

Citadelle ★★★ *(at the far end of the Côte de la Citadelle; ☎694-2815)*. Québec City's citadel represents three centuries of North American military history and is still in use. Since 1920, it has housed the Royal 22nd Regiment of the Canadian Army, a regiment distinguished for its bravery during World War II. Within the circumference of the enclosure are some 25 buildings, including the officers' mess, the hospital, the prison, and the official residence of the Governor General of Canada, as well as the first observatory in Canada. The citadel's history began in 1693, when Engineer Dubois Berthelot de Beaucours had the Cap Diamant redoubt built at the highest point of Québec City's defensive system, some 100m above the level of the river. This solid construction is today included inside the King's bastion.

Throughout the 18th century, French and then British engineers developed projects for a citadel that remained unfulfilled.

Chaussegros de Léry's powderhouse of 1750, which now houses the Museum of the Royal 22nd

Regiment, and the temporary excavation works to the west (1783) are the only works of any scope accomplished during this period. The citadel that appears today was built between 1820 and 1832 by Colonel Elias Walker Durnford. Dubbed the "Gibraltar of America," and built according to principles expounded by Vauban in the 17th century, the citadel has never borne the brunt of a single cannonball, though it has acted as an important element of dissuasion.

Musée du Royal 22ᵉ Régiment
($5.50; Apr to mid-May, every day 10am to 4pm; mid-May to mid-Jun, every day 9am to 5pm, mid-Jun to early Sep, every day 9am to 6pm; Sep 9am to 4pm, Oct 10am to 3pm; ☎694-2815). This museum offers an interesting collection of arms, uniforms, insignia and military documents spanning almost 400 years. It is possible to go on a guided tour of the whole installation, to witness the changing of the guard, the retreat, and the firing of the cannon. The changing of the guard lasts 35min and takes place every day from mid-June until the beginning of September, weather permitting.

Small panes of glass

Why do the windows of the old houses in Québec City and in all over the province have many small panes instead of large pieces of glass? You might think it is because of the cold and the snow. But the answer is even more down-to-earth. During colonial times, glass was imported from France. Needless to say, much of it broke en route. As a result, the merchants decided to import smaller pieces of glass so there would be less risk of breakage. Even so, in order to protect the glass it was sometimes transported in large barrels of molasses!

The retreat lasts 30min and can be seen through July and August, on Tuesday, Thursday, Saturday, and

Sunday at 7pm, weather permitting. The firing of the cannon takes place every day at noon and at 9:30pm at the Bastion du Prince de Galles.

Tour B: Petit-Champlain to Vieux-Port

(two days)

Québec's port and commercial area is a narrow *U*-shaped piece of land wedged near the waters of the St. Lawrence. This area is sometimes called the Basse-Ville of Vieux-Québec because of its location just at the foot of the Cap Diamant escarpment. The cradle of New France, Place-Royale is where, in 1608, Samuel de Champlain (1567-1635) founded the settlement he called "Abitation," which would become Québec City. In the summer of 1759, three quarters of the city was badly damaged by British bombardment. It took 20 years to repair and rebuild the houses. In the 19th century, the construction of multiple embankments allowed the expansion of the town and the linking by road of the area around Place-Royale with the area around the intendant's palace. The decline of the port at the beginning of the 20th century led to the gradual abandonment of Place-Royale; restoration work began in 1959. The Petit-Champlain district has been reclaimed by artisans who have set up shop here, especially on the Rue du Petit-Champlain. This area now caters mostly to tourists, who visit the numerous studios to watch the craftspeople at work and to buy their wares.

This walking tour begins at Porte Prescott, which straddles Côte de la Montagne. Those who do not enjoy walking would be well advised to take the funicular from Terrasse Dufferin and to begin the tour at the start of Rue Petit-Champlain.

The **Funiculaire (Funicular)** *($1; ☎692-1132)* began operating in November 1879. It was put in place by entrepreneur W. A. Griffith in order to bring the lower and upper towns closer together. When the funicular was first built, water was transferred from one reservoir to another to make it function. It was converted to electricity in 1906, at the same time that Terrasse

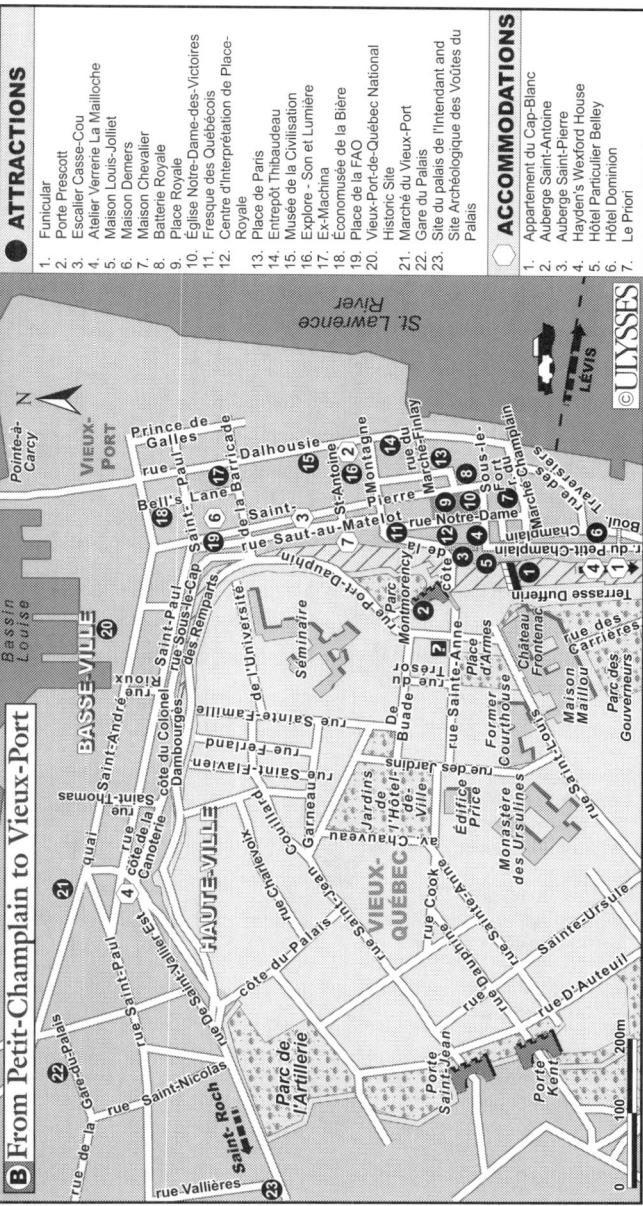

B From Petit-Champlain to Vieux-Port

ATTRACTIONS

1. Funicular
2. Porte Prescott
3. Escalier Casse-Cou
4. Atelier Verrerie La Mailloche
5. Maison Louis-Jolliet
6. Maison Demers
7. Maison Chevalier
8. Batterie Royale
9. Place Royale
10. Église Notre-Dame-des-Victoires
11. Fresque des Québécois
12. Centre d'interprétation de Place-Royale
13. Place de Paris
14. Entrepôt Thibaudeau
15. Musée de la Civilisation
16. Explore - Son et Lumière
17. Ex-Machina
18. Économusée de la Bière
19. Place de la FAO
20. Vieux-Port-de-Québec National Historic Site
21. Marché du Vieux-Port
22. Gare du Palais
23. Site du palais de l'Intendant and Site Archéologique des Voûtes du Palais

ACCOMMODATIONS

1. Appartement du Cap-Blanc
2. Auberge Saint-Antoine
3. Auberge Saint-Pierre
4. Hayden's Wexford House
5. Hôtel Particulier Belley
6. Hôtel Dominion
7. Le Priori

Dufferin was illuminated. It is an outdoor elevator that obviates the need to take the *Escalier Casse-Cou*, "break-neck stairway," or to go around Côte de la Montagne. Due to an unfortunate accident that occurred in the summer of 1996, the funicular has been completely overhauled. The area's merchants have also set up a shuttle service between the two neighbourhoods.

Porte Prescott *(Côte de la Montagne)* can be reached from Côte de la Montagne or from Terrasse Dufferin by means of a stairway and a charming footbridge on the left of the funicular's entryway. This discreetly postmodern structure was built in 1983 by the architectural firm of Gauthier, Guité, Roy, which sought to evoke the 1797 gate by Gother Mann. It allows pedestrians to cross directly from Terrasse Dufferin to Parc Montmorency.

Descend Côte de la Montagne and take the Escalier Casse-Cou on the right.

The **Escalier Casse-Cou** *(Côte de la Montagne)*, which literally means "the break-neck strairway," has been here since 1682. Until the beginning of the 20th century, it had been made of planks that were in constant need of repair or replacement. It connects the various businesses situated on different levels. At the foot of the stairway is **Rue du Petit-Champlain**, a narrow pedestrian street flanked by charming craft shops and pleasant cafés located in 17th and 18th cen tury houses. Some of the houses at the foot of the cape were destroyed by rockslides prior to the reinforcement of the cliff in the 19th century.

Tour B: Petit-Champlain to Vieux-Port

At the foot of the Escalier Casse-Cou, a small *économusée* (economuseum) unveils the secrets of glass-blowing. At **Atelier Verrerie La Mailloche** *(free admission; end Jun to early Oct every day 9am to 10pm, rest of the year 9:30am to 5:30pm; 58 Rue Sous-le-Fort, G1K 3G8, ☎694-0445 or 694-1571)*, visitors can observe the fascinating spectacle of artisans shaping molten glass according to traditional techniques. The finished products are sold in a shop on the second floor.

Maison Louis-Jolliet ★ *(16 Rue du Petit-Champlain)* is one of the earliest houses of Vieux-Québec (1683) and one of the few works of Claude Baillif still standing. The house was built after the great fire of 1682, which destroyed Basse-Ville. It was this tragedy that prompted the authorities to require that stone be used in all buildings. The fire also paved the way for some improvements in urban planning: roads were straightened and Place-Royale was created. Louis Jolliet (1645-1700) was the man who, along with Father Marquette, discovered the Mississippi and explored Hudson Bay. During the last years of his life, he taught hydrography at the Séminaire de Québec. The interior of the house was completely gutted and now contains the lower platform of the funicular (see above).

Follow Rue du Petit-Champlain as far as the stairway on the left leading to Boulevard Champlain. Looking back up from the base of the stairs provides an interesting perspective of the Château Frontenac.

Maison Demers ★ *(28 Boulevard Champlain)* was built in 1689 by mason Jean Lerouge. This impressive residence is an example of the bourgeois style of Québec's Basse-Ville. A two-storey residential facade gives on to Rue du Petit-Champlain while the rear, which was used as a warehouse, extends down another two storeys to open directly onto l'Anse du Cul-de-Sac. Although it is now filled and built-up, one can still distinguish traces of this natural harbour by examining the older urban arrangement.

The cove called l'Anse du Cul-de-Sal, also known as the Anse aux Barques, was Québec City's first port. In 1745, Intendant Gilles Hocquart ordered the construction of a major shipyard in the western part of the cove. Several French battleships were built there using Canadian lumber.

In 1854, the terminus of the Grand Trunk railway was built on the embankments, and in 1858 the Marché Champlain went up, only to be destroyed by fire in 1899. Although it is now filled in and built-up, one can still distinguish traces of this natural harbour by examining the older urban arrangement. The location is presently occupied by administrative buildings and by the **terminus of the Québec-Lévis ferry**. A short return trip on the ferry provides a spectacular view of the ensemble of Vieux-Québec. Taking the ferry in the winter affords a rare chance to come face to face with the ice floes of the St. Lawrence (see p 45).

Québec-Lévis ferry

Follow Boulevard Champlain east as far as Rue du Marché-Champlain. The ferry boards from the south end of this road.

Hôtel Jean-Baptiste-Chevalier ★★ *(60 Rue du Marché-Champlain)* is not a hotel but rather the townhouse of a wealthy family. The first building in the Place-Royale area to be restored, the hôtel is really three separate houses from three different periods: **Maison de l'Armateur Chevalier** (home of Chevalier the Shipowner), built in a square in 1752; **Maison Frérot**, with a mansard roof (1683); and **Maison Dolbec**, dating from 1713. These houses were all repaired or partially rebuilt after the British Conquest. As a group, they were rescued from deterioration in 1955 by Gérard Morisset, the director of the Inventaire des Oeuvres d'Art, who suggested that they be purchased and restored by the government of Québec. This decision had a domino effect and prevented the demolition of Place-Royale.

Maison Chevalier *(free admission; end of Jun to early Sep every day 10am to 6pm; May to end of Jun and early Sep to end of Oct Tue to Sun 10am to 6pm; Nov to May Sat and Sun 10am to 5pm; 60 Rue du Marché-Champlain, ☎643-2158)* harbours an annex of the Musée de la Civilisation, where an interesting exhibit, "Habiter au Passé" (Living in the Past) portrays the daily lives of the merchants of New France. The exhibit features, furniture as well as everyday items. The original, stately Louis XV woodwork (circa 1764) can also be seen.

Take Rue Notre-Dame, and turn right onto Rue Sous-le-Fort.

With no walls to protect Basse-Ville, other means of defending it from the cannon-fire of ships in the river had to be found. Following the attack by Admiral Phipps in 1690, it was decided to set up the **Batterie Royale** ★ *(at the far end of Rue Sous-le-Fort)*, according to a plan drawn up by Claude Baillif. The strategic position of the battery allowed for the bombardment of any enemy ships foolhardy enough to venture into the narrows in front of the city. The ruins of the battery, long hidden under storehouses, were discovered in 1974. The crenellations, removed in the 19th century, were reconstructed, as was the wooden portal, discernible in a sketch from 1699.

The two rough stone houses on Rue Saint-Pierre, next to the battery, were built for Charles Guillemin in the early 18th century. The narrowness of the house on the left shows just how precious land was in the Basse-Ville during the French Regime. Each lot, irregular or not, had to be used. A little further along, at number 25 Rue Saint-Pierre, is the Louis-Fornel house, where a number of artefacts are on display in vaults. This vaulted basement was built in the 17th century from the ruins of Champlain's stronghold, and extends right under the square.

Continue along Rue Saint-Pierre, and turn left on Rue de la Place to go up to Place-Royale.

Place-Royale ★★★ is the most European quarter of any city in North America. It resembles a village in north-

Place-Royale

western France. Place-Royale is laden with symbolism, as it was on this very spot that New France was founded in 1608. After many unsuccessful attempts, this became the official departure point of French exploits in America. Under the French Regime, Place-Royale was the only densely populated area in a vast, untamed colony. Today, it contains the most significant concentration of 17th- and 18th-century buildings in the Americas north of Mexico.

"S" or linchpins

You have perhaps noticed the S-shaped peices of iron that decorate the walls of some of this neighbourhood's old houses. These objects, called "linchpins," hold the stones of the walls on which the weight of the roof rests.

The square itself was laid out in 1673 by Governor Frontenac as a market. It took the place of the garden of Champlain's Abitation, a stronghold that went up in flames in 1682, along with the rest of Basse-Ville. In 1686, Intendant Jean Bochart de Champigny erected a **bronze bust of Louis XIV** in the middle of the square, hence the name of the square, Place-Royale. In 1928, François Bokanowski, then the French Minister of Commerce and Communications, presented Québécois Athanase David with a bronze replica of the marble bust of Louis XIV in the Gallerie de Diane at Versailles to replace the missing statue. The bronze, by Alexis Rudier, was not set up until 1931, for fear of offending England.

Small, unpretentious **Église Notre-Dame-des-Victoires ★★** *(free admission; May to mid-Oct Mon to Sat 9am to 4:30pm, closed Sat during weddings and christenings, Sun 9:30am to 4:30pm, mid-Oct to early May Tue to Sat 9am to noon, Sun 9am to 1pm; Place-Royale)* is the oldest church in Canada. Designed by Claude Baillif, it dates from 1688. It was built on the foundations of Champlain's *Abitation* and incorporates some of its walls. Beside the church, black granite marks the foundation remains from the second Abitation de Champlain. These vestiges were discovered in 1976.

Initially dedicated to the Baby Jesus, it was rechristened Notre-Dame-de-la-Victoire after Admiral Phipp's attack of 1690 failed. It was later renamed Notre-Dame-des-Victoires (the plural) in memory of the misfortune of British Admiral Walker, whose fleet ran aground on Île-aux-Oeufs during a storm in 1711. The bombardments of the conquest left nothing standing but the walls of the church, spoiling the Levasseur's lovely interior. The church was restored in 1766, but was not fully rebuilt until the current steeple was added in 1861. Raphaël Giroux is responsible for most of the present interior, which was undertaken between 1854 and 1857, but the strange "fortress" tabernacle of the main altar is a later work by David Ouellet (1878). Lastly, in 1888, Jean Tardivel painted the historical scenes on the vault and on the wall of the chancel. What are most striking, though, are the various pieces in the church: the *ex-voto* (an offering) that hangs from the centre of the vault depicting the *Brézé*, a ship that came to Canada in 1664 carrying soldiers of the Carignan Regiment; and the beautiful tabernacle in the Sainte-Geneviève chapel, attributed to Pierre-Noël Levasseur (circa 1730). Among the paintings are

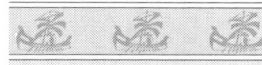

Vaults

The houses in Vieux-Québec often had vaulted cellars to support the building and were used to keep the food and drink cool. Some of these cellars have survived the times and you can visit them to day. Maison Fornel, which houses the Association Québec-France on Place-Royale, opens its vaults to visitors (9am to 4pm) and even presents small exhibitions. The entrances are at 25 Rue Saint-Pierre and 9 Place-Royale.

works by Boyermans and Van Loo, originally from the collection of Abbot Desjardins.

Under the French Regime, the square attracted many merchants and ship owners who commissioned the building of attractive residences. The tall house on the southwest corner of the square and on Rue de la Place, **Maison Barbel**, was built in 1754 for the formidable businesswoman Anne-Marie Barbel, widow of Louis Fornel. At the time, she owned a pottery factory on Rivière Saint-Charles and held the lease on the lucrative trading post at Tadoussac.

Maison Dumont *(1 Place-Royale)* was designed in 1689 by the tireless Claude Baillif for the vintner Eustache Lambert Dumont. The house incorporated elements of the old store of the Compagnie des Habitants (1647). Visitors can see its huge vaulted basement now used, as it was in the past, to store casks and bottles of wine. Turned into an inn in the 19th century, the house was the favourite stopping place of U.S. President Howard Taft (1857-1930) on his way to his annual summer vacation in La Malbaie.

Maison Bruneau-Rageot-Drapeau, at number 3A, is a house built in 1763 using the walls of the old Nicolas Jérémie house. Jérémie was a Montagnais interpreter and a clerk at the fur-trading posts of Hudson Bay.

Maison Paradis, on Rue Notre-Dame, houses the **Atelier du Patrimoine Vivant** *(free admission; late Jun to mid-Oct, every day 10am to 5pm; 42 Rue Notre-Dame, ☎647-1598)*. In these studios, various artisans hone their skills using traditional methods.

If you continue on Rue Notre-Dame towards Côte de la Montagne and then turn around, you will be surprised by the coloured spectacle. On the blind wall of Maison Soumande, in front of Parc de la Cetière, the colours of the **Fresque des Québécois** ★★ are displayed. In fact, if they're not careful, passersby may actually miss the fresco: it is a *trompe l'œil*. A team of French and Québec artists created this fresco with the guidance of specialists (historians, geographers, etc.) who made sure the painting was realistic and instructive. They brought together on 420m^2 Québec City's architecture and famous sites such as the Cap Diamant, the ramparts, a bookshop, houses of Vieux-Québec, in short, different places that the town's inhabitants encounter every day. Just like the crowd of admiring onlookers that gathers rain or shine, you can amuse yourself for quite a while trying to identify the historical figures and the role they played. From top to bottom and from left to right, you will see Marie Guyart, Catherine de Longpré, François-Xavier Garneau, Louis-Joseph Papineau, Jean Talon, le Comte de Frontenac, Marie Fitzbach, Marcelle Mallet, Louis Jolliet, Alphonse Desjardins,

Lord Dufferin, Félix Leclerc and finally, Samuel de Champlain, with whom it all started.

Return to Place-Royale and visit the **Centre d'Interprétation de Place-Royale** ★★ *($3, $11 ticket includes admission to Musée de la Civilisation and Musée de l'Amérique Française; end of Oct to end of Jun Tue to Sun 10am to 5pm, end of Jun to end of Oct every day 10am to 5pm; 27 Rue Notre-Dame, ☎646-3167, www.mcq.org)*, which was inaugurated in the fall of 1999. To accommodate the centre, both the Hazeur and Smith houses, which had burned down, were rebuilt in a modern style while using a large portion of the original materials. The omnipresent glass lets you admire the exposed rooms as well as the buildings' architecture from all angles. Along by the glass walls between the two houses, a stairway goes down Côte de la Montagne to Place-Royale. From the staircase, you can see some of the centre's treasures. On each of the three levels, an exhibition presents a chapter of Place-Royale's history. There are also artifacts that were discovered during archaeological digs under the square. Whether they are whole objects or tiny pieces that are difficult to identify, they are all instructive. You can also watch a multimedia show and admire scale models such as the one representing the second Abitation de Champlain in 1635.

You will learn, among other things, that the first hotel to be established in Québec City was opened in 1648 by a Mr. Boidon, a fated name (*Bois donc* means "have a drink!"). The hotel tradition continued on Place-Royale until

Rue des Pain-Bénits

If you visit the city during the holidays, consider making a visit to Place-Royale, especially on January 3. This is the feast day of Saint Geneviève, patron saint of the chapel adjoining Église Notre-Dame-des-Victoires. Every year since the colony was established, blessed bread rolls are distributed to the people to celebrate this event. The little street that runs along the east side of the church is called Rue des Pains-Bénits. While eating your bread, take a look at the nativity scene inside the church.

the middle of the 20 century when the last hotel was destroyed by fire. Visitors had been welcomed, lodged and nourished there for 300 years.

In the basement, the vaults of the house are transformed into a playroom where young and old can dress up as one of the former occupants. A great (and original) idea!

Continue along Rue de la Place until it opens onto Place de Paris.

Place de Paris ★ *(along Rue du Marché-Finlay)* is an elegant and sophisticated mix of contemporary art and traditional surroundings conceived by Québécois architect Jean Jobin in 1987. A large sculpture by French artist Jean-Pierre Raynault dominates the centre of the square. The work was presented by Jacques Chirac, the mayor of Paris, on behalf of his city, when he visisted Québec City. Entitled *Dialogue avec l'Histoire* (Dialogue with History), the black granite and white marble work is said to evoke the first human presence in the area and forms a pair with the bust of Louis XIV, visible in the background. Québécois have dubbed it the Colossus of Québec because of its imposing dimensions. From the square, which was once a market, there is a splendid view of the Batterie Royale, the Château Frontenac and the St. Lawrence River.

Entrepôt Thibaudeau *(215 Rue du Marché-Finlay)* is a huge building whose stone facade fronts onto Rue Dalhousie. It represents the last prosperous days of the area before its decline at the end of the 19th century. The Second Empire building is distinguished by its mansard roof and by its segmental arch openings. It was built in 1880, following the plans of Joseph-Ferdinand Peachy, for Isidore Thibaudeau, president and founder of the Banque Nationale and importer of European novelties.

Head back up the street towards Rue Saint-Pierre and turn right.

Further along at number 92 is yet another imposing merchant's house, **Maison Estèbe** (1752). It is now part of the Musée de la Civilisation, whose smooth stone walls can be seen along the Rue Saint-Pierre. Guillaume Estèbe was a businessman and the director of the Saint-Maurice ironworks at Trois-Rivières. Having participated in a number of unsavoury schemes with Intendant Bigot during the Seven Years' War, he was locked-up in the Bastille for a few months on embezzlement charges. The house, where he lived for five years with his wife and 14 children, is built on an embankment that used to front onto a large private wharf corresponding today to the courtyard of the museum. The courtyard is accessible through the gateway on the left. The 21-room interior escaped the bombardments of 1759. Some of the rooms feature handsome Louis XV woodwork. On the corner of Rue Saint-Jacques is the old **Banque de Québec** building (Edward Staveley, architect, 1861). Across the street, the old **Banque Molson** occupies an 18th-century house.

Turn right onto Rue Saint-Jacques. The entrance to the Musée de la Civilisation is on Rue Dalhousie, on the right.

The **Musée de la Civilisation** ★★ *($7; $11 package with Musée de l'Amérique Française and Centre d'Interprétation de la Place-Royale; Tue free admission, except in summer; late Jun to early Sep, every day 10am to 7pm; early Sep to late Jun, every day 10am to 5pm; 85 Rue Dalhousie, ☎643-2158, ≠646-9705, www.mcq.org)* is housed in a building, completed in 1988, in the traditional architectured style of Québec City, with its stylized roof, dormer windows and a belltower like those common to the area. Architect Moshe Safdie, who also designed the revolutionary Habitat '67 in Montreal, Ottawa's National Gallery and Vancouver's Public Library, designed a sculptural building with a monumental exterior staircase at its centre. The lobby provides a charming view of Maison Estèbe and its wharf while preserving a contemporary look that is underlined by Astri Reuch's sculpture, **La Débâcle**.

The Musée de la Civilisation presents a great variety of temporary exhibitions. Themes such as humour, circus and song, for example, have been the object of very lively displays. Travelling exhibitions also tell about the world's great civilizations, while permanent exhibitions provide a portrait of civilizations from the region. "Mémoires" recounts the history of the Québec people; "Grandir" is about children; "Nous les Premières Nations," developed in collaboration with First Nations peoples, is a large exhibition tracing the history of the 11 nations that originally inhabited Québec. You can view many objects as well as audiovisual materials such as the work of filmmaker Arthur Lamothe. Some of the more remarkable items are the Aboriginal artifacts, the large French Regime fishing craft unearthed during excavations for the museum itself, some highly ornate 19th-century horse-drawn hearses, and some Chinese objets d'art and pieces of furniture, including an imperial bed, from the collection of the Jesuits. You can also visit the museum's vaulted cellar, which dates from the 18th century.

Explore - Son et Lumière *($6.25; Jun to end of Sep every day 10am to 5pm; spring and fall, every day 10am to 5pm; 63 Rue Dalhousie, ☎692-2175)* uses multimedia technology to recount the voyages of such great European explorers of the Americas as Cartier and Champlain.

Head northeast, towards the Vieux Port, through Rue Dalhousie.

Beside the Musée de la Civilisation is a lavish beaux-arts fire station dating from 1912 that now houses **Ex Machina**, a multi-disciplinary artistic production centre founded by Robert Lepage. Note the high tower with a copper dome rising on the southeast corner like a church spire, which was inspired by the tower of the Hôtel du Parlement. Firemen used to hang up their hoses in the tower to dry and to prevent them from damage since in those days hoses were made out of fabric. The building has been expanded and in order to keep its character, a false wall similar to the original stone wall – but made of plastic – has been erected in front of the new part.

Vieux-Port ★ *(160 Rue Dalhousie).* The old port is often criticized for being overly American in a city with European sensibility. It was refurbished by the Canadian government on the occasion of the maritime celebration, "Québec 1534-1984." There are various metallic structures designed to enliven the promenade, at the end of which is the handsome **Édifice de la Douane** (1856), the old customs building, designed by William Thomas of Toronto.

The entire port area between Place-Royale and the entrance of **Bassin Louise** is known as **Pointe-à-Carcy**. At the beginning of the year 2000, the Commission du Vieux-Port started a new phase to renovate completely Pointe-à-Carcy and turn it into a veritable harbour for pleasure boats

An **Économusée de la Bière** *(free admission; $5 tours with sampling, every day noon to 3pm; 37 Quai Saint-André, ☎692-2877)* has been set up in an established Vieux-Port bar, L'Inox. By reading the information panels on the walls, you will learn more about the long and glorious history of beer. You can also discover the secrets of beer-brewing by taking a guided tour. Since L'Inox is a micro-brewery it is possible to have the master brewer take you behind the scenes which are visible from the bar through a glass wall (reservations are necessary). And not only will he explain how he makes the beer, he will offer you a taste of his work.

Place de la FAO is located at the intersection of Rue Saint-Pierre, Saint-Paul and Sault-au-Matelot. This square honours the United Nations Food and Agriculture Organisation whose first meeting was held at the Château Frontenac in 1945. The sculpture at the centre of the square represents the prow of a boat as it emerges from the waves, its female figurehead, *La Vivrière*, firmly grasping all kinds of fruit, vegetables and grains.

In the square at the corner of Rue Saint-Pierre stands an imposing building with a large round portico which formerly housed the **Imperial Bank of Commerce**. Today it houses the Le Portal art gallery.

Take Rue Sault-au-Matelot to Rue de la Barricade. This street is named in honour of the barricade set up against invading revolutionaries coming from what was to become the United States. They attempted to take Québec City on December 31, 1775.

On the right, Rue de la Barricade leads to **Rue Piétonnière Sous-le-Cap**. This narrow passage was once wedged between the St. Lawrence and Cap Diamant escarpment. At the end of the 19th century, the street housed working-class families of Irish origin. Today's inhabitants, finding the houses too small, have renovated the little cottages on the side of the cliff and connected them to their houses by walkways crossing the street at clothesline height. One almost enters Rue Sous-le-Cap on tiptoe because of the feeling that you're walking into another world. At the end of the street is Côte du Colonel-Dambourgès and then Rue Saint-Paul.

Rue Saint-Paul is a most pleasant street, lined with antique shops overflowing with beautiful Québec heritage furniture.

To get to the Centre d'Interprétation du Vieux-Port-de-Québec, take Rue Rioux or

Rue des Navigateurs which both meet up with Rue Quai Saint-André.

Old Port of Quebec Interpretation Centre *($3; May 3 to Sep 3 every day 10am to 5pm, Sep 3 to Oct 8 1pm to 5pm, rest of the year open for groups with reservations; 100 Rue Saint-André, ☎648-3300).* In the days of sailboats, Québec City was one of the most important gateways to America, since many vessels could not make their way any farther against the current. Its bustling port was surrounded by shipyards that made great use of plentiful and high-quality Canadian lumber. The first royal shipyards appeared under the French Regime in the cove known as l'Anse du Cul-de-Sac. The Napoleonic blockade of 1806 forced the British to turn to their Canadian colony for wood and for the construction of battleships. This gave the impetus to a number of shipyards and made fortunes for a number of their owners. The interprative centre at this national historic site concentrates on these flourishing days of navigation in Québec.

Marché du Vieux-Port ★ *(corner of Rue Saint-Thomas and Rue Saint-André).* Most of Québec City's public markets were shut down in the 1960s because they had become obsolete in an age of air-conditioned supermarkets and frozen food. However, people continued to want fruit and vegetables fresh from the farm as well as the contact with the farmers. Moreover, the market was one of the only non-aseptic places people could congregate. Thus, the markets gradually began to reappear at the beginning of the '80s. Marché du Vieux-Port was built in 1987 by the architectural partners Belzile, Brassard, Galienne and Lavoie. It is the successor to two other markets, Finlay and Champlain, that no longer exist. In the summer, the market is a pleasant place to stroll and take in the view of the Marina Bassin Louise at the edge of the market.

Walk back towards Rue Saint-Paul, and continue on to the corner of Rue Saint-Nicolas in the heart of the Palais quarter on either side of Palais de l'Intendant.

For over 50 years, the citizens of Québec City clamoured for a train station worthy of their city. Canadian Pacific finally fulfilled their wish in 1915. Designed by New York architect Harry Edward Prindle in the same style as the Château Frontenac, the **Gare du Palais** ★ *(Rue de la Gare)* gives visitors a taste of the romance and charm that await in Québec City. The 18m-high arrival hall that extends behind the giant window of the facade is bathed by sunlight passing through the leaded glass skylight of the roof. The faïence tiles and multicoloured bricks in the walls lend a striking aspect to the whole. The station was closed for almost 10 years (from 1976 to 1985) at the time when railway companies were imitating airlines and moving their stations to the suburbs. Fortunately, it was reopened, with great pomp, and now houses the bus and train stations. The building on the right is Raoul Chênevert's 1938 post office. It illustrates the persistence of the Château style of architecture that is so emblematic of the city.

L'Îlot Saint-Nicolas *(Rue Saint-Paul at the corner of Rue Saint-Nicolas).* The block bordered by Ruelle de l'Ancien-Chantier, Rue Saint-Vallier Est, Rue Saint-Paul and Rue Saint-Nicolas is known as l'Îlot Saint Nicolas. It was restored with verve by architects De Blois, Côté, Leahy.

The handsome stone building on the corner and the two others behind it on Rue Saint-Nicolas housed the famous **Cabaret Chez Gérard** from 1938 to 1978. It was here that Charles Trenet, Rina Ketty and many other famous French singers performed. Charles Aznavour actually got his start here. In the bohemian days of the 1950s, he sang here every night for many months for a mere pittance.

The big Scottish-brick building with the pinnacle inscribed "**Les Maisons Lecourt**" was put up across from l'Îlot Saint-Nicolas using the remnants of Intendant Bigot's "royal store." Nicknamed *La Fripone* (The Rogue's) because of the extortionary prices exacted from the miserable populace by Bigot and his accomplices, the location was one of only two in the city during the French Regime where one could moor a boat (the other being l'Anse du Cul-de-Sac). In the 17th century, warehouses and wharfs were built along the estuary of the Saint-Charles, as was a shipyard with a drydock that bequeathed the street its name, Rue de l'Ancien-Chantier, meaning "old shipyard."

Gare du Palais

Walk back up Rue Saint-Nicolas, turn right on Rue Saint-Vallier Est, and take the pedestrian path on the right.

The **Site du Palais de l'Intendant** ★ and the **Centre d'Interprétation Archéologique** are part of **l'Îlot des Palais** *(free admission; end of Jun to early Sep, and every day 10am to 5pm, rest of the year with reservations only; 8 Rue Vallière, ☎691-6092)* and the **Site Archéologique des Voûtes du Palais**, (the palace vaults archeological site). The intendant oversaw the day-to-day affairs of the colony. The royal stores, the few state enterprises and the prison were located near his residence. With so many opportunities to make himself rich, it was only natural that his should be the most splendid mansion in New France. The remains of one wing of the palace can still be seen in the shape of the segment of brown brick foundation wall that is now aboveground. The location was originally that of the brewery set up by the first intendant, Jean Talon (1625-1694). Talon took great effort to populate and develop the colony. For his trouble, he was made secretary of the king's cabinet upon his return to France. His brewery was replaced by a palace designed by engineer La Guer Morville in 1716. This elegant building had a classical entrance in cut stone that gave onto a horseshoe-shaped staircase. Twenty or so ceremonial rooms, arranged in a row one after the other, served for receptions and for the meetings of the Conseil Supérieur.

The palace was spared British cannon-fire only to be burned to the ground during the American invasion of 1775-76. The arches of its cellars were used as the foundation of the Boswell brewery in 1872, bringing the site full circle. Visitors are free to inspect the cellars, where the **Centre d'Interprétation Archéologique** (archeological information centre) is located. The centre displays artifacts and ruins of the site itself.

To return to Haute-Ville, climb Côte du Palais at the end of Rue Saint-Nicolas.

Tour C: Grande Allée

(one day)

Grande Allée appears on 17th-century maps, but it was not built up until the first half of the 19th century, when the city grew

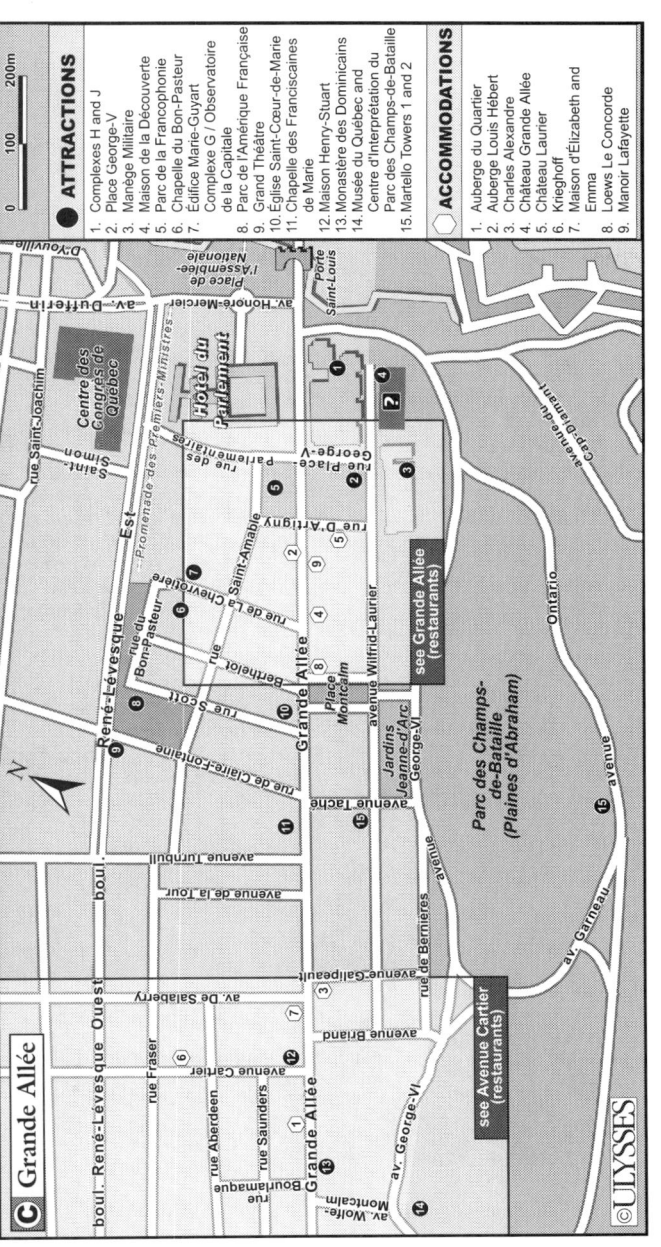

beyond its walls. Grande Allée was originally a country road linking the town to Chemin du Roi and thence to Montréal. At that time, it was bordered by the large agricultural properties of the nobility and clergy of the French Regime. After the British Conquest, many of the domains were turned into country estates by English merchants who set their manors well back from the road. The neoclassical town then spilled over into the area before the Victorian city had a chance to stamp the landscape with its distinctive style. Today's Grande Allée is the most pleasant route into the downtown area and the focus of extramural Haute-Ville. Although it links the capital's various ministries, it is a cheery street, as many of the bourgeois houses on it have been converted into restaurants and bars.

This walking tour starts at Porte Saint-Louis and gradually works its way from the walled city.

On the right is Paul Chevré's monument to historian François-Xavier Garneau. On the left is the *Croix du Sacrifice* where Remembrance Day services are held every year on November 11.

The **Hôtel du Parlement** ★★★ *(free admission; guided tours late Jun to early Sep Mon to Fri 9am and 4:30pm, Sat to Sun 10am to 4:30pm; early Sep to Jun, Mon to Fri, 9am to 4:30pm; at the corner of Honoré-Mercier and Grande Allée Est,* ☎*643-7239)* is known to Québécois as l'Assemblée Nationale, the National Assembly. The seat of the government of Québec, this imposing building was

Assemblée Nationale

erected between 1877 and 1886. It has a lavish French Renaissance Revival exterior intended to reflect the unique cultural status of Québec in the North American context. Eugène-Étienne Taché (1836-1912) looked to the Louvre for his inspiration in both the plan of the quadrangular building and its decor. Originally destined to incorporate the two houses of parliament characteristic of the British system of government, as well as all of the ministries, it is today part of a group of buildings on either side of Grande Allée.

The numerous statues of the parliament's main facade constitute a sort of pantheon of Québec. The 22 bronzes of important figures in the history of the nation were cast by such well-known artists as Louis-Philippe Hébert and Alfred Laliberté. A raised inscription on the wall near the central passage identifies the statues. In front of the main entrance a bronze by Hébert entitled *La Halte dans la Forêt* (The Pause in the Forest) depicts an Aboriginal family. The work, which is meant to honour the original inhabitants of Québec, was displayed at Paris's World's Fair in 1889. *Le Pêcheur à la Nigog* (Fisherman at the Nigog), by the same artist, hangs in the niche by the fountain.

Halte dans la Forêt (Hébert)

The building's interior is a veritable compendium of the icons of Québec's history. The handsome woodwork is in the tradition of religious architecture.

The members of parliament called *députés*, sit in the National Assembly, or Salon Bleu (Blue Chamber), where Charles Huot's painting, *La Première Séance de l'Assemblée Législative du Bas-Canada en 1792* (The First Session of the Legislative Assembly of Lower Canada in 1792), hangs over the chair of the president of the Assembly. A large work by the same artist covers the ceiling and evokes the motto of Québec, *Je me souviens* (I remember). The Salon Rouge (Red Chamber), intended for the Conseil Législatif, an unelected body eliminated in 1968, is now used for parliamentary commissions. A painting entitled *Le Conseil Souverain* (The Sovereign

Council), a reminder of the mode of government in the days of New France, graces this chamber.

Several of the windows of the parliament building boast gorgeous Art Nouveau stained glass by master glazier Henri Perdriau, a native of Saint-Pierre de Montélimar in Vendée, France. Undeniably, the most spectacular is the arch that adorns the entrance to the elegant Le Parlementaire restaurant (see p 224). This feature was designed by architect Omer Marchand in 1917. National Assembly debates are open to the public, but a pass is required.

In the Parc de l'Hôtel du Parlement, there are two important monuments: one in honour of Honoré Mercier, premier of Québec from 1887 to 1891, and the other in honour of Maurice Duplessis, premier during the *grande noirceur* or "great darkness" (1936-1939 and 1944-1959), as well as the one representing René Lévesque, who holds a special place in the hearts of Québécois and who was the premier from 1976 to 1985.

As you pass the front of the Assemblée Nationale, notice beautiful Avenue Honoré-Mercier, which was recently redesigned. On the other side, many events are hosted on Place du Parlement throughout the year. In July, a stage is erected for the Summer Festival and in February, the Ice Palace, the focus of carnival festivities, is located here.

The dizzying growth of the civil service during the Quiet Revolution of the 1960s compelled the government to construct several modern buildings to house its various ministries. A row of beautiful Second Empire houses was demolished to make way for *Complexes H and J (on Grande Allée opposite the Hôtel du Parlement)*. Dubbed "the bunker" by the Québécois, Pierre Saint-Gelais's 1970 building houses the premier's office.

Take Grande Allée westward, leaving Vieux-Québec. On the left you will come to Rue Place-George-V which runs along the square of the same name. Take this street to Avenue Wilfrid-Laurier.

Place George V and the **Manège Militaire** ★ *(Avenue Wilfrid-Laurier)*. This expanse of lawn is used as the training area and parade ground of the military's equestrians. There are cannons and a statue in memory of the two soldiers who perished attempting to douse the flames of the 1889 fire in the suburb of Saint-Sauveur. Otherwise, the grounds serve mainly to highlight the amusing Château-style facade of the Manège Militaire, (military riding academy), built in 1888 and designed by Eugène-Étienne Taché, who also designed the Hôtel du Parlement.

The Centre d'Interprétation du Parc des Champs-de-Bataille is on Avenue Wilfrid-Laurier behind the H and J Buildings, which border the Plains of Abraham. Newly opened in one of the Citadelle buildings, **Maison de la Découverte** ★ *(835 Avenue Wilfrid-Laurier, G1R 2L3, ☎649-6157)* should please Québec City natives as much as visitors. Upstairs, at the Office du Tourisme de la Communauté Urbaine de Québec, travellers can get help finding their way around. And on the ground floor, questions are answered about the Parc des Champs-de-Bataille, its history and the many activities that go on here. There are also a few services and an entrance to the Plains of Abraham. Various guided tours leave from here. One of them takes place on board the "Bus d'Abraham" guided by Abraham Martin in person!

Go back towards Grande Allée.

Parc de la Francophonie *(between Rue Saint-Augustin and Rue d'Artigny)* and **Complexe G**, which appears in the background, both occupy the site of the old Saint-Louis quarter, today almost entirely vanished. Parc de la Francophonie was laid out for open-air shows. It also takes the name Le Pigeonnier, (dovecote) from the interesting concrete structure placed in the middle, based on an idea by landscape architects Schreiber and Williams, in 1973.

Continue west on Grande Allée, along the liveliest section.

A little further to the west, the fabric of the old city is again in evidence. **Terrasse Stadacona** *(numbers 640 to 664)*, on the right, is a neoclassical row of townhouses on the English model: the multiple houses share a common facade. These houses date from 1847 and have been turned into bars and restaurants with terraces sheltered by multitudes of parasols. Opposite *(numbers 661 to 695)* is a group of Second Empire houses that dates from 1882, a period when Grande Allée was the fashionable street in Québec City. These houses show the influence of the parliamentary buildings on the residential architecture of the quarter. Three other houses on Grande Allée are worth mentioning for the eclecticism of their facades: **Maison du Manufacturier de Chaussures W. A. Marsh** *(number 625)*, house of a prominent shoe manufacturer, designed in 1899 by Toronto architect Charles John Gibson; **Maison Garneau-Meredith** *(numbers 600 to 614)* of the same year; and **Maison William Price**, a little Romeo-and-Juliet-style place which is, unfortunately, dwarfed by the hotel **Le Concorde**. The revolving restaurant (see p 230) of this hotel affords a magnificent view of Haute-Ville and the Plains of Abraham (see p 130).

In little **Parc Montcalm**, next to the hotel, is a statue commemorating the general's death on September 13, 1759, at the Battle of the Plains of Abraham. The **statue of French General Charles de Gaulle** (1890-1970), which faces away from Montcalm, created quite a controversy when it was erected in the spring of 1997. Farther along, at the entrance to the Plains of Abraham, **Jardin Jeanne-d'Arc** boasts magnificent flowerbeds and a statue of Joan of Arc astride a spirited charger. Note that you are now standing on a huge drinking-water reservoir located under this part of the Plains of Abraham!

Return to Grande Allée and go east, then turn left on Rue de La Chevrotière.

Behind the austere facade of the mother house of the Soeurs du Bon-Pasteur, a community devoted to the education of abandoned and delinquent girls, is the charming, Baroque Revival-style **Chapelle du Bon-Pasteur** ★★ *(free admission; Jul and Aug Tue to Sat, 1:30pm to 4:30pm; 1080 Rue de la Chevrotière)*. Designed by Charles Baillargé in 1866, this tall, narrow chapel houses an authentic baroque tabernacle dating from 1730. Pierre-Noël Levasseur's masterpiece of New France carving is surrounded by devotional miniatures hung on pilasters by the nuns.

Atop the 31 storeys of **Édifice Marie-Guyart** in Complexe G, the **Observatoire de la Capitale** *($4; Jun to Sep every day 10am to 7pm, Jul and Aug 10am to 10pm, Oct to May every day 10am to 5pm; 1037 Rue De La Chevrotière, ☎644-9841)*, provides a splendid view of Québec City and the surrounding area. At 221m in altitude, it is the highest observation point in the city. For an even better view, use the telescopes.

Go back and turn a right on Rue Saint-Amable. Walk as far as Parc de l'Amérique Française.

The **Parc de l'Amérique Française** is a fairly recent creation. It faces the head office of the Laurentien Insurance Company and is centered around a collection of flags of the various francophone communities of America.

The **Grand Théâtre** *(269 Boulevard René-Lévesque Est, ☎643-8131)* is located at the far end of the park. Inaugurated in 1971, the theatre of Polish architect Victor Prus was to be a meeting place for members of Québec City's high society. There was quite a scandal, therefore, when Jordi Bonet's mural was unveiled and the assembled crowd read the lines from a poem by Claude Péloquin: *"Vous êtes pas tannés de mourir, bande de caves,"* (Aren't you suckers tired of dying?). The theatre has two halls (Louis-Fréchette and Octave-Crémazie) and presents symphony orchestra concerts as well as theatre, dance and variety shows.

Go back as far as Rue Scott where you turn right to return to Grande Allée.

Église Saint-Cœur de Marie *(530 Grande Allée Est)* was built for the Eudists in 1919 and designed by Ludger Robitaille. It looks more martial than devotional because of its bartizans, machicolations and towers. Its large archways are reminiscent of a Mediterranean fortress. Across the road is the most outlandish row of Second Empire houses still standing in Québec City *(455-555 Grande Allée Est)*, **Terrasse Frontenac**. The product of Joseph-Ferdinand Peachy's imagination (1895), its slender, fantastical peaks look like something from a fairy tale

Chapelle des Franciscaines de Marie ★ is the chapel of a community of nuns devoted to serving God. They commissioned the Sanctuaire de l'Adoration Perpétuelle (Sanctuary of Perpetual Adoration) in 1901. This exuberant Baroque Revival chapel invites the faithful to prayer and celebrates the everlasting presence of God. It features a small columned cupola supported by angels and a sumptuous marble baldaquin.

Several handsome, bourgeois houses dating from the early 20th century face the chapel. Among them, at numbers 433-435, is the residence of John Holt, proprietor of the Holt Renfrew stores. Both this and the neighbouring house, number 425, are designed like Scottish manors. Undeniably the most elegant in its mild Flemish and Oriental eclecticism is the house of Judge P. A. Choquette, designed by architect Georges-Émile Tanguay.

Maison Henry-Stuart

($5; end of Jun to early Sep, every day 11am to 5pm; Sep to Jun, Sun 1pm to 5pm; guided tours 11am, noon, 1pm, 2pm, 3pm, 4pm in the summer; winter Sun 1pm, 2pm, 3pm, 4pm; 82 Grande Allée Ouest and Avenue Cartier, ☎647-4347), on the corner of Cartier and Grande Allée, is one of the few remaining Regency style Anglo-Norman cottages in Québec City. This type of colonial British architecture is distinguished by a large pavilion roof overhanging a low veranda surrounding the building. The house was built in 1849 and used to mark the border between city and country; its original garden still surrounds it. The interior features several pieces of furniture from the Saint-Jean-Port-Joli manor and has been practically untouched since 1911. More or less closed to the public for a number of years, Maison Henry-Stuart and its garden, which belongs to the organisation "Jardins du Québec," now welcome

Maison Henry-Stuart

visitors. The house is home to the Conseil des Monuments et Sites de Québec. Tea is now served here on summer afternoons.

Avenue Cartier is one of the most attractive shopping streets in town. The main artery of the Montcalm residential neighbourhood, it is lined with restaurants, shops and specialty food stores that attract the yuppie clientele strolling around here.

In the area of the American-style **Maison Pollack** *(1 Grande Allée Ouest)* is the Renaissance Revival **Maison des Dames Protestantes** *(111 Grande Allée Ouest)*, built in 1862 by architect

Michel Lecourt. Also nearby is **Maison Krieghoff** *(115 Grande-Allée Ouest)*, which was occupied in 1859 by the Dutch painter Cornelius Krieghoff.

Monastère des Dominicains ★ *(175 Grande Allée Ouest, closed to the public)* and its church are relatively recent realizations that testify to the persistence and historical exactitude of 20th century Gothic Revival architecture. This sober British-style building promotes reverence and meditation.

Turn left on Avenue Wolfe-Montcalm the entrance to both Parc Champs-de-Bataille and the Musée du Québec.

Located at the roundabout is the **Monument to General Wolfe**, victor of the decisive Battle of the Plains of Abraham. It is said to stand on the exact spot where he fell. The 1832 monument has been the object of countless demonstrations and acts of vandalism. Toppled again in 1963, it was rebuilt, this time with an inscription in French.

The **Musée du Québec** ★★★ *($7; early Jun to early Sep, every day 10am to 5:45pm, Wed to 9:45pm; early Sep to late May, Tue to Sun 11am to 5:45pm, Wed to 8:45pm; Parc des Champs de Bataille, ☎644-6460, ≈646-3330, www.mdq.org)* was renovated and expanded in 1992. The older, west-facing 1933 Classical revival building is on the right. The entrance, parallel to Avenue Wolfe-Montcalm, is dominated by a glass tower similar to that of the Musée de la Civilisation. The first building is subterraneously linked with the old prison on the left. The latter has been cleverly restored to house exhibits and has been rebaptized Édifice Ballairgé in honour of its architect. Some of the cells have been preserved.

A visit to this important museum allows one to become acquainted with the painting, sculpture and silverwork of Québec from

Musée du Québec

the time of New France to today. The museum recently inaugurated a gallery (Salle 3) in honour of painter Jean-Paul Riopelle in which his huge mural (42m) *Hommage à Rosa Luxembourg* is installed. The collections of religious art gathered from Québec's rural parishes are particularly interesting. Also on display are official documents, including the original surrender of Québec (1759). The museum frequently hosts temporary exhibits from the United States and Europe. Many cultural activities are held here, such as conferences, films and concerts.

On the first floor of the museum's Édifice Baillargé is the **Centre d'Interprétation du Parc des Champs-de-Bataille Nationaux (National Battlefield Park Interpretive Centre)** *($2; mid-May to early Sep, every day 10am to 5:30pm, early Sep to mid-May, Tue to Sun 11am to 5:30pm; Édifice Baillargé, level 1, ☎648-5641)*, which exhibits a reconstruction of the Battle of the Plains of Abraham and a model of the subsequent development of the area through a multi-media show.

Turn left on Avenue Georges VI and right on Avenue Garneau.

Parc des Champs-de-Bataille ★★★ *(free admission; ☎648-4071)* takes visitors back to July 1759: commanded by General Wolfe, the British fleet arrives in front of Québec City. The attack is launched almost immediately. Almost 40,000 cannonballs crash down on the besieged city. As the summer draws to a close, the British must come to a decision before they are surprised by French reinforcements or trapped in the December freeze-up. On the 13th of September, under cover of night, British troops scale the Cap Diamant escarpment west of the fortifications. The ravines which here and there cut into the otherwise uniform mass of the escarpment allow them to climb and to remain concealed. By morning, the troops have taken position in the fields of **Abraham Martin**, hence the name of the battlefield and the park. The French are surprised, as they had anticipated a direct attack on the citadel. Their troops, with the aid of a few hundred Aboriginal warriors, throw themselves against the British. The generals of both sides are slain, and the battle draws to a close in bloody chaos. New France is lost!

Parc des Champs-de-Bataille, where the battle took place, was created in 1908 to commemorate the event. At 101ha, the park is a superb recreational space. Previously occupied by a military training ground, the Ursulines and a few farms, the park was laid out between 1929 and 1939 by landscape architect Frederick Todd. This project provided work for thousands of Québécois during the Depression. Today, the plains are a large green space crisscrossed by paths for all kinds of winter and summer activities. You will find beautiful landscaping here as well as historical and cultural sites such as the **Kiosque Edwin-Bélanger**, which presents outdoor entertainment. At the park's eastern entrance, Maison de la Découverte (see p 125) presents a good introduction to the Plains: various exhibitions and activities interpret its history and natural environment.

Tour Martello

The **Tours Martello no.1 and no. 2** ★ *($3.50 for no. 1; no. 2 closed to the public; mid-Jun to early Sep every day 10am to 5:30pm, Sat and Sun Jun to Sep and Oct to Thanksgiving 11am to 5:30pm)*, are characteristic of British defenses at the beginning of the 19th century. Tower number 1 (1808) is visible on the edge of Avenue Ontario; number 2 (1815) blends into the surrounding buildings on the corner of Avenue Laurier and Avenue Taché. Inside the first one, an exhibition recounts some of the military strategies used in the 19th century.

*This is the end of the Grande Allée walking tour. To return to the walled city, follow Avenue Ontario east to Avenue Georges VI or take Avenue du Cap-Diamant (in the hilly part of the park) to **Promenade des Gouverneurs**. The promenade follows the citadel and overlooks the Cap Diamant escarpment, winding up at Terrasse Dufferin. This route affords stunning views of the city, the St. Lawrence River and the south shore.*

Tour D: Saint-Jean-Baptiste

(two hours)

A student hangout complete with bars, theatres and boutiques, the Saint-Jean-Baptiste quarter is perched on a hillside between Haute-Ville and Basse-Ville. The abundance of pitched and mansard roofs is reminiscent of parts of the old city, but the orthogonal layout of the streets is quintessentially North American. Despite a terrible fire in 1845, this old Québec City suburb retains several examples of wooden constructions, forbidden inside the walls of the city.

Capitole de Québec

The Saint-Jean-Baptiste tour begins at Porte Saint-Jean, near Place d'Youville. It threads along Rue Saint-Jean, the neighbourhood's main artery.

At the beginning of the 20th century, Québec City was in dire need of a new auditorium, its Académie de Musique having burnt to the ground in March 1900. With the help of private enterprise, the mayor undertook the search for a new location. The Canadian government, owner of the fortifications, offered to furnish a strip of land along the walls of the city. While narrow, the lot grew wider toward the back, permitting the construction of a fitting hall, the **Capitole de Québec** ★ *(972 Rue Saint-Jean)*. W. S. Painter, the ingenious Detroit architect already at work on the expansion of the Château Frontenac, devised a plan for a curved facade, giving the building a monumental air despite the limited size of the lot. Inaugurated in 1903 as the Auditorium de Québec, the building is one of the most impressive beaux-arts realizations in the country.

In 1927, the famous American cinema architect Thomas W. Lamb converted the auditorium into a sumptuous 1,700-seat cinema. Renamed the Théâtre Capitole, the auditorium nevertheless served as a venue for shows until the

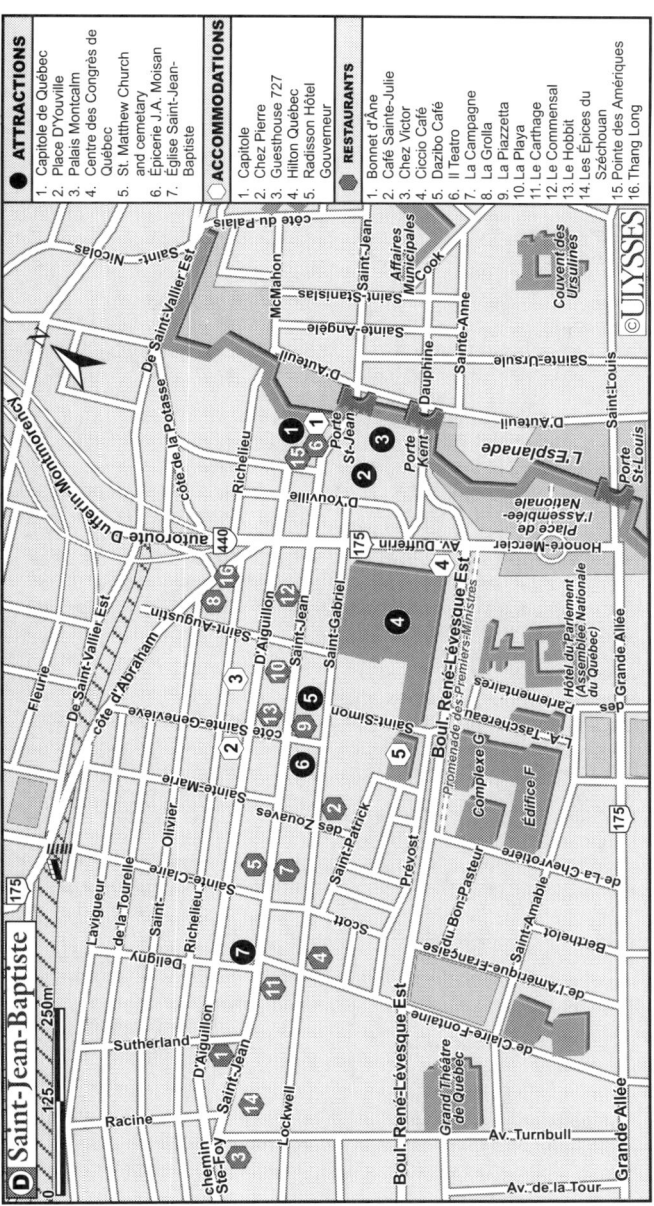

construction of the Grand Théâtre in 1971. Abandoned for a few years, the Capitole was entirely refurbished in 1992 by architect Denis Saint-Louis. The building now houses a dinner-theatre in the hall, and a luxury hotel (see p 192) and restaurant (see p 233) in the curved facade. The Capitole has recently acquired the adjoining cinema, on front of which is an imposing round sign. The cinema has been converted into a nightclub.

Place d'Youville is the public space at the entrance of the old section of town. Formerly an important market square, it is today a bustling crossroads and cultural forum. A recent redevelopment has given the square a large promenade area with trees and benches. The counterscarp wall, part of the fortifications removed in the 20th century, has been highlighted by the use of black granite blocks. Since the end of 1999, important work has once again been carried out to transform the area surrounding the square. A large highrise hotel has been built to the northwest.

The Montcalm Market was levelled in 1932 in order to build the multifunctional space called the **Palais Montcalm** *(995 Place d'Youville)*. Also known as the Monument National, this is the venue of choice for political rallies and demonstrations of all kinds. The auditorium has a sparse architecture which draws on both neoclassical and Art Deco schools. Today, visitors come here for concerts or exhibitions.

Chapelle du Couvent des Soeurs de la Charité (1856) is visible on leaving Place d'Youville. Its delicate Gothic Revival facade is dwarfed by two huge towers.

Cross Avenue Dufferin. Higher up at the corner of Rue Saint-Joachim is a large network of buildings that includes the Centre des Congrès, the Place Québec shopping centre and the Hilton and Radisson Gouverneur hotels.

Centre des Congrès de Québec *(900 Boulevard René-Lévesque Est, 2nd floor, C.P. 37060, ☎644-4000)* was inaugurated in 1996 and is situated north of the Hôtel du Parlement. This large, modern building features glass walls that let the daylight stream in. It has an exhibition hall, several conference rooms and even a ballroom and it is connected to the Place Québec shopping centre and the Hilton and Radisson Gouverneur hotels (see p 193). Its creation has revived this previously dreary part of Boulevard

René-Lévesque (formerly Boulevard Saint-Cyrille). The wall that divided the boulevard has been taken down and trees have been planted. On the other side of the boulevard is **Promenade Desjardins**, erected in honour of Alphonse Desjardins, founder of the Caisse Populaire Desjardins. At the entrance to the Centre des Congrès is the lively sculpture *Le Quatuor d'airain*.

From Rue Saint-Joachim, take Rue Saint-Augustin, which will lead you to Rue Saint-Jean where you turn left.

There has been a cemetery on the site of the **Church and Cemetery of Saint Matthew ★** *(755 Rue Saint-Jean)* since 1771, when Protestants, whether French Hugenot, English Anglican or Scottish Presbyterian, banded together to found a Protestant graveyard. Several 19th-century tombstones are still standing. The gravestones were carefully restored recently, and the cemetery is now a public garden.

Located next to it, along Rue Saint-Jean, is a lovely Anglican church. Its Gothic Revival architecture was influenced by the Ecclesiologists, an influential school of Anglican thought that sought to re-establish ties with the traditions of the Middle Ages. In its design, and even in its materials, it looks more like an ancient village church than a Victorian church with a Gothic decor. The nave was first erected in 1848; then, in 1870, William Tutin Thomas, the Montréal architect who designed the Canadian Centre for Architecture's Shaughnessy House, drafted an enlargement, giving the church its present bell tower and interior. Québec's Anglican community dwindled in the 20th century, leading to the abandonment of the church. In 1980, it was cleverly converted into a branch of the municipal library. Several of the adornments crafted by British artists have been retained: Percy Bacon's handsome oak choir enclosure, Felix Morgan's alabaster pulpit, and Clutterbuck's beautiful stained glass. The sober vault with its exposed beams is also noteworthy.

Continue along Rue Saint-Jean.

At number 699, **Épicerie J.-A.-Moisan** *(699 Rue St-Jean)* was founded in 1871 and claims to be the "oldest grocery store in North America." It does in fact look like a general store from yesteryear, with its wooden floor and shelves, old advertisements and many tin cans. Relish the past by stocking up on its fresh, appetizing products.

The **Église Saint-Jean-Baptiste** ★ *(Rue Saint-Jean on the corner of Rue de Ligny)* stands out as Joseph Ferdinand Peachy's masterpiece. A disciple of French eclecticism, Peachy was an unconditional admirer of the Église de la Trinité in Paris. The resemblance here is striking, as much in the portico as in the interior. Completed in 1885, the building caused the bankruptcy of its architect, who was, unfortunately for him, held responsible for cracks that appeared in the facade during construction.

For a beautiful view of the city, climb the Rue Claire-Fontaine stairs up to the corner of Rue Lockwell on the right. The climb is steep but the view is worth the effort, especially in the evening when the Basse-Ville lights dance at your feet behind the imposing church. When strolling through this neighbourhood's attractive streets, you will have many opportunities to catch a glimpse of this great view. For example, you can go down Rue Sainte-Claire to the stairs leading to the Saint-Roch neighbourhood, which you will be able to see with the Laurentian mountains in the background.

Tour E: chemin Sainte-Foy

(half a day)

At the end of the 18th century, the Haute-Ville walls could no longer contain the expanding city. Suburbs were created around Saint-Jean-Baptiste church and Grande Allée. There was, however, an area that kept its pastoral charm up until the beginning of the 20th century: the farmland along an old country road, Chemin Sainte-Foy, leading to the village of the same name. Since 1950, **Sainte-Foy** has become Québec City's largest suburb. Because of its large shopping centres and exclusively low-rise housing, Sainte-Foy was known mainly as a dormitory suburb. But over the past few years, it has attempted to shed that reputation by creating civic and cultural facilities that could make more than one Québec town envious. Described for a long time as a city of "progress," it has conserved little of its past. The tour travels first through the Montcalm and Saint-Sacrement neighbourhoods where the relatively well-to-do population lives on shaded streets that at times recall the outskirts of

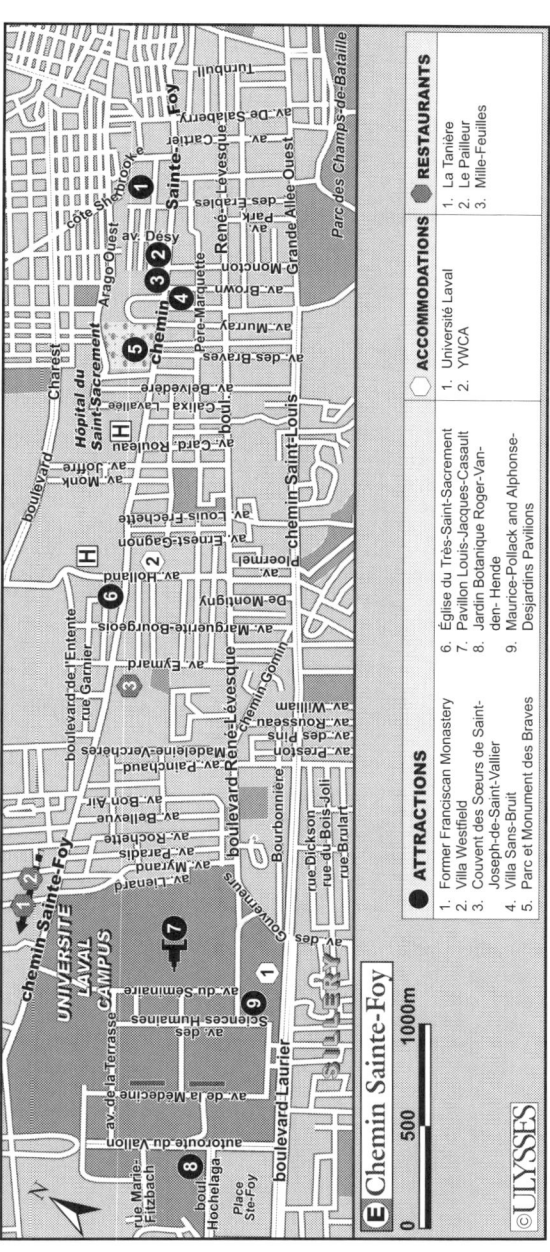

London. The tour then takes you to the modern campus of Université Laval.

The tour starts on Chemin Sainte-Foy at the corner of Avenue Cartier and heads west. Turn right on Avenue de l'Alverne.

The **Former Franciscan Monastery** *(on the northeast corner of Avenue Alverne and Rue des Franciscains)* today converted into a housing complex, was built in 1901 and was designed around a cloister inspired by the French Regime's monastery style. It is a remnant of one of several religious communities that settled along Chemin Sainte-Foy at the beginning of the 20th century. At that time, great stretches of land, far from the noise of the city, could be bought for a song.

Turn left on Rue des Franciscains, then left again on Avenue Désy. Turn right on Chemin Sainte-Foy, heading west.

Villa Westfield *(430 Chemin Sainte-Foy).* The land along Chemin Sainte-Foy was granted to notable people and Québec religious communities in the early part of the 17th century, but, shortly after the Conquest, a number of these huge properties were handed over to British dignitaries. Following the example of the domains in Sillery (see p 235), several of them would be turned into country gardens with villas. These domains were divided up in the 20th century and residential developments and institutional buildings replaced most of the villas. However, a few of these residences have survived. Such is the case of the Villa Westfield, built around 1825 for Charles Grey Stewart, a Lower Canada customs inspector. Its monumental-English-style architecture features neoclassical ornamentation. It was once surrounded by a magnificent English garden (private, no visiting).

A little further west is the **Couvent des Sœurs de Saint-Joseph-de-Saint-Vallier** *(560 Chemin Sainte-Foy),* which was formerly the residence of Andrew Thompson, at which time it was called "Bijou." The house, which forms the central part of the convent, was build in 1874 in the Second Empire style and can be recognized by its mansard roof and curved segmental openings. The wings added by the religious order fit admirably well with the architecture of the house. In 1927, a neo-Romanesque chapel was built in the eastern part of the convent.

Turn left on Avenue Brown.

Here you can see the **Villa Sans-Bruit** *(874 Avenue Brown)*, constructed around 1850. The mansard roof was added in 1880 at the time when the house belonged to the Laurie family. Until recently, this area of the Haute-Ville was considered the bastion of Québec City's small anglophone community.

Head south on Avenue Brown. Turn right on Rue du Père-Marquette where you will find the Église des Saints-Martyrs-Canadiens (1929), then turn right again on Avenue des Braves.

Avenue des Braves ★ is in line with the monument of the same name (see below). When the avenue was planned in 1912, it was to be Québec City's most prestigious residential street. Today, you can still see a few opulent stone and brick houses from the 1920s and 1930s. They were built for Québec City bourgeoisie who at the time were leaving their staid homes in the old city for the more open spaces of the suburbs.

The beautiful residence at number 1080 belonged to Roger Lemelin, author of *Les Plouffe*, from 1953 to 1972. And briefly, between 1994 and 1996, it was the official residence of Québec's premier at the time, Jacques Parizeau.

Go back up Avenue des Braves to the monument at the corner of Chemin Sainte-Foy.

Parc and Monument des Braves ★. On April 27, 1760, the Chevalier de Lévis arrived from Montréal leading 3,800 men and tried to capture Québec City, which had fallen to the British Army the previous autumn. Although they failed to enter the city, they succeeded in defeating General Murray's troops in Sainte-Foy, making this battle one of the only French victories of the Seven Years' War in New France. Parc des Braves was created on the exact site of the battle. Weapons have been found here as well as skeletons of soldiers killed in action. Its name pays tribute to the courage of these valiant young men who made this rash move while waiting for help from a fleet of French reinforcements that would never arrive. In 1855, a monument designed by Charles Baillairgé was erected in their memory in the park. The statue of Bellone, an ancient war goddess standing atop a cast-iron column, was a gift from Prince Jérôme-Napoléon Bonaparte.

In 1930, landscape architect Frederick Todd redesigned Parc des Braves and as a result, wealthy families from the old city moved to the surrounding area. The park has lovely views of Basse-Ville and the Laurentian Mountains.

Continue west on Chemin Sainte-Foy.

At the corner of Chemin Sainte-Foy and Rue Belvédère is the **Emplacement de la Terre de Jean Bourdon**. Bourdon was an engineer in New France during the first half of the 17th century and owned the Pointe-aux-Trembles (Neuville) Seigneury as well. Around 1645, Bourdon had a farm built on this land, which he fortified with stone. The farm had a small and a large dwelling, a chapel, two barns and three storehouses. Unfortunately, these buildings disappeared during the upheaval that followed the Conquest.

Large institutions such as the imposing Saint-Sacrement Hospital (number 1050) can be found along Chemin Sainte-Foy.

Église du Très-Saint-Sacrement *(1330 Chemin Sainte-Foy)* is a late neo-Romanesque work of the 1920s by architects Charles Bernier of Montréal and Oscar Beaulé of Québec City. Influenced by late medieval architecture, they gave the church a slender, rather austere nave. However, the stained-glass windows by Marius Plamondon, installed in 1954, add a bit of colour. The noviciate of the Très-Saint-Sacrement is in the back.

From here, take bus number 7 along Chemin Sainte-Foy to reach the university campus 2km further west. Get off at the corner of Avenue du Séminaire to reach the centre of campus.

Université Laval Campus *(south of Chemin Sainte-Foy and west of Avenue du Séminaire).* Université Laval was founded in 1852, making it the oldest French-speaking university in America. It was first established in the heart of the old city, near the seminary and Catholic cathedral before being moved to its current site 100 years later. The university was named in honour of Monseigneur de Laval, the first bishop of New France. Each year this vast campus welcomes some 40,000 students. It features good examples of modern and postmodern Québec architecture: one of the more interesting buildings is the **PEPS** (sports and physical education building) on the right, built in 1971, which blends well with the landscape.

A little further to the left, **Pavillon Louis-Jacques-Casault** closes off the symmetrical

Tour E: chemin Sainte-Foy   141

perspective of the campus *(1210 Avenue du Séminaire)*. This building was constructed in 1954-1958 according to the designs of Ernest Cormier who also created the Université de Montréal's main building. In the beginning, Pavillon Louis-Jacques-Casault was to be the "Great Seminary" for training priests, which explains the presence of the central chapel adorned with medieval-inspired towers. With the approach of the Révolution Tranquille (Quiet Revolution), such a building was considered a dinosaur, reflecting the architecture of the past despite its recent construction. Since 1980, it has housed the **Direction Générale des Archives Nationales du Québec** (☎643-8904) as well as the interesting **Centre Muséographique de l'Université Laval** *($3; Tue-Thu noon to 4pm, 1st Sun of the month noon to 4pm;* ☎656-7111). This institution's collections are grouped in four themes: Universe, Earth, Life and Man. The nearby **Pavillon Alexandre-de-Sève** and **La Laurentienne** are clearly more modern.

Centre d'Accueil et de Renseignements de l'Université Laval (reception and information centre) *(closed weekends, mid-Jun to mid Aug 8:30am to noon, 1:30pm to 4:30pm, Fri 8:30am to noon, 1:30pm to 4pm, rest of the year 8am to 5:30pm; Pavillon Alphonse-Desjardins, room 1106,* ☎656-3333). Here visitors can obtain information on campus activities. Finally, west of Avenue des Sciences-Humaines on Avenue de la Médecine is the **Musée de Géologie du Pavillon Adrien-Pouliot** *(free admission; every day 8:30am to 5pm;* ☎656-2193) exhibiting fossils and minerals from around the world.

Cross the Vallon Highway to reach the Roger-Van den Hende Botanical Gardens.

One of the most interesting gardens in Québec City is found on the university campus. **Jardin Roger-Van den Hende ★** *(free admission; early May to late Sep, every day 9am to 8pm; 2480 Boulevard Hochelaga,* ☎656-3410) is named after the Université Laval scientist who created it from scratch. Used for

Pont de Québec

research and teaching, the garden is also open to visitors. The arboretum, herbacetum, rose garden and water garden are all worth a visit. Guided tours are also offered.

To return to the old part of Québec City, take Métrobus no. 800 or 801 in front of the newly renovated and expanded **Maurice-Pollack** *and* **Alphonse-Desjardins** *pavilions in the southern part of the campus, on the east side of the Vallon Highway. Note that nearly all the university buildings are connected by a series of long underground passageways that may be worth a visit for those interested in this kind of subterranean architecture!*

Tour F: Saint-Roch

(four hours)

Québec City's working-class, Basse-Ville, is laid out on both sides of Rivière Saint-Charles, a contrast to the walled Haute-Ville. There is no tourist attraction as such here, but the neighbourhood bustles with people going about their daily business. Saint-Roch, Saint-Sauveur and Limoilou are familiar names to Québécois but unknown to visitors who seldom venture down to Basse-Ville. The Saint-Roch neighbourhood, located at the foot of the northern cliff of Cap Diamant, is nevertheless considered as Québec City's commercial centre.

Originally settled by potters and tanners at the end of the French Regime, Saint-Roch slowly developed along Rue Saint-Vallier. Then, when the Napoleonic blockade forced Great Britain to rely on its colonies for its wood supply, huge shipyards were created on the banks of Rivière Saint-Charles. This attracted a large working-class population to Saint-Roch. A cholera epidemic in 1832 ravaged the area and almost a quarter of its inhabitants died. Floods then devastated it in both 1845 and 1866. The neighbourhood saw its largest industry disappear in a few years following the return to normal French-British relations and the creation of metal hulls on ships (1860-1870).

This marked the beginning of a complete transformation that would make Saint-Roch the main industrial quarter in French Canada. Interestingly, the factory owners were French Canadian, as were the workers, something that was rarely seen in Canada at that time.

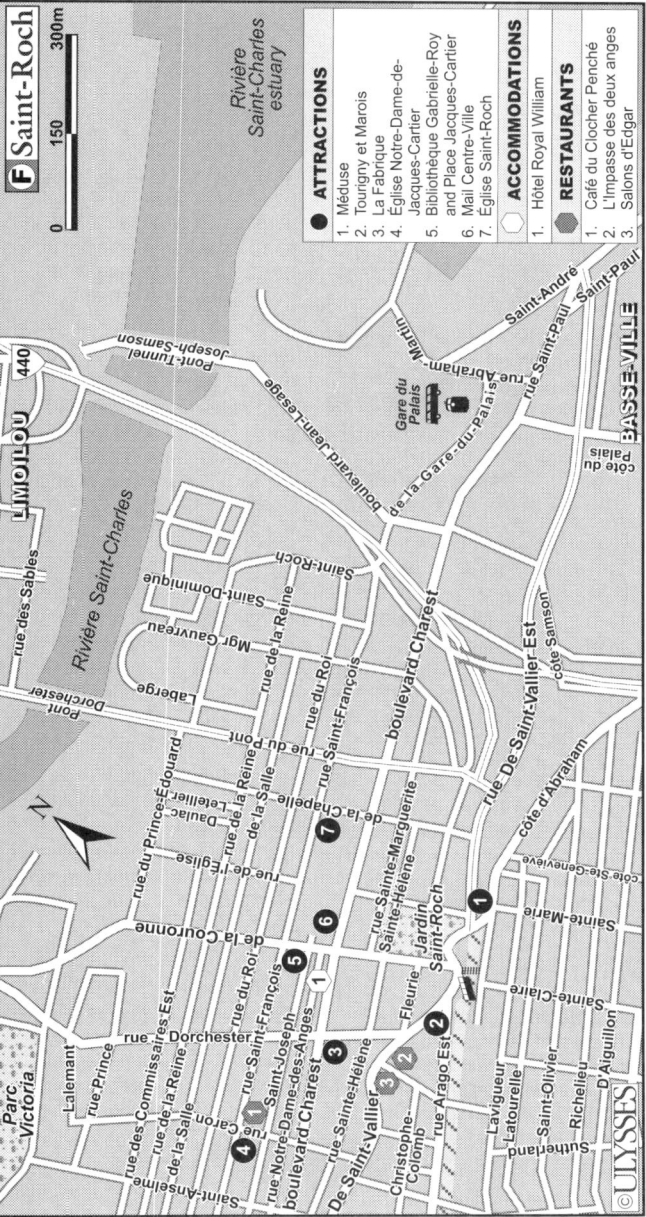

From the Haute-Ville, go down the Côte du Palais to leave the walled city, then turn left on Rue Saint-Vallier Est, which travels under the Dufferin-Montmorency Highway. You can join the Saint-Roch tour to the Vieux-Québec (Basse-Ville) tour, which ends nearby.

Rue Saint-Vallier Est between Côte du Palais and Côte d'Abraham is a thoroughfare from the French Regime located outside the boundaries of the historic quarter. It has been disfigured in many places, particularly by the construction of the Dufferin-Montmorency Highway ramps in 1970; nevertheless, it shows evidence of a very interesting past.

At number 870, you can see the ruins of the **Maison Blanche,** the secondary residence of Charles-Aubert de la Chesnaye, a wealthy merchant. The house was built in 1679 by architect Claude Baillif. In 1845, fire caused it great damage; only the arches and a few sections of wall remain from the original house, later, only half of it was salvaged.

A little further along are two cast-iron and wood staircases designed by Charles Baillairgé. One was constructed in 1883 and the other in 1889, allowing to connect the geographically and socially separate, worlds of the city below and the city above. At number 715, a group of well-preserved buildings belongs to the Lépine-Cloutier Funeral Home, which has been in operation since 1845.

Wedged between Rue Saint-Vallier Est and Côte d'Abraham, **Méduse** *(541 Rue Saint-Vallier Est, ☎640-9218)* houses various artists' associations that support and promote Québec culture. Made up of restored houses and modern buildings that integrate the city's architecture, the complex is perched on the side of Cap Diamant linking Haute-Ville and Basse-Ville. Associations in various fields such as photography, printmaking, and video, are installed here, as well as studios and galleries. Radio Basse-Ville, a community radio station, and L'Abraham-Martin bistro are also located here. Running along the east side is a stairway which links Côte d'Abraham to Rue Saint-Vallier Est.

At the foot of the stairway is **Îlot Fleuri**, a park where contemporary sculpture is exhibited to add a bit of spice to this green space.

Since 1993, the corner of Côte d'Abraham has been embellished with a rock garden and waterfall that was named **Jardin de Saint-Roch**.

Cross Côte d'Abraham.

Tourigny et Marois *(at the corner of Rue Saint-Vallier Est and Rue Arago)*. During the last quarter of the 19th century, Saint-Roch saw its shipyards shut down one by one. At the same time, manufacturers of goods such as tobacco, shoes, clothing and furniture opened up, following the tradition of the potters and tanners of the 18th century. But over the past few years, most of these factories have shut down, contributing to the neighbourhood's impoverishment. The Tourigny et Marois factory is one of the last shoe manufacturers still operating in Saint-Roch. The present building, built on an unusual lot, was erected in 1914.

The section of Rue Saint-Vallier Est between Rue de la Couronne and Boulevard Charest is livelier now that a few friendly bars and restaurants have sprung up; as well, several projects are currently being developed to render this part of town a little more attractive.

Turn right on Rue Dorchester.

La Fabrique ★ *(295 Boul. Charest Est at the corner of Rue Dorchester)* is located in the former Dominion Corset factory which, as its name indicates, was a manufacturer of corsets and brassieres. President Georges Amyot built this enormous factory between 1897 and 1911, creating jobs for the abundant workforce of young unmarried women. Because Amyot believed a married woman's place was in the home and not the factory, marriage ment immediate dismissal.

The former Dominion Corset factory was restored and renamed "La Fabrique" in 1993. It now houses an interpretation centre of Québec City's rich industrial past, the **Centre de Développement Urbain de Québec**, as well as the **École des Arts Visuels de l'Université Laval**. Take a look at the facade's complex brickwork, the clocktower and the water tower, elements that are reminiscent of American factory architecture at the end of the 19th century.

Cross Boulevard Charest.

Boulevard Charest was created in 1928 to relieve this neighbourhood's congested narrow streets, since the roads built between 1790 and 1840 were no longer able to handle commercial and industrial traffic. There are a few prominent buildings on Boulevard Charest which once were Québec City's department stores. Today they are all closed. Number 740, the former Pollack store dating from 1950, now has a shopping centre on the ground floor. The back of the old Paquet store can still be found at the corner of the Rue de l'Église, and at the corner of Rue de la Couronne, you can see the Syndicat de Québec, rebuilt in 1949 and shut down in 1981.

Turn left on Rue Saint-Joseph, then right on Rue Caron.

Église Notre-Dame-de-Jacques-Cartier ★ *(Rue Caron)* was originally the Saint-Roch Congregationalists' chapel. It was built in 1853 and expanded in 1875. In 1901, it brought together an entire parish. Its interior was richly decorated by Raphaël Giroux and includes lateral rood screens adorned with gold columns. At the back of the church is the stately embossed-stone presbytery constructed in 1902.

Turn right on Rue La Salle then right again on Rue de la Couronne.

Maisons Ouvrières de Saint-Roch ★ **(Saint-Roch workers' houses)** are unique to Québec City's Basse-Ville. Compact and erected at the edge of the sidewalk, they are made of brownish brick or, occasionally, wood. They have sloping or mansard roofs and shuttered French windows. The architecture could be described as a kind of hybrid between North American working-class and French industrial-town architecture.

At the beginning of the 19th century, as Saint-Roch was rapidly developing, people quickly built their houses of wood and inspired by the French Regime's country houses. But the great fire of 1845 reduced the neighbourhood to ashes and changed the rules of the game. After the fire, brick or stone construction became mandatory and wood ornamentation was discouraged. These rules were softened at the end of the 19th century and several houses were then decorated with Victorian wood trim. But the face of Saint-Roch did not change significantly and has kept its quaint, old-time image to this day.

Bibliothèque Gabrielle-Roy (library) *(Mon noon to 9pm, Tue-Fri 10:30 to 9pm, Sat-Sun noon to 5pm; 350 Rue Saint-Joseph Est, ☎529-0924)* and **Place Jacques-Cartier**. This is the heart of Saint-Roch. In 1831, the creation of a marketplace was planned for this location but it was only in 1857 that two of its halls were actually built. One of them burned down in 1911 and the other was demolished around 1930 to create Place Jacques-Cartier. The statue of the famous explorer, which can be seen at the centre of the square, was a gift from the City of Saint-Malo, France.

At the far end, Bibliothèque Gabrielle-Roy (municipal library) (1982-83) was named for one of French Canada's most famous writers. In her novels, this author describes the extreme poverty of people living in working-class neighbourhoods during the Depression. The library also offers special exhibition spaces to promote the work of contemporary artists.

Turn left on Rue Saint-Joseph Est to enter Mail Centre-Ville.

Mail Centre-Ville (mall) *(along Rue Saint-Joseph Est between Rue Dorchester and Rue du Pont, ☎648-1986)* is a pedestrian street that occupies part of this neighbourhood's main commercial artery. This window-covered mall sheltering pedestrians from bad weather was constructed at the beginning of the 1980s to counter Rue Saint-Joseph's commercial decline caused by suburban shopping centres. It was formerly known as "Mail Saint-Roch."

However, this undertaking did not prevent an exodus to the suburbs and Mail Centre-Ville has become less and less popular. Numerous critics have stated that the roof disfigures the artery and even the neighbourhood as a whole. This is why the city has decided to remove the mall's roof between Rue du Pont and Rue de la Couronne. Work began in March 2000 and entails several phases. For now though, the mall is in quite bad shape.

Église Saint-Roch ★ *(590 Rue Saint-Joseph Est)*. Surprisingly, none of the working-class neighbourhoods have kept their old churches. Fire and the rapidly-increasing population have meant that larger and more modern buildings have replaced the old churches. The first Église Saint-Roch was erected around 1811 and was replaced by two other buildings before the present church was built between 1916 and 1923 by architects Talbot and Dionne. It is an immense neo-Romanesque structure with two steeples and a rather austere interior; however, it features interesting stained-glass windows made by the Montréal firm Hobbs (around 1920).

Turn right on Rue du Pont to get to Boulevard Charest and go east on Boulevard Charest to return to Côte du Palais.

Rue du Pont was named as such when the first Pont Dorchester was inaugurated in 1789 at the north end of the street. The bridge crosses Rivière Saint-Charles and links Limoilou (see below) and the northern sector of Québec City, and has been rebuilt many times. You can still find remains of the French Regime settlement east of Rue du Pont. This area, which reaches as far as the columns of the Dufferin-Montmorency Highway, is where the Récollet Fathers' Saint-Roch Hermitage was situated, giving its name to the area.

In 1692, after having given up their Saint-Sauveur monastery to Monseigneur de Saint-Vallier so that it could be turned into a hospital, the Récollets settled in the east where they built a hermitage (retreat) for their priests. The hermitage consisted of a large house with an adjoining chapel; both have since disappeared. Later, a small village was created and businesses were started, thus beginning to populate the area.

Tour G: Limoilou

(half a day)

As the winter of 1535 approached, Jacques Cartier, who was on his second exploration trip to Canada, had to find the proper spot to anchor his fleet before it was trapped by ice in the middle of the St. Lawrence River. He discovered a well-protected harbour in the bend of Rivière Saint-Charles and had a small log fort built. Towering above it, was erected a wooden cross with the coat of arms of François I. And so, Limoilou became the first French settlement in Canada. However, after Jacques Cartier left, the fort disappeared. Today, the Cartier-Brébeuf National Historic Site marks the area.

In 1625, the territory was granted to the Jesuits. They created the Seigneurie de Notre-Dame-des-Anges here and had colonists settle and cultivate the land. It was only in the middle of the 19th century that Limoilou began to be urbanized, taking advantage of the prosperity of Saint-Roch's shipyards on the other side of Rivière Saint-Charles.

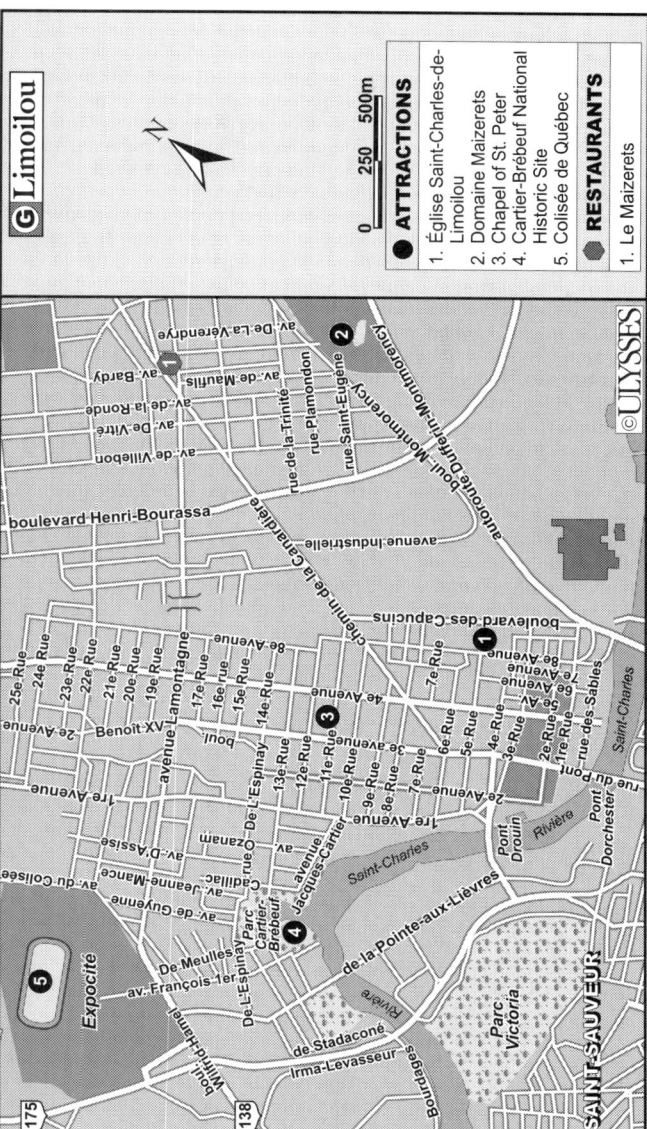

There then appeared large estates, each with fields, warehouses, a working-class village and, on the outskirts, the owner's residence surrounded by a landscaped garden. Little of this period remains. It is only at the beginning of the 20th century that the present neighbourhood took shape and acquired its name. Limoilou refers to the Manoir de Limoilou near Saint-Malo, France, where Cartier retired after his numerous trips to New France.

To get to Limoilou from Vieux-Québec, take bus no. 3 from Place d'Youville. It runs along Rue du Pont and then crosses Rivière Saint-Charles. Get off at the corner of 3e Rue, which you take on the right (going east).

Aboriginal Peoples called the river *Kabir Kouba,* meaning "river with many bends," and in 1535, Cartier renamed it "Rivière Saint-Croix." The Récollets who settled on the southern banks in 1615 gave the river its present name, **Rivière Saint-Charles**, in honour of Pontoise priest Charles de Boves who had financed their establishment in New France. The river crosses the rich alluvial plane at the foot of Cap Diamant, going through the centre of Basse-Ville and isolating Limoilou from other working-class neighbourhoods. The river is made up of numerous loops that used to end in a swampy estuary, but now makeup the Port de Québec and Bassin Louise.

During the Conquest in 1763 the Jesuits lost their right to teach in Canada. The last of them died in Québec City at the end of the 18th century, and the Notre-Dame-des-Anges seigneury was taken over by the King of England who redistributed the land. Around 1845, William Hedley Anderson created **Hedleyville** in his southern portion. It was the first Limoilou village to specialize in naval construction and the commerce of wood. Only a few of the buildings remain from the village, which was located between 1re and 3e Rues and between 4e and 7e Avenues. Number 699 3e Rue is the former **École d'Hedleyville** *(private, no visiting)*, constructed in 1863 to give the workers' children a basic education. The school's architecture is not much different from the neighbourhood's wooden dwellings and was converted to housing quite a while ago.

Go to the end of the 3e Rue, more precisely to the corner of Boulevard des Capucins, where you can admire between the pillars of the Dufferin-Montmorency Highway the view of the former **Anglo Canadian Paper Mills**, today the property of the Daishowa Company. This gigantic red-brick industrial complex looks like an impregnable stronghold and was erected in 1928 on the landfilled Rivière Saint-Charles estuary.

Return to 8e Avenue and go north (turn right if you have gone as far as Boulevard des Capucins).

Beautiful **Église Saint-Charles-de-Limoilou** ★ *(8e Avenue)* stands at the corner of 5e Rue, offering a pleasant perspective. The church and conventional buildings surrounding it were all erected on a strip of land that once belonged to Québec City's Hôtel-Dieu. Build with a typical neo-Romanesque façade (1917-1920), the nave of the Limoilou mother church has a double row of medieval-looking arches designed by architect Joseph-Pierre Ouellet. Its interior is representative of Québec City's parish churches which are generally narrower and taller than most churches in other Québec regions. In this manner, the influence of Notre-Dame de Québec Cathedral, a tall, long, narrow Baroque work from the mid-18th century, seems to have been felt locally right up until the Second World War.

Along the 5e Rue are several of Limoilou's civic buildings such as the beautiful Beaux-Arts fire station constructed in 1910 by the City of Québec. The City had annexed the formerly autonomous Limoilou municipality the previous year, making it part of Québec City.

An option here is to explore the eastern part of Limoilou as far as Domaine Maizerets. Plan a good 30min walk to get there. Continue on 8e Avenue as far as Chemin de la Canardière and turn right. Turn right again on Avenue de la Vérendrye and go as far as Boulevard Montmorency. To follow the main tour, go back to 8e Avenue and then turn left on 12e Rue where you will see the Chapel of St. Peter.

On **Domaine Maizerets** ★ *(free admission; every day 9am to 9pm; 2000 Boul. Montmorency, ☎691-2385)* is the Maizerets house, one of the former summer residences of the Séminaire de Québec. The first house was built in 1697 and has been expanded three times since. It was first known as the Domaine de la Canardière because of the innumerable birds that nested on the nearby sandbars. Then the house was given the name Domaine de Maizerets as a way of paying homage to Louis Ango de Maizerets, the Québec City seminary's superior at the time. The house, its farm and park are a rare group of rural buildings dating back to the 18th century in the Québec City region that are still intact. Its gardens, part of the Association des Jardins du Québec, are a pleasant place to relax.

The **Chapel of St. Peter** *(corner of 12e Rue and 3e Avenue)* is a witness of the Anglo-Saxon Anglican presence in Limoilou during the 1920s and 1930s. Most worshippers were managerial staff or owners of the nearby factories and the Anglican bishop had this chapel built especially for them. However, they were never sufficient in number to justify transforming the chapel into a large church.

The streets around the chapel are good examples of the **architecture of Limoilou houses**; their resemblance to those in Montréal is not accidental. In fact, Limoilou saw itself as a "modern" town – later a neighbourhood – modelling itself after other North American towns at the beginning of the 20th century. Developers from Montréal and the United States as well sold lots requiring Montréal-style constructions such as flat roofs, multi-level galleries, exterior metal staircases, parapets, alleyways and sheds. Even the names of the shaded streets and avenues were given numbers instead of names, in all-American fashion.

Continue along 12e Rue to 1re Avenue where you turn right and then left onto 13e Rue, which runs into Rue Cadillac and Rue de l'Espinay. This is the main entrance to the Cartier-Brébeuf National Historic Site.

Cartier-Brébeuf National Historic Site ★ *($3 exhibit; 175 Rue de l'Espinay, ☎648-4038)* is located near the spot where Jacques Cartier and his crew spent the winter of 1535-1536. The difficult conditions of this forced winter stay resulting in the death of 25 sailors are explained at the reception and interpretation centre *(admission prices and hours vary)*. A scale model of Cartier's fort is also displayed there. One must remember that Cartier's plan was not to establish a colony on Canadian soil but rather to make more lucrative discoveries, such as a passage to China or minerals as precious as the gold of the Spanish colonies.

This historic site is a pleasant green space spread out around an inlet of Rivière Saint-Charles. There was a time when this was the mouth of the Rivière Lairet, but today it has been filled in. You can see a **replica of the Grande Hermine**, Cartier's main ship, as well as a reconstructed **Iroquois Long House** showing Aboriginal living arrangements in the St. Lawrence Valley at the time of the first explorers. But Cartier is not the only person whose memory is honoured at this historic site. Saint Jean de Brébeuf (1593-1649), a Jesuit missionary martyred by the Iroquois, arrived here in 1625 to establish the Notre-Dame-des-Anges seigneury. A monument commemorating both men was inaugurated in 1889. Cartier-Brébeuf National Historic Site has a pleasant walkway that runs along the meandering Rivère Saint-Charles to the south.

You can take Avenue Jeanne-Mance to get to Parc de l'Exposition. However, it is a good distance on foot and you must cross a rather uninteresting area to get there. This excursion is particularly worthwhile if there are special events going on at the Centre de Foire (fairgrounds) during your visit. To return, take bus no. 12 going east to the corner of 1e Rue and Avenue Lamontagne (18e Rue), then transfer to bus no. 801 for Haute-Ville.

The **Colisée de Québec** is an indoor skating rink where the home-team favourites, the Québec Nordiques, used to play hockey. The Colisée was built in 1950 by an architect of Swiss origin, Robert Blatter, who is also responsible for several attractive international-style houses in Sillery. However, the Colisée's expansion and renovation during the 1970s was not a great success.

The Colisée is located at the centre of what is called **ExpoCité** *(250 Boulevard Wilfrid-Hamel, ☎691-7110)*. Very popular before the arrival of television, regional exhibitions were presented annually in various cities on the continent so that everyone could learn about recent discoveries and view fragments of an exotic, faraway world. These fairs also offered workers a place to relax and gave children a fun place to play. The Centre de Foire de Québec's new large functional pavilions are designed to receive the many exhibitions and fairs that are of interest to the people of Québec City and surrounding area.

The Parc de l'Exposition de Québec includes the Colisée and the **Hippodrome de Québec** *(☎524-5283)* as well as some of the former pavilions that housed the annual provincial exhibitions presented here since 1892. The **Pavillon des Arts** (1913) and the **Palais Central** (1916) are two Beaux-Arts buildings that are reminiscent of the Chicago World's Fair pavilions of 1893.

Tour H: Saint-Sauveur

(half a day)

Québec writer Roger Lemelin (1919-1994) has made the neighbourhood of his childhood and romances well known through his work. His novels *Au pied de la pente douce* (1944) and *Les Plouffe* (1948) have been made into television series as well as films. He describes the harsh, ordinary day-to-day life of the Saint-Sauveur people while showing their shortcomings and kind-heartedness. At the time, this working-class quarter of Basse-Ville located west of Saint-Roch was Québec City's poorest sector and had the highest rate of unemployment.

The history of Saint-Sauveur began in 1615 when the Récollets came to the banks of Rivière Saint-Charles. These reformed Franciscans had great plans for their land. They anticipated bringing 300 families from France who would settle in a town called "Ludovica." In 1621, they built the first stone church in New France. Unfortunately, when the Kirke brothers captured Québec City in 1629, the project was brought to a halt and despite the return to French rule in 1632, the Récollets' colonisation project was never mentioned again. Only their monastery was rebuilt before being bought by the Bishop of Québec City to create the Hôpital Général (1693).

It was only after the great fire destroyed the neighbouring quarter of Saint-Roch (1845) that Saint-Sauveur became urbanized. In great confusion, hundreds of small wooden houses were built on meagre and often insalubrious land. In 1866 and again in 1889, major fires ravaged a good part of the neighbourhood which nevertheless continued to attract a number of general workers. These days, Saint-Sauveur is known as a neighbourhood where a deep-seated spirit of Québec City can be found in its narrow streets and doll-like houses.

Leaving Haute-Ville, take bus no. 2 from Place d'Youville. Get off at the corner of Boulevard Langelier and Boulevard Charest. Take Boulevard Langelier to the left, then turn right on Rue Arago.

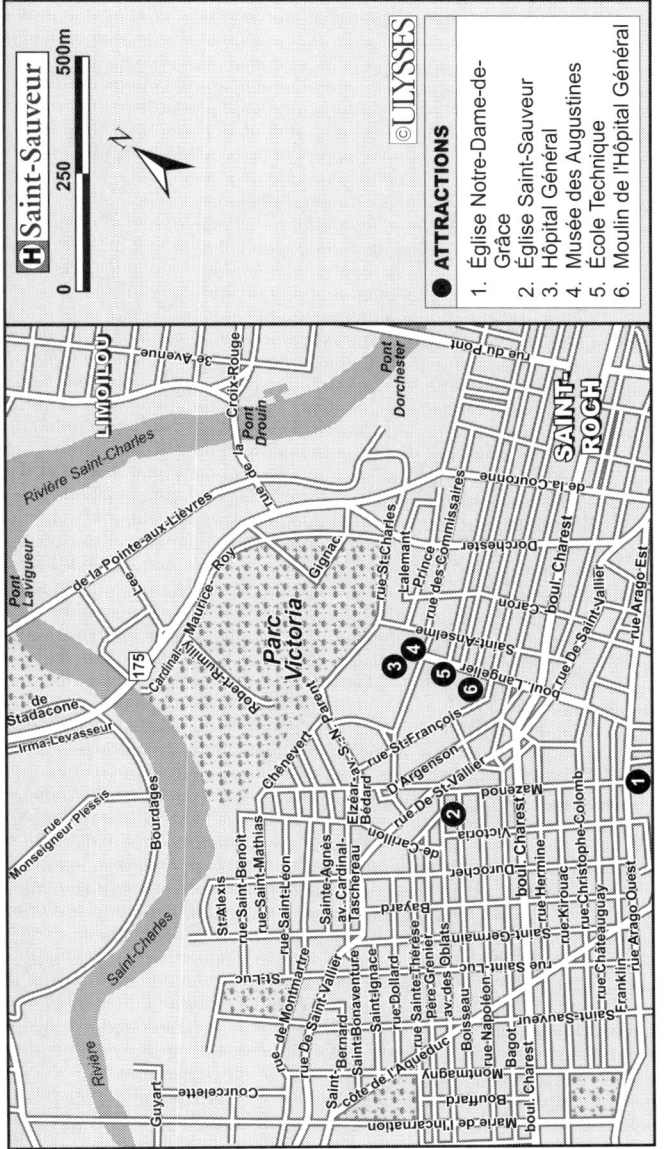

Église Notre-Dame-de-Grâce *(Rue Arago at the corner of Colbert)* is situated at the foot of the Haute-Ville cliff. It is an eclectic late work (1925) inspired by medieval architecture, built by Abbé Jean-Thomas Nadeau and notary Gérard Morisset. The latter also played an important role in saving Place-Royale many years later.

Turn right on charming Rue Victoria.

The small houses with mansard roofs on Rue Victoria and surrounding streets give the neighbourhood a friendly village atmosphere. These dwellings were constructed on the tiniest plots of land marked by owners who wanted to fit a maximum number of families into a minimum space. At the beginning of the 20th century, some houses were expanded with extra storeys along with balconies and richly-ornamented bay windows.

Église Saint-Sauveur ★ stands at the north end of Rue Victoria. It was erected in 1867, re-using the original burnt walls of the first church built in 1851. Architect Joseph-Ferdinand Peachy designed a neo-Romanesque facade with a spire to give it a Baroque look. Abundantly decorated at the end of the 19th century, the interior has a slender nave and is surrounded by high lateral galleries. Note the windows by Beaulieu and Rochon (1897).

Cross the square in front of the church to get to Avenue des Oblats, turn right and go along to Rue Saint-Vallier Ouest where you turn left.

This street is the heart of the Saint-Sauveur neighbourhood, with snack bars, Asian restaurants, second-hand dealers and workshops. There are also a few former residences of prominent personalities, which are adorned with balconies and towers. **Rue Saint-Vallier** runs through several neighbourhoods in Basse-Ville as a winding path that ends at Bassin Louise.

Take Rue de Carillon north, then turn right on Rue Elzéar-Bédard. Next, almost in front of you, take Avenue Simon-Napoléon-Parent which was named after a mayor at the end of the last century. There are several interesting Second Empire and Queen Anne-style Victorian residences along this avenue leading to Parc Victoria.

Parc Victoria was created in 1897 to provide the neighbourhoods of Saint-Roch and Saint-Sauveur with some green space, an element that had been missing until then. Pathways and rustic log structures were built and became very popular among city dwellers. But the park lost most of its appeal when the bend in Rivière Saint-Charles was filled in since the river had almost completely encircled the park at that time. The construction of Police Headquarters also contributed to the transformation of this green space.

Walk along Avenue Simon-Napoléon-Parent beside the park, then turn right on Avenue Saint-Anselme and again right on Avenue des Commissaires. Go around the walls of the Hôpital Général because the entrance is at the end of Boulevard Langelier.

Hôpital Général ★★
(260 Boulevard Langelier). The Récollets built the first stone church in New France in 1621 on the site of the Hôpital Général. Their plan was to bring 300 families from France and settle on the banks of Rivière Saint-Charles in a village called "Ludovica." Although this project never came through, the institution slowly grew and took root. The present chapel was built in 1673 and in 1682, the Récollets added an arched cloister to their monastery. A few elements remain and have been integrated into the subsequent additions.

In 1693, Monseigneur Jean-Baptiste de la Croix de Chevrières de Saint-Vallier, the second Bishop of Québec City, bought the monastery from the Récollets to establish a hospital. The Augustine Hospitaller Order of the Hôtel-Dieu took charge of the institution which looked after destitute, disabled and elderly people. Today the Hôpital Général is a modern institution with the modern equipment, emergency and operating rooms, and is open to everyone. However, a great deal has been preserved. In fact, more than any other institution of its kind in Québec City. There are many elements from the 17th and 18th centuries such as the Récollets' cells, woodwork, dispensary cupboards and painted panelling. Fortunately, the hospital was never damaged by flames and only a little by the Conquest bombardments, a rarity in Québec City.

It is not possible to visit these vestiges, but you can take a tour of the **Musée des Augustines** *(free admission; open by appointment and guided tour only)* and the small chapel that was redecorated in 1770 by Pierre Émond and where the preciously guarded tabernacle made in 1722 by François-

Noël Levasseur has been kept. There are some beautiful paintings such as *L'Assomption de la Vierge* by Frère Luc, painted here during the artist's visit to Canada in 1670, and several paintings by Joseph Légaré bought in 1824.

Take Boulevard Langelier, leaving the hospital and museum behind you.

École Technique

(310 Boulevard Langelier), or École des Métiers, is a good example of Québec City's Beaux-Arts architecture. This is a major architectural work by René Pamphile Lemay that was built from 1909 to 1911. The long redbrick and stone building had a 22m-high central tower but unfortunately was demolished around 1955.

The **Moulin de l'Hôpital Général** stands in the middle of a small park at the corner of Avenue Langelier and Rue Saint-François. This old windmill is the only one of about 20 that have survived the harshness of Québec weather. Its stone tower was erected on earlier foundations in 1730 for the nuns and patients of the Hôpital Général. It milled grain until 1862 when a fire destroyed it completely. The mill was then integrated into an industrial building and was concealed so that it disappeared from view. Only in 1976 was the tower, or what remained of it, uncovered and given a new roof.

To end this tour and return to the Haute-Ville, take Rue Saint-François going east and continue for a while until you reach Rue Dorchester. At the corner of these two streets is a bus stop where you can take Métrobus no. 800 or 801.

Tour I: from Sillery to Cap-Rouge

(half a day)

This tour goes up and down along the cliff reaching from Cap Diamant to Cap-Rouge. It begins in Sillery, the affluent Québec City suburb, goes through Sainte-Foy (see p 136) and ends at the Cap-Rouge cliff. You will never be too far from the river and at times will be able to enjoy magnificent panoramas.

Sillery

(pop. 13,082)

Sillery retains many traces of its colourful past, influenced by the town's dramatic topography. There

Tour I: from Sillery to Cap-Rouge

are actually two sections to Sillery, one at the base and the other at the top of a steep cliff which runs from Cap Diamant to Cap-Rouge. In 1637, the Jesuits built a mission in Sillery, on the shores of the river, with the idea of converting the Algonquins and Montagnais who came to fish in the coves upriver from Québec City. They named the fortified community in honour of the mission's benefactor, Noël Brûlart de Sillery, an aristocrat who had recently been converted by Vincent de Paul.

By the following century, Sillery was already sought after for its beauty. The Jesuits converted their mission into a country house, and the bishop of Samos built Sillery's first villa (1732). Following the British Conquest, Sillery became the favoured town of administrators, military officers and British merchants, all of whom built luxurious villas on the cliff in architectural styles that were fashionable in England at the time. The splendour of these homes and their vast English gardens were in stark contrast to the simple workers houses that were clustered at the base of the cliff. The occupants of these houses worked in the shipyards where a fortune was being made building ships out of wood coming down the Outaouais region to supply the British navy during Napoleon's blockade, which began in 1806. The shipyards, set up in Sillery's sheltered coves, had all disappeared before Boulevard Champlain, now running along the river's edge, was built in 1960.

The tour begins at the entrance to Parc du Bois-de-Coulonge, on Chemin Saint-Louis, which is the extension of Grande Allée just before it branches off towards the south and becomes Boulevard Laurier.

The **Bois-de-Coulonge** ★★ *(free admission; 1215 Chemin Saint-Louis, ☎528-0773)* borders Chemin Saint-Louis to the east. This English park once surrounded the residence of the lieutenant-governor of Québec. The stately home was destroyed in a fire in 1966, though some of its buildings survived, notably the guard's house and the stables. The Saint-Denys stream flows through the eastern end of the grounds at the bottom of a ravine, and marks the spot where British troops gained access to the Plains of Abraham where a historic battle decided the future of New France. Now Bois de Coulonge, member of the Jardins du Québec, features magnificent gardens and an attractive arboretum.

Villa Bagatelle ★ *($2.50; Mar to Dec, Tue to Sun noon to 5pm; 1563 Chemin Saint-Louis, ☎688-8074)* was once home to an attaché of the British governor, who lived on the neighbouring property of Bois-de-Coulonge. Built in 1848, the villa is a good example of 19th-century Gothic-Revival residential architecture, as interpreted by American Alexander J. Davis. The house and its Victorian garden were impeccably restored in 1984 and are now open to the public. There is an interesting information centre providing background on the villas and large estates of Sillery.

On Avenue Lemoine, which runs along the south side of Bagatelle, is the **Spencer Grange Villa**, built in 1849 for Henry Atkinson *(1321 Avenue Lemoine)*. During the Second World War, was occupied by Zita de Bourbon-Parme, the dethroned Empress of Austria.

Continue on Chemin Saint-Louis as far as the corner of Avenue Maguire and Côte de l'Église. Avenue Maguire is the neighbourhood's main shopping area. Turn left on Côte de l'Église.

A short side trip leads the **Cimetière de Sillery**, Sillery's Catholic cemetery, where René Lévesque, founder of the Parti Québécois and Premier of Québec from 1976 to 1984, is buried. To get there, turn right on Avenue Maguire, then left on Boulevard René-Lévesque Ouest. The cemetery is just a little further.

Église Saint-Michel ★ *(at the corner of Chemin du Foulon and Côte de l'Église)* was erected in 1852 by architect George Browne. Inside are five paintings from the famous Desjardins collection. These originally hung in Parisian churches until they were sold in 1792 following the French Revolution and brought to Québec by Abbé Desjardins.

From the **Observatoire de la Pointe-à-Puiseaux**, opposite the church square, you can take a look at the vast panorama of the St. Lawrence River and south shore. On the right are the bridges that link the north and south shores. The first, to the east, is the **Pont de Québec**, a cantilever bridge that was deemed an engineering morrel when it was first built. However, its construction was marked by a tragic event: the central span collapsed when workers were attempting to put it in place for the first time in August 1907. The other bridge with great white arches is named **Pont Pierre-Laporte** in memory of the provincial government minister who was abducted and killed by members of the Front de Libération du Québec (FLQ) during the 1970 October Crisis.

At the foot of the hill, turn right on Chemin Foulon, which takes its name from a mill that was used for carding and fulling wool in the old days.

The **Maison des Jésuites de Sillery** ★★ *(donation; Jun to Sep 11am to 5pm, Oct to May 1pm to 5pm, closed Mon; 2320 Chemin du Foulon, ☎654-0259, ≠654-0991)* built of stone and covered with white plaster, occupies the former site of a Jesuit mission, a few ruins of which are still visible. In the 17th century, the mission included a fortified stone wall, a chapel, a priest's residence as well as aboriginal housing. As European illnesses such as smallpox and measles devastated the Aboriginal population, the mission was transformed into a hospice in 1702. At the same time, work began on the present house, a building with imposing chimney stacks. In 1763, the house was rented to John Brookes and his wife, writer Frances Moore Brookes, who immortalized it by making it the setting for her novel *The History of Emily Montague*, published in London in 1769. It was also during this time that the structure was lowered and the windows were made smaller, in the New England saltbox tradition. The house now has two storeys in front and one in back, covered with a catslide roof.

By 1824 the main building was being used as a brewery and the chapel had been torn down. The house was later converted into an office complex for various shipyards. In 1929, the Maison des Jésuites became one of the first three buildings designated as historic by the government of Québec. Since 1948, it has housed a museum detailing the 350-year history of the property.

Continue along Chemin du Foulon then take Côte à Gignac up the embankment on the right. At the top of the hill turn right on Chemin Saint-Louis.

Domaine Cataraqui ★ *(5$; all year every day 10am to 5pm, Sep to May closed Mon; 2141 Chemin Saint-Louis, ☎681-3010)* is the best-kept property of its kind still in existence in Sillery. It includes a large neoclassical residence, designed in 1851 by architect Henry Staveley, a winter garden and numerous outbuildings scattered across a beautiful, restored garden. The house was built after a wood merchant

Exploring

named Henry Burstall, whose business operated at the bottom of the cliff on which the house stands. In 1935, Cataraqui became the residence of painter Henry Percival Tudor-Hart and his wife Catherine Rhodes. They sold the property to the Québec government to prevent it from being divided, as many others had been. Today it is open to public as are its superb gardens where exhibits and concerts are regularly presented. In early fall, many concerts take place during the **Festival de Musique Ancienne de Sillery**.

Head west on Chemin Saint-Louis.

Maison Hamel-Bruneau *(free admission; Tue to Sun 12:30pm to 5pm, Wed to 9pm; 2608 Chemin Saint-Louis, ☎654-4325)* is a beautiful example of Regency architecture, popular in British colonies at the beginning of the 19th century. This style is characterized by hip roofs with flared eaves covering low wraparound verandas. Graced with French windows, Maison Hamel-Bruneau has been carefully restored and transformed into a cultural centre by the town of Sainte-Foy.

Turn left on Avenue du Parc to get to the Aquarium du Québec.

The **Aquarium du Québec** *($9.50; every day 9am to 5pm; 1675 Avenue des Hôtels, Sainte-Foy, ☎659-5264)*, home to some 250 species of fish, marine mammals and reptiles, is full of fascinating sights. Of particular interest among the indigenous animals are the three species of seal. The vast grounds surrounding the aquarium feature walking paths and picnic tables with a view of the river.

Seals

Take Chemin Saint-Louis west towards Cap-Rouge, then take Rue Louis-Francœur to the right before turing left down Côte de Cap-Rouge.

Cap-Rouge

(pop. 14,738)

Jacques Cartier and the Sieur de Roberval tried to establish a French colony in Cap-Rouge in 1541. They called their encampments Charlesbourg-Royal and France-Roy. But the unfortunate who accompanied them, having no idea of how cold Canada could get in January, built frail wood buildings with paper windows! Most died during the winter, victims of the cold or of scurvy, a disease caused by a lack of vitamin C. The others returned to France in the spring.

A plaque has been placed at the **Site Historique de Cap-Rouge** *(at the end of Côte de Cap-Rouge)*, an historic site commemorating the first French colony in America. Cartier and Roberval had intended to make the site a base camp for expeditions heading out in search of a passage to the Orient.

Tour J: Heading North

(one day)

The tour begins in Charlesbourg, one of the first areas of New France to be populated. It stops at Wendake, a Huron-Wendat village, then continues northward to the Réserve Faunique des Laurentides. A word to great-outdoors enthusiasts: the Réserve Faunique des Laurentides is one of the entry points to the wonderful Saguenay-Lac-Saint-Jean region, which you can explore with the *Ulysses Charlevoix Saguenay-Lac-Saint-Jean travel guide*.

Charlesbourg

(pop. 73,962)

In New France, seigneuries were usually shaped in long rectangles marked out in squares that ran up and down hills. Most of them were set up perpendicular to a significant waterway as well. Charlesbourg is the only real exception to this system, but what an exception! In 1665, when looking for different ways to populate the colony and assure its prosperity and security, the Jesuits developed an original plan to urbanize their land: the Notre-Dame-des-Anges seigneury. It is a huge square, that was divided into angled plots of land converging towards the centre where the dwellings were situated. The houses faced a square defined by a road called the Trait-Carré where there was a church, cemetery and community pasture. This concentric plan assured a better defence against the Iroquois and is still visible today in the old part of Charlesbourg. Two other initiatives of this kind, Bourg Royal to the east and Petite Auvergne to the south, did not have the same success, however, little remains of them today.

The Notre-Dame-des-Anges seigneury was granted to the Jesuits in 1626, making it one of the first permanent settlements inhabited by Europeans in Canada. Despite this early settlement and original seigneurial design, few buildings built before the 19th century remain in Charlesbourg. The fragility of early buildings and the push to modernize are possible explanations for this. Since 1950, Charlesbourg has become one of the main suburbs of Québec City and has lost much of its original character.

It is best to park near the church and explore the Trait-Carré on foot. You can also take Métrobus no. 801 to get to Charlesbourg. This bus goes as far as the Jardin Zoologique.

ÉgliseSaint-Charles-Borromée ★★ *(135 80ᵉ Rue Ouest)* revolutionized the art of building in rural Québec. Architect Thomas Baillargé, influenced by the Palladian movement, showed particular innovation in the way he arranged the windows and doors of the facade, to which he added a large pediment. Construction of the church began in 1828 and the original design has remained intact since. The magnificent interior decor by Baillargé was done in 1833.

At the back of the choir, narrower than the nave, is the Arch de Triomphe-style retable and in the centre is the tabernacle evoking St. Peter's Basilica in Rome. A 17th century painting by Pierre Mignard entitled *Saint Charles Borromée distribuant la communion aux pestiférés de Milan* (St. Charles Borromée giving communion to plague victims in Milan) also hangs there. Two beautiful statues by Pierre-Noël Levasseur, dating from 1742, complete the ensemble. When you step out, you can see the huge Second Empire-style 1876 presbytery, showing the village priest's privileged status in the 19th century, and the Bibliothèque Municipale (municipal library) in the former Collège Saint-Charles (1904).

Take 1re Avenue south then turn left on Rue du Trait-Carré Est, which leads to Chemin Samuel.

Maison Éphraïm-Bédard *(free admission; end of Jun to mid Aug Wed-Sun noon to 7pm, early Sep to end of Jun Tue and Thr 1:30pm to 4pm; 7655 Chemin Samuel, ☎628-8278)* is one of the rare surviving houses in old Charlesbourg. The local historical society has been installed there since 1986 and presents an exhibition

Tour J: Heading North   165

on the evolution of the Trait-Carré. Old maps and aerial photographs show the particular physical layout of Charlesbourg. Guided tours of the area are offered as well.

If you return to Rue Trait-Carré Est, you can see **Maison Magella-Paradis** *(Thu-Fri 7pm to 9pm, Sat-Sun 1pm to 5pm, ☎623-1877)* at number 7970. Built in 1833, it sometimes hosts exhibitions. A little farther along at number 7985, **Maison Pierre-Lefevbre**, built in 1846, houses **Galerie d'Art du Trait-Carré** *(free admission; Thu-Fri 7pm to 9pm, Sat-Sun 1pm to 5pm ☎623-1877)*. Works by local artists are featured here.

Turn right on 80e Rue Est. At the corner of Boulevard Henri-Bourassa is the Jesuits old mill.

Polar Bear

The **Moulin des Jésuites** ★ *(free admission; mid-Jun to mid-Aug, every day 10pm to 7pm; mid-Aug to mid-Jun, Sat and Sun 10am to 5pm; 7960 Boulevard Henri-Bourassa, ☎624-7720)*. This pretty mill, in roughcast rubble stone, is the oldest building in Charlesbourg. It was built in 1740 by the Jesuits who were the landowners at the time. After several decades of neglect, the two-storey building was restored in 1990 and now houses the **Centre d'Interprétation du Trait-Carré** and a tourist bureau. Concerts and exhibits are also presented here.

To get to the zoo, take the Autoroute Laurentienne (Laurentian Highway) (73) north and exit at Rue de la Faune.

A visit to the zoo is always guaranteed to fill both adults and children with wonder. The **Jardin Zoologique du Québec** ★ *($9.50; year-round, every day 9am to 5pm; 9300 Rue de la Faune, Charlesbourg, ☎622-0312, ≠644-9004, www.spsnq.qc.ca)* is an attractive site filled with greenery and flowers. In winter the area can be discovered on cross-country skis. The buildings that house the animals are made of stone, reminiscent of Quebec's old constructions, and include the **Maison des Insectes** (insect house), aviaries with over 150 species of birds and a pavilion for felines and primates. You can also attend seal performances and see many other mammals. All of this can be explored along three trails: the Hibou (owl), Ours (bear) and Orignal (moose). Many educational activities are organized throughout the year.

Take Autoroute Laurentienne (73), this time going south to return to the vicinity of 80e Rue, which becomes Boulevard Saint-Joseph. Take Boulevard Saint-Joseph going west until it becomes Boulevard Bastien.

Wendake

(pop. 1,035)

Forced off their land by the Iroquois in the 17th century, 300 Huron families moved to various places around Québec before settling in 1700 in Jeune-Lorette, today known as Wendake. Visitors will be charmed by the winding village roads in this Aboriginal reserve located on the banks of the Rivière Saint-Charles. The museum and gift shop provide a lot of information on the culture of this peaceful and sedentary people.

The **Église Notre-Dame-de-Lorette** ★ *(140 Boulevard Bastien)*, the Huron-Wendat church completed in 1730, is reminiscent of the first churches of New France. This humble building with a white plaster facade conceals unexpected treasures in its chancel and in the sacristy. Some of the objects on display were given to the Huron-Wendat community by the Jesuits, and come from the first chapel in Ancienne-Lorette (late 17th century). Among the works are several statues by Noël Levasseur created between 1730 and 1740, an altar-facing depicting an Aboriginal village by Huron-Wendat sculptor François Vincent (1790) and a beautiful *Vierge à l'Enfant* (Madonna and Child) sculpture by a Parisian goldsmith (1717). In addition, the church features a reliquary that was made in 1676, chasubles from the 18th century and various liturgical objects by Paul Manis (1715). However, the most interesting element remains the small, Louis XIII-style gilded tabernacle on the high altar sculpted by Levasseur in 1722. Maison Aroüanne (see below) offers guided tours.

Located near the church, **Maison Aroüanne** *(free admission; early May to late Sep every day 9am to 4pm, early Oct to late Apr with reservations; 10 Rue Chef-Alexandre-Duchesneau, ☎845-1241)* tells about Huron-Wendat culture and traditions through the presentation of traditional garments and everyday objects. There are also temporary exhibitions and cultural events.

Onhoüa Chetek8e ★ *($6; every day 9am to 5pm; 575 Rue Stanislas-Koska, ☎842-4308)* is a replica of a Huron-Wendat village from the time of early colonization. The traditional design includes wooden longhouses and fences. Visitors are given an introduction to the lifestyle and social organization of the ancient Huron-Wendat nation. Various Aboriginal dishes are also served and are worth a taste.

Parc de la Falaise et de la Chute Kabir Kouba has several short paths running along the cliff about 40m above Rivière Saint-Charles. The Aboriginal people called this river *Kabir Kouba*, which means "the river with many twists and turns."

Take Highway 73, which becomes Highway 175 and passes through the towns of **Lac-Beauport**, **Lac-Delage**, **Stoneham** *and* **Tewkesbury**. *Further along this highway is the entrance to* **Parc de la Jacques-Cartier** *(see p 64).*

To return to Québec City, take Highway 173 south.

Tour K: Côte-de-Beaupré and Île d'Orléans

(one to two days)

This long, narrow strip of land nestled between the St. Lawrence and the undeveloped wilderness of the Laurentian massif, is the ancestral home of many families whose roots go back to the beginning of the colony. It illustrates how the spread of the population was limited to the riverside in many regions of Québec, and recalls the fragility of development in New France. From Beauport to Saint-Joachim, the colony's first road, the Chemin du Roy (king's road) built under orders from Monseigneur de Laval during the 17th century, follows the Beaupré shore. Along this road, housea re built in a style characterized by a raised main floor covered in stucco, long balconies with intricately carved wood balusters and lace-curtained windows. As for Île d'Orléans, it is a 32km by 5km island in the middle of the St. Lawrence River downstream from Québec City. The island is close to the hearts of this region's inhabitants and has been for many years. You will quickly understand why when you visit the island and see the superb countryside, as well as Québec's heritage treasures that appear along Chemin Royal.

Beauport

(pop. 72,259)

Three types of urban development have shaped Beauport over the course of its history. Originally an agricultural settlement, it became in the 19th century an important industrial town, evolving into one of the main suburbs of Québec City in the 1960s. In 1634, the Beauport seigneury from which the present city grew, was granted to Robert Giffard, a doctor and surgeon from the Perche region of France. During the next few years he enthusiastically set about building a manor house, a mill and a small village, establishing one of the largest seigneuries in New France. Unfortunately, wars and fires have claimed several of these buildings.

The large white house known as **Manoir Montmorency** *(2490 Avenue Royale, ☎663-3330)* was built in 1780 for British governor Sir John Haldimand. At the end of the 18th century, the house became famous as the residence of the Duke of Kent, son of George III and father of Queen Victoria. The manor which once housed a hotel, was severely damaged by fire in May 1993. It has been restored according to the original plans and now features an information centre, a few shops and a restaurant (see p 237) which offers an exceptional view of the Montmorency Falls, the St. Lawrence and Île d'Orléans. The small Sainte-Marie chapel on the property and the gardens are open to the public.

Manoir Montmorency

The Manoir Montmorency is nestled in the **Parc de la Chute Montmorency** ★★ *(parking $7, free in winter, cablecar $7 return; accessible all year; for opening hours and parking ☎663-2877, ≠663-1666, www.chute montmorency.qc.ca)*. Rivière Montmorency, with its source in the Laurentians, flows peacefully until it reaches a sudden 83m drop and tumbles into a void, creating one of the most impressive natural phenomena in Québec. One and a half times the height of Niagara Falls, the Montmorency Falls flow at a rate that can reach 125,000 litres-per-second during spring thaw. To take in this magnificent spectacle, a park has been created and a tour of the falls is offered. From the manor, follow the pretty cliff path, location of the Baronne lookout. You'll soon reach two bridges, the Pont Au-dessus de la Chute and the Pont Au-dessus de la Faille, which cross the falls and the fault respectively and offer spectacular views. Once in the park you'll find picnic tables and a playground. The bottom of the falls can be reached by the 487-step panoramic staircase or the trail. The cable car provides a relaxing and picturesque way to go back to the top. During winter, steam freezes into ice cones called "sugar-loaves" that adventurous souls can climb.

Samuel de Champlain, founder of Québec City, was impressed by the falls and named them after the viceroy of New France, Charles, Duc de Montmorency. During the 19th century, the falls became a fashionable leisure area for the well-to-do of the region who would arrive in horse-drawn carriages or sleighs.

The lower part of the park, situated opposite the falls, is accessible by a long wooden staircase or by cable car. To reach the lower part of the park by car, you must make a complicated detour: continue along Avenue Royale, turn right on Côte de l'Église, then right again on Highway 40. The parking lot is on the right. To get back to Avenue Royale, take Boulevard Sainte-Anne west, Côte Saint-Grégoire and finally Boulevard des Chutes to the right.

To get to Sainte-Anne-de-Beaupré, take Boulevard Sainte-Anne (Highway 138) going east or take Chemin Royal, which travels through the bucolic countryside and pretty villages.

Among these villages, **Château-Richer** is charming and picturesque, highlighted by the striking placement of the church on a promontory. Hundred-year-old root cellars and stone ovens are visible from the road and are still used occasionally. Throughout the village, small wooden signs have been posted in front of historical buildings indicating any distinctive architectural features and when they were built. Here you can find the **Centre d'Interprétation de la Côte de Beaupré** ★ *($2; Jun to mid-Oct, every day 10am to 5pm; 7007 Avenue Royale, ☎824-3677)*, located in the Petit-Pré mill. It features an interesting exhibition on the history and geography of the Côte de Beaupré.

Sainte-Anne-de-Beaupré

(pop. 3,298)

This long, narrow village is one of the largest pilgrimage sites in North America. In 1658, the first Catholic church on the site was dedicated to Saint Anne after sailors from Brittany, who had prayed to the Virgin Mary's mother, were saved from drowning during a storm on the St. Lawrence. Soon, a great number of pilgrims began to visit the church. The second church, built in 1676, was replaced in 1872 by a huge temple, which was destroyed by fire in 1922. Finally work began on the present basilica which stands at the centre of a virtual compound of chapels, monasteries and facilities as varied as they are unusual. Each year, Sainte-Anne-de-Beaupré welcomes more than a million pilgrims, who stay in the hotels and visit the countless souvenir boutiques, of perhaps questionable taste, along Avenue Royale.

The **Basilique Sainte-Anne-de-Beaupré** ★★★ *(information counter is loctated near the entrance, early May to mid-Sep, every day 8:30am to 5pm; 10018 Avenue Royale, ☎827-3781)*, towering over the small, metal-roofed wooden houses that line the winding road, is surprising not only for its impressive size, but also for the feverish activity it inspires all summer long. The church's granite exterior, which takes on a different colour depending on the lighting, was designed in French Romanesque Revival style by Parisian architect Maxime Roisin, who was assisted by Quebecer Louis Napoléon Audet. Its spires rise 91m high, while the nave is 129m long and the transepts over 60m wide.

The wooden statue gilded with copper sitting atop the church's facade was taken from the 1872 church.

The basilica's interior is divided into five naves, supported by heavy columns with highly sculpted capitals. The vault of the main nave is adorned with sparkling mosaics designed by French artists Jean Gaudin and Auguste Labouret, recounting the life of Saint Anne. Labouret also created the magnificent stained glass, found all along the perimeter of the basilica. The left transept contains an extraordinary statue of Saint Anne cradling Mary in her right arm. Her tiara reminds visitors that she is the patron saint of Québec. In a beautiful reliquary in the background, visitors can admire the Great Relic, part of Saint Anne's forearm sent over from the San Paolo Fuori le Mura in Rome. Finally, follow the ambulatory around the choir to see the ten radiant chapels built in the 1930s, whose polychromatic architecture is inspired by the Art Deco movement. The Basilica is open all year.

Material retrieved after the demolition of the original church in 1676 was used to build the **Chapelle Commémorative** ★ *(free admission; May to mid-Sep, every day 8am to 8pm; Avenue Royale, ☎827-3781)* in 1878. The steeple (1696) was designed by Claude Bailiff, an architect whose numerous other projects in 17th-century New France have all but disappeared because of war and fire. Inside, the high altar comes from the original church built during the French Regime. It is the work of Jacques Leblond-dit-Latour (1700). The chapel is adorned with paintings from the 18th century. The water from the Fontaine de Sainte-Anne, at the foot of the chapel, is said to have healing powers.

La Scala Santa ★ *(free admission; May to mid-Sep, every day 8am to 8pm; to the right of the Chapelle Commémorative)*, an unusual yellow and white wooden building (1891) covers a staircase which pilgrims climb on their knees while reciting prayers. It is a replica of the Scala Santa, the sacred staircase conserved in Rome at San Giovanni in Laterano that Christ climbed to get to the court of Pontius Pilate. An image of the Holy Land is inlaid in each riser.

The **Chemin de la Croix** *(behind the Chapelle du Souvenir)* is located on the side of the hill and leads to the **Monastère des Laïcs**. The Chapelle de Saint-Gérard is worth a short visit. The life-size statues were cast in bronze at Bar-le-Duc, France.

The **Cyclorama de Jérusalem** ★★ *($6; late Apr to late Oct every day 9am to 6pm, Jul and Aug every day 9am to 8pm, 8 Rue Régina, near the parking lot; ☎827-3101)*. This round building with oriental features houses a 360° panorama of Jerusalem on the day of the crucifixion. This immense *trompe l'œil* painting, measuring 14m by 100m, was created in Chicago around 1880 by French artist Paul Philippoteaux and his assistants. A specialist in panoramas, Philippoteaux produced a work of remarkable realism. It was first exhibited in Montréal before being moved to Sainte-Anne-de-Beaupré at the very end of the 19th century. Very few panoramas and cycloramas, so popular at the turn of the century, have survived to the present day.

The **Musée de Sainte Anne** ★ *($5; late Apr to mid-Oct, every day 10am to 5pm; early Oct to late Apr, Sat-Sun 10am to 5pm; 9803 Boulevard Ste-Anne, ☎827-6873)* is dedicated to sacred art honouring the mother of the Virgin Mary. These interestingly diverse pieces were acquired over many years from the basilica but have only recently been put on display for the public. Sculptures, paintings, mosaics, stained-glass windows and goldworks are dedicated to the cult of Saint Anne, as well as written works expressing prayers or thanks for favours obtained. The history of pilgrimages to Sainte-Anne-de-Beaupré is also explained. The exhibition is attractively presented and spread over two floors.

*You can continue along Avenue Royale to **Cap-Tourmente National Wildlife Area** ★ (see p 70), or take Highway 360 Est to **Station Mont-Sainte-Anne** ★ (see p 65). Continuing further east on this highway, you will approach the magnificent Charlevoix region that you can visit with Ulysses Charlevoix Saguenay-Lac-Saint-Jean travel guide. To continue the present tour on Île d'Orléans, take Highway 138 west and you will soon see signs for the bridge that takes you over to the island.*

Île d'Orléans

(pop. 7,660)

Île d'Orléans is synonymous with old stones. In fact, of all Québec regions, it is the most evocative of life in New France. When Jacques

Cartier arrived in 1535, the island was covered in wild vines which inspired its first name: Île Bacchus. However, it was soon renamed in homage to the Duc d'Orléans. With the exception of Sainte-Pétronille, the parishes on the island were established in the 17th century. The colonization of the entire island followed soon after. In 1970, the government of Québec declared Île d'Orléans a historic district. The move was made in part to slow down the development that threatened to turn the island into yet another suburb of Québec City, and also as part of a widespread movement among Québécois to protect the roots of their French ancestry by preserving old churches and houses. Since 1936, the island has been linked to the mainland by a suspension bridge, the Pont de l'Île. Île d'Orléans is also known as the country of Félix Leclerc (1914-1988), the most famous Québec poet and *chansonnier*.

This tour around Île d'Orléans will allow you to enjoy its many charms. Depending on the season, you may also be able to pick fruit (see p 69). Don't be surprised if, along the way, you see enclosed llamas or ostriches. Barely ten years ago, this island only had old-fashioned black and white cows, but today, new kinds of farming have developed, multiplying the number of discoveries you can make here!

Begin the tour of the island by taking Chemin Royal to the right on top of the hill by the bridge.

★
Sainte-Pétronille

Paradoxically, Sainte-Pétronille was the site of the first French settlement on Île d'Orléans and is also its most recent parish. In 1648, François de Chavigny de Berchereau and his wife Éléonore de Grandmaison established a farm and a Huron-Wendat mission here. However, constant Iroquois attacks forced the colonists to move further east to a spot facing Sainte-Anne-de-Beaupré. It was not until the middle of the 19th century that Sainte-Pétronille was consolidated as a village, as its beautiful location began attracting numerous summer visitors. Anglophone merchants from Québec City built beautiful second homes here, many of which are still standing along the road. A word to music lovers: chamber music concerts are presented at the Église de Sainte-Pétronille on Sundays in the summer.

During her life, Éléonore de Grandmaison had four husbands. After the death of François de Chavigny, she married Jacques Gourdeau who gave his name to the estate, his wife's property. Overlooking the river from the top of a promontory, **Manoir Gourdeau** *(137 Chemin Royal)* has been given this name even though the house's construction date does not quite coincide with the time the couple was together. The long building was very likely built at the end of the 17th century but has been considerably expandedand changed since then.

Turn right on Rue Horatio-Walker, which leads to the river banks and a promenade.

Maison Horatio-Walker ★ *(11 and 13 Rue Horatio-Walker)*. The red brick building and the stucco house beside it were, respectively, the workshop and residence of painter Horatio Walker from 1904 to 1938. The British-born artist liked the French culture and the meditative calm of Île d'Orléans. His workshop, designed by Harry Staveley, remains a good example of English Arts and Crafts architecture.

The Porteous family, of English origin, settled in Québec City at the end of the 18th century. In 1900, they built the **Domaine Porteous** ★ *(253 Chemin Royal)*. This vast country house surrounded by superb gardens was christened "La Groisardière". Designed by Toronto architects Darling and Pearson, the house revived certain aspects of traditional Québec architecture. The most notable of these is the Louis XV-inspired woodwork, and the general proportions used in the design of the house which are similar to the Manoir Mauvide-Genest in Saint-Jean. Inside, are many remounted paintings by William Brymner and Maurice Cullen depicting countryside scenes on Île d'Orléans. The building also incorporates *art nouveau* features. The property, which today belongs to the Foyer de Charité Notre-Dame-d'Orléans, a seniors' residence, was expanded between 1961 and 1964 when a new wing and a chapel were added.

Saint-Laurent

Until 1950, Saint-Laurent's main industry was the manufacturing of *chaloupes*, boats and sailboats that were popular in the United States and Europe. Though production of these boats has ceased, some traces of the industry, such as abandoned boatyards, can still be seen off the road near the banks of the river. The village was founded in 1679 and still has some of its older buildings, such as the beautiful **Maison Gendreau** built in 1720 *(2387 Chemin Royal, west of the village)* and the **Moulin Gosselin**, which was turned into a restaurant *(758 Chemin Royal, east of the village)*.

★★
Saint-Jean

In the mid-19th century, Saint-Jean was the preferred homebase of nautical pilots who made a living guiding ships through the difficult waters and rocks of the St-Lawrence. Some of their

French Regime Dwelling

Parc Maritime de Saint-Laurent ★ *($2; mid Jun to early Sep every day 10am to 5pm; 120 Chemin de la Chalouperie, ☎828-9672)* has been developed on the site of the Saint-Laurent shipyard. Here you can visit the Godbout *chalouperie* workshop, a family business established around 1840. They have a collection of nearly 200 craftsmen's tools. A path behind the building leads to the water where you can rent a small boat and go on a tour.

neoclassical or Second Empire houses can still be seen along Chemin Royal and provide evidence of the privileged place held by these seamen who were indispensable to the success of commercial navigation.

The most impressive manor from the French Regime still standing is in Saint-Jean. **Manoir Mauvide-Genest** ★★ *(1451 Chemin Royal)* was built in 1734 for Jean Mauvide, the Royal Doctor, and his wife Marie-Anne

Genest. This beautiful stone building is coated with white roughcast in traditional Norman architectural style. The property officially became a seigneurial manor in the middle of the 18th century, when Mauvide, who had become rich doing business in the Caribbean, bought the southern half of the Île d'Orléans seigneury.

In 1926, Camille Pouliot, descendant of the Genest family, bought the manor house. He then restored it, adding a summer kitchen and a chapel and later transformed the house into a museum, displaying furniture and objects from traditional daily life. Pouliot was one of the first people to be actively interested in Québec's heritage. The manor was bought back in 1999 and although it will remain a museum, it will be closed for renovation until the summer of 2001.

★ Saint-François

This, the smallest village on Île d'Orléans, retains many buildings from its past. Some, however, are far from the Chemin Royal and are therefore difficult to see from Route 368. The surrounding countryside is charming and offers several pleasant panoramic views of the river, of Charlevoix and of the coast. The famous wild vine that gave the island its first name, Île Bacchus, can also be found in Saint-François.

As you leave the village, you will find an **observation tower** ★ which offers excellent views to the north and east. Visible are the Îles Madame et Au Ruau which mark the meeting point of the fresh water of the St. Lawrence and the salt water of the gulf. Mont Sainte-Anne's ski slopes, Charlevoix on the north shore and the Côte-du-Sud seigneuries on the south shore can also be seen in the distance.

★ Sainte-Famille

The oldest parish on Île d'Orléans was founded by Monseigneur de Laval in 1666 in order to establish a settlement across the river from Sainte-Anne-de-Beaupré for colonists who had previously settled around Sainte-Pétronille. Sainte-Famille has retained many buildings from the French Regime. Among them is the town's famous church, one of the greatest accomplishments of religious architecture in New France, and the oldest two-towered church in Québec.

The beautiful **Église Sainte-Famille** ★★ *(3915 Chemin Royal)* was built between 1743 and 1747 to replace the original church built in 1669. Inspired by the Église des Jésuites in Québec City, which has since been destroyed, Father Dufrost de la Jemmerais ordered the construction of two towers with imperial roofs, which explains the single steeple sitting atop the gable. Other unusual elements such as five alcoves and the sundial by the entrance (which has since been destroyed) made

Église Sainte-Famille

the building even more unique. In the 19th century, new statues were installed in the alcoves and the imperial roofs gave way to two new steeples, bringing the total number of steeples to three.

Although modified several times, the interior decor retains many interesting elements. Sainte-Famille was a wealthy parish in the 18th century, thus allowing the decoration of the church to begin as soon as the frame of the building was finished. In 1748, Gabriel Gosselin installed the first pulpit and in 1749 Pierre-Noël Levasseur completed construction of the high altar's present tabernacle. Louis-Basile David, inspired by the Quévillon school, designed the beautiful coffered vault in 1812. Many paintings adorn the church, such as *La Sainte Famille* (The Holy Family) painted by Frère Luc during his stay in Canada in 1670, the *Dévotion au Sacré Coeur de Jésus* (Devotion to the Sacred Heart of Jesus, 1766) and *Le Christ en Croix* (Christ on the Cross) by François Baillargé (1802). The church grounds offer a beautiful view of the coast.

Most of the French Regime farmhouses on Île d'Orléans were built a good distance from the road. Today these properties are much sought after and their owners jealously guard their privacy, which makes any visiting unlikely. Fortunately, a foundation has been set up by residents so that **Maison Drouin** ★★ *($2, end of Jun to mid Oct every day 11am to 6pm, ☎829-0330)* is open every summer to interested visitors. It is one of the oldest houses on the island and in Québec, dating from the 17th century. It stands by a bend on Chemin Royal and was build with large fieldstones and wooden beams. You will learn about its history from guides dressed in period costume acting out the daily life of its former inhabitants. The three rooms on the ground floor as well as the upstairs recall the environment of the first colonists. Antique furniture and tools are also displayed to help illustrate pioneer life, making it a lovely place to visit.

Saint-Pierre

The most developed parish on Île d'Orléans had already lost some of its charm before the island was declared a historic site. Saint-Pierre is particularly important to the people of Québec, since it was the home of the renowned poet and singer Félix Leclerc (1914-1988) for many years. The singer and songwriter, who penned *P'tit Bonheur* was the first musician to introduce Québécois music to Europe. He is buried in the local cemetery.

Église Saint-Pierre ★
(1249 Chemin Royal),a lowly building erected in 1716, is the oldest village church still standing in Canada. The church is also a rare survivor of this kind of architecture, which was widespread in New France. It only has one portal and an oculus window on the facade. Most of these little churches with pointed roofs were destroyed in the 19th century and replaced with more elaborate structures. Pillaged during the Conquest, the interior of Église Saint-Pierre was rebuilt at the end of the 18th century. Note in particular the altars by Pierre Émond (1795) embellished with the papal coat of arms. The paintings above the altars are by François Baillairgé.

This church was abandoned in 1955 when the larger church nearby was inaugurated, but, threatened by demolition was taken over by the Québec government. Conserved intact, it displays equipment no longer found in most Québec churches such as a central stove with long iron stovepipe. The pews have doors which allowed these closed spaces to be posted as private property and in winter, the owners warmed with hot bricks and furs.

The tour is now over. At the traffic light, turn right, go down the hill and return to Québec City on Highway 138 Ouest.

Accommodations

Québec City has all kinds of accommodations to offer: two youth hostels, plenty of bed and beakfasts, inns and luxury hotels.

You will certainly find a suitable place to stay, whether it is for one night or one week.

Rates may vary from one season to another. Rooms are more expensive during the summer or high season, and the weeks of the Festival d'Été (Summer Festival) in July and Carnaval in February are the busiest of the year. We recommend that you reserve well in advance if you plan to visit Québec City during these periods. The prices mentioned here are for a standard room for two people in high season, unless otherwise indicated. However, there may be rooms of different prices in the same hotel. The following accommodations are classified according to price starting with the least expensive. Remember

to add the 7% federal tax and the 7.5% Québec sales tax to the given rate when making your calculations. These taxes are refundable to non-residents (see p 56). A non-refundable tax called

"Taxe Spécifique sur l'Hébergement" (accommodation tax) is also applied to accommodation costs. It was introduced in 1997 to support the tourist infrastructure in the Québec City region. The amount is $2 per night regardless of the total bill or the type of accommodation.

Symbols accompanying the description of each establishment will help you choose the location that suites you best. Note that these symbols do not necessarily apply to all rooms. The key to the symbols can be found at the beginning of this book. While most accommodations provide private bathrooms, there are exceptions where bathrooms must be shared. This will be mentioned in our descriptions.

Although comfort may be a little rudimentary in the smaller inns, the comfort level in hotels is generally high and includes many services. There are quite a few bed and breakfasts in Québec City. Their prices are reasonable and their advantage is they offer a home-style atmosphere. In Québec, bed and breakfasts are known as gîtes du passant The *gîtes du passant* are members of the Fédération des Agricotours du Québec and must conform to their regulations and standards to ensure a high level of quality. A *Ulysses Gîtes du Passant au Québec* travel guide is available and lists the various accommodations and services for each Québec region.

Hospitalité Canada Tours is a free telephone service operated by the Maison du Tourisme de Québec *(12 Rue Ste-Anne;* ☎*800-665-1528 or from Montreal* ☎*514 252-3117;* ≠*(514 393-8942)*. Depending on what kind of accommodations you're looking for, the staff will suggest various places belonging to the network and even make reservations for you.

Ulysses's Favourites

For history buffs:
Château Frontenac (p 187),
Hôtel Clarendon (p 186),
Le Vieux-Presbytère (p 199)
Auberge Baker (p 197)

For the view:
Château Frontenac (p 187),
Hôtel Loews Le Concorde (p 191),
Hôtel Dominion 1912 (p 189),
Château Bellevue (p 186)
Château de Pierre (p 186)
La Goéliche (p 199)

For the décor:
Auberge Saint-Antoine (p 189),
Hôtel du Théâtre Capitole (p 192),
Hôtel Dominion 1912 (p 89)
Auberge Saint-Pierre (p 189)

For the warm welcome:
Auberge du Quartier (p 190)
Auberge du Petit Pré (p 196)

For peace and quiet:
Château Bonne-Entente (p 193),
Le Canard Huppé (p 199),
La Chaumière Juchereau-Duchesnay (p 195)

For the friendly atmosphere:
Auberge de la Paix (p 182),
Café Krieghoff B&B (p 190),
La Marquise de Bassano (p 184)
Hôtel Belley (p 187)

For business people:
Québec Hilton (p 192),
Hôtel Loews Le Concorde (p 191)
Radisson Hôtel Gouverneur (p 193)

Tour A: Vieux-Québec

Centre International de Séjour (Hostelling International)
$17 members
$19.50 non-members
19 Rue Ste-Ursule
G1R 4E1
☎*800-461-8585*
☎*694-0755*
from Montréal
☎*(514) 252-3117*

The Centre International de Séjour is a youth hostel with 250 beds for young people during the summer months. The rooms can accommodate from three to eight people, the dormitories from 10 to 12, and there are also private double rooms.

Auberge de la Paix
$19 bkfst incl.
plus $2 for bedding
if you don't have your own
sb, K
31 Rue Couillard
G1R 3T4
☎*694-0735*

Behind its lovely white facade in Vieux-Québec, Auberge de la Paix has a youth-hostel atmosphere. It has 59 beds in rooms able to accommodate from two to eight people, as well as a kitchenette and a living room. This inn lives up to its name by providing a friendly and fun place to relax. In the summer, a lovely garden is filled with flowers. Children are welcome!

Manoir LaSalle
$50
pb/sb
18 Rue Sainte-Ursule
G1R 4C9
☎*692-9953*

Manoir LaSalle is a small hotel with 11 rooms, one of which has a private bathroom. This red brick building is exemplary of the architectural style of some of the first homes built in the city.

Auberge Saint-Louis
$55
$85 bkfst incl.
ℜ, ≡
48 Rue Saint-Louis
G1R 3Z3
☎*692-2424*
☎*888-692-4105*
≈*692-3797*

Located on busy Rue Saint-Louis, Auberge Saint-Louis is a small pleasant, hotel. Room prices vary according to amenities offered. Less expensive rooms do not have private bathrooms. The hotel is well maintained.

Au Jardin du Gouverneur
$60 bkfst incl.
≡
16 Rue Mont-Carmel
G1R 4A3
☎*692-1704*
≈*692-1713*

Au Jardin du Gouverneur is a charming little hotel a in

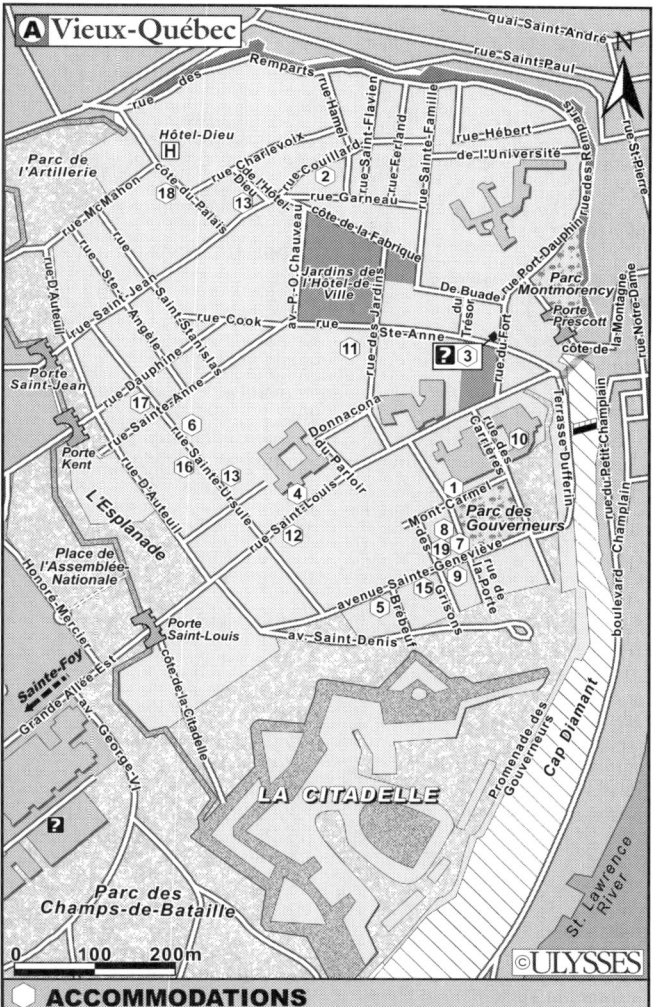

A Vieux-Québec

ACCOMMODATIONS

1. Au Jardin du Gouverneur
2. Auberge de la Paix
3. Auberge du Trésor
4. Auberge Saint-Louis
5. Cap-Diamant
6. Centre International de Séjour
7. Château Bellevue
8. Château de Léry
9. Château de Pierre
10. Château Frontenac
11. Clarendon
12. Clos Saint-Louis
13. Hôtel du Vieux-Québec
14. Maison Acadienne
15. Maison Sainte-Geneviève
16. Maison Sainte-Ursule
17. Manoir LaSalle
18. Manoir Victoria
19. Marquise de Bassano

small blue and white house opposite Parc des Gouverneurs. Rooms are a good size but there is nothing special about the decor. No smoking.

Marquise de Bassano
$65 bkfst incl.
sb
15 Rue des Grisons
G1R 4M6
☎*692-0316*
www.total.net/~bassano

Vieux-Québec has been home to some colourful characters throughout its history. At the corner of the Rue des Grisons and Avenue Sainte-Geneviève is a small Victorian house which, it is said, was built for one of them. The dark panelling that decorates the inside surely guards some secrets of the Marquise de Bassano. The house has been transformed into a welcoming bed and breakfast, with charming rooms and cheerful sitting room with a piano and a fireplace. During breakfast, which sometimes lasts into the afternoon, the young hosts take pleasure in animating the discussions!

Maison du Fort
$75 bkfst incl.
≡
21 Avenue Ste-Geneviève
G1R 4B1
☎*692-4375*
⇌*692-5257*

Maison du Fort is tucked away in a quiet neighbourhood around Parc des Gouverneurs. This small residence offers adequate rooms, and the service is quite welcoming.

Maison Acadienne
$77
⊛, ≡, *K*
43 Rue Ste-Ursule
G1R 4E4
☎*694-0280*

A number of old houses on Rue Sainte-Ursule have been made into hotels. Among these, Maison Acadienne is easily noticed by its large, white facade. The rooms are rather lacklustre, although some of them have been renovated.

Manoir Victoria
$79
≡, ≈, ☉, △, ℜ, *K*
44 Côte du Palais
G1R 4H8
☎*692-1030 or 692-3822*
☎*800-463-6283*

Manoir Victoria is a 145-room hotel nestled on Côte du Palais. Decorated in true Victorian style, it succeeds in being both chic and very comfortable. The lobby, at the top of a long flight of stairs, is inviting and contains both a bar and a dining room. Manoir Victoria offers well-equipped suites and a number of cultural and sports packages.

Tour A: Vieux-Québec

Cap-Diamant
$80
≡, *tv*, ℝ
39 Avenue Ste-Geneviève
G1R 4B3
☎*694-0313*

The Cap-Diamant hotel is located in an old house in Vieux-Québec. This is the kind of house where even the walls have secrets… and many stories to tell. It is the perfect place to immerse yourself in family life of the past. The long staircase, the creaking floors, and even the wallpaper contribute to its quaint look and make it quite charming. In the summer you can enjoy the porch or wander in the flower-filled garden and sit by the stream.

Château de Léry
$85 bkfst incl.
≡
8 Rue Laporte
G1R 4M9
☎*692-2692*
☎*800-363-0036*
≠*692-5231*

Located next to Parc des Gouverneurs and overlooking the river, the Château de Léry has comfortable rooms. Rooms facing the street have a good view. This hotel is in a quiet neighbourhood in the old part of the city, but is just a few minutes walk from the bustle of downtown.

Auberge du Trésor
$105
ℜ
20 Rue Sainte-Anne
G1R 3X2
☎*694-1876*
☎*800-566-1876*

Auberge du Trésor was built in 1676. Renovated many times since then, it maintains an impressive appearance. Rooms are modern and comfortable. All rooms have private bathrooms and colour televisions.

Le Clos Saint-Louis
$105 bkfst incl.
sb/pb, ⊛, ≡, ℜ
71 Rue St-Louis
G1R 3Z2
☎*694-1311*
☎*800-461-9411*
≠*694-9411*

Le Clos Saint-Louis is lodged in two imposing Victorian houses dating from 1844 on Rue St-Louis. Located close to Vieux-Québec attractions, this hotel has 50 rooms spread out on three floors and there are even plans to renovate the attic soon. The rooms have all been arranged to make their historic aspect especially welcoming: some have four-poster beds with canopies, others old-fashioned bookcases or fireplaces. The rooms on the second floor are particularly attractive with their stone walls and exposed wooden beams. Even if some of the bathrooms must be shared, they are all modern and well equipped. In the morning, coffee and croissants are served in the cellar.

Hotel Clarendon
$119
≡, ℜ
57 Rue Ste-Anne
G1R 3X4
☎*692-4652*
☎*888-554-6001*
≠*692-4652*

Built in 1870, the Hotel Clarendon is one of the oldest hotels in the city. The hotel has an unpretentious exterior while the elegant interior is decorated in Art Deco style. The entrance hall is very attractive. The rooms in this hotel have been renovated many times over the years and are spacious and comfortable. This a very good place to stay in Vieux-Québec (see also p 89). Its restaurant, Le Charles-Baillargé (see p 215), serves elegant meals, and you can also has a lively bar, L'Emprise (see p 243), which plays jazz music.

Château Bellevue
$129
16 Rue Laporte
G1R 4M9
☎*692-2473*
☎*800-463-2617*
≠*692-4876*

The Château Bellevue has an impressive view of the river. The rooms are reasonable but equipped with uninteresting modern furniture.

Château de Pierre
$135
≡
17 Avenue Ste-Geneviève
G1R 4A8
☎*694-0429*

The Château de Pierre is housed in an old colonial-style house. The ostentatious entrance of this hotel is quite striking and somewhat flashy. The rooms are comfortable.

Hôtel du Vieux-Québec
$139
≡, K, P
1190 Rue St-Jean
☎*692-1850*
☎*800-361-7787*
≠*692-5637*

Hôtel du Vieux-Québec is a modern establishment that exudes a kind of coolness often associated with modernism. Although the decor is not extravagant, it is quite comfortable and friendly. The rooms are spacious and several of them have kitchenettes. There also is a terrace.

Tour B: Petit-Champlain to Vieux-Port

Château Frontenac
$375
ℜ, ≡, &., ⊛, ≈, ⊘
1 Rue des Carrières
G1R 4P5
☎*692-3861*
☎*800-268-9420*
⇄*692-1751*

The Château Frontenac is by far the most prestigious hotel in Québec City (see p 83). Enter its elegant lobby with its wood panelling and warm colours and let yourself be transported back in time. Château Frontenac was built in 1893 and over the years has been the setting of several historic events. The decor exudes a classic, refined richness that is truly worthy of a castle. Its restaurant also offers a taste of luxury (see Le Champlain, p 216). The sumptuous rooms offer visitors the most comfortable environment possible, and although the size and benefits of the hotel's 600 rooms vary greatly, they are all quite pleasant. The rooms overlooking the river have beautiful bay windows and, of course, the view is magnificent.

Hôtel Belley
$75
K
249 Rue St-Paul
G1K 3W5
☎*692-1694*
☎*888-692-1694*
⇄*692-1696*

The pleasant Hôtel Belley stands opposite the market at the Vieux-Port. A hotel since 1877, this handsome building will leave you with fond memories for years to come. It has eight simply decorated, cozy rooms, some with exposed brick walls, others with wooden beams and skylights. The ground floor is home to a bar called Taverne Belley (see p 244), whose breakfasts and lunches, served in two lovely rooms, are very popular with locals. A number of extremely comfortable and attractively decorated lodgings, some with terraces, are also available in another house across the street. These may be rented by the night, by the week or by the month.

Hayden's Wexford House
$85 bkfst incl.
450 Rue Champlain
G1K 4J3
☎ *524-0524*
≈ *648-8995*

Located on a magnificent street between Cap Diamant and the river, Hayden's Wexford House proudly heralds its facade and has done so since 1832. Its name, in fact, is inscribed in the brickwork. This house has kept all of its former charm. The four small rooms nestled on the top floor have lovely views from the dormer windows and are tastefully decorated with wood trim and floral patterns. The bathrooms have been recently renovated and are modern. To add to the guests' comfort, quality mattresses have been made to measure. Breakfast is served in a charming dining room with stone walls that is also in keeping with the character of the house. No smoking.

Appartements du Cap-Blanc
$125
ℑ
444 Rue Champlain
G1K 4J3
☎ *524-6137*
≈ *648-8995*

Do you want to spend a few days in Québec City in a well-situated *pied-à-terre* with all the necessary conveniences? Appartements du Cap-Blanc will surely please you since they are right next door to the owner's bed and breakfast (see Hayden's Wexford House). Each apartment occupies one floor of a renovated old house. Two of them have fireplaces so you can spend pleasant moments in front of the fire in this cozy stone and wood setting. Each apartment has a living room, well-equipped kitchenette, dining room, bathroom and closed bedroom, all attractively decorated. You'll never want to leave! There is a minimum stay of two nights and no smoking.

Le Priori
$145 bkfst incl.
⊛, ℜ
15 Rue du Saul-au-Matelot
G1K 3Y7
☎ *522-8108*
☎ *800-351-3992*
≈ *692-0883*

Le Priori is located on a quiet street in Basse-Ville. The building is very old but has been renovated in a very modern style. The decor successfully contrasts the old stone walls of the building with up-to-date furnishings. The appearance is striking and even the elevator is distinctive. Le Priori is highly recommended.

Auberge Saint-Pierre
$169 bkfst incl.
K
79 Rue St-Pierre
G1K 4A3
☎694-7981
☎888-268-1017
≠694-0406

A lovely inn has recently opened in a building that had housed Canada's first insurance company since the end of the 19th century. The historic charm of the Auberge Saint-Pierre was conserved when the building was renovated. The rooms make you think of the neighbouring apartments, with their various landings and narrow hallways. Each room has beautiful, dark hardwood floors and sumptuously coloured walls. Those on the lower floors have lovely high ceilings, while those higher up have a wonderful view.

Auberge Sainte-Antoine
$219 bkfst incl.

⊛, ≡
10 Rue St-Antoine
G1K 4C9
☎692-2211
☎888-692-2211
≠692-1177

Auberge Sainte-Antoine is located near the Musée de la Civilisation. This lovely hotel is divided into two buildings. Guests enter through a tastefully renovated old stone building. The entrance hall is distinguished by exposed wooden beams, stone walls and a beautiful fireplace. The hotel serves breakfast. Each room is decorated according to a different theme and has its own unique charm.

Escalier Casse-Cou

Hôtel Dominion 1912
$219 bkfst incl.
126 Rue St-Pierre
G1K 4A8
☎692-2224
☎888-833-5253
≠692-4403

One of the beautiful buildings on Rue Saint-Pierre, this one dating from 1912, has been newly renovated into a hotel that charms its chic clientele. The luxurious Hôtel Dominion 1912 has a modern aspect with materials such as glass and wrought iron, but still maintains its original character. Elements of interior decoration such as cream and sand coloured draperies and cushions, and luxuriously soft sofas and bedspreads make the place extremely comfortable. Black and white photographs of the neighbourhood hang in each room, inviting you to go out and visit it. The upper floors have magnificent views of the river on one side and of the city on the other.

Tour C: Grande Allée and Avenue Cartier

La Maison d'Elizabeth et Emma
$65 bkfst incl.
$55 without bkfst
sb, K
10 Grande Allée Ouest
G1R 2G6
☎647-0880

Over the last few years, residents of Grande Allée have established several places for visitors to stay. You will easily recognize the warm colours of Maison d'Elizabeth et Emma. Located at the corner of Rue De Salaberry, the house's entire second floor is given over to guests. There are four rooms, including a large one in front that may be a little noisy, and a small former maid's room at the back. However, they are all adorned with period furniture and beautiful dark woodwork. Large windows make the place very bright and there is a small reading area and kitchen. When the weather is nice, breakfast is served on the balcony.

Café Krieghoff
$65 bkfst incl.
ℜ, ℝ, ≡
1091 Avenue Cartier
G1R 2A6
☎522-3711
⇌647-1429

Café Krieghoff offers travellers a bed and breakfast combination. The novelty, however, is that breakfast is served in the café itself (see p 224) which guarantees both good food and pleasant surroundings! The friendly staff makes sure to include visitors in the family-like atmosphere. The five rooms nestled above the restaurant are modest and clean. Each one has access to a private bathroom (even if it is not connected to the room), and they all share a small sitting room and balcony with a view of lively Avenue Cartier.

Manoir Lafayette
$89
≡, ℜ
661 Grande Allée Est
G1R 2K4
☎522-2652
⇌522-4400

Manoir Lafayette is attractive and elegant. The hotel was recently renovated and some rooms are equipped with comfortable antique furniture. The Lafayette has an excellent location.

Auberge du Quartier
$90 bkfst incl.
170 Grande Allée Ouest.
G1R 2G9
☎525-9726
☎800-782-9441
⇌521-4891

Looking for a charming little neighbourhood inn? Situated opposite the imposing Église Saint-Dominique, just 5min from the Plaines d'Abraham and the Musée du Québec, Auberge du Quartier should please you. This large white, well-lit house has a dozen clean, attractive and modern rooms. They are spread out on three floors, with a suite in the attic. Reception by the owner and staff is very friendly.

Hôtel Château Laurier
$94
≡, ℜ, ⊛, P
1220 Place George-V Ouest
G1R 5B8
☎*522-8108*
☎*800-463-4453*
≈*524-8768*
www.vieux-quebec.com/Laurier
For several years, Château Laurier has been situated in an old house with a beautiful stone facade on the corner of Grande Allée. The hotel recently adopted a new image. The small guestrooms have been renovated, retaining their original character, while a large modern wing with classical decor has been added at the back. Nevertheless, they are fairly cramped and some have a view of the parking lot. They will suit people looking for fresh new accommodations as well as business people, since some of the rooms offer Internet access.

Hôtel Loews Le Concorde
$125
&, ≡, ≈, ⊘, △, ℜ
1225 Place Montcalm
G1R 4W6
☎*647-2222*
≈*647-4710*
Just outside Vieux-Québec is the Hôtel Loews Le Concorde. It is part of the Loews hotel chain and has spacious, comfortable rooms with spectacular views of Québec City and the surrounding area. There is a revolving restaurant on top of the hotel (see L'Astral p 230).

Château Grande Allée
$130
601 Grande Allée Est
G1R 2K4
☎*647-4433*
≈*646-7553*
The Château Grande Allée is a recent addition to busy Grande Allée. The well-kept rooms are so large that they look under-furnished. Making up for this slight shortcoming are various features, including large bathrooms.

Tour D: Saint-Jean-Baptiste

Guesthouse 727
$69 bkfst incl.; sb, bp;
727 Rue d'Aiguillon, G1R 1M8
☎ *648-6766*
≈ *648-1474*

In the heart of the gay neighbourhood, Guesthouse 727 is a friendly place, which offers people from the milieu a pleasant and relaxed atmosphere. A few of the rooms are furnished with antiques and some are equipped with VCRs.

Chez Pierre
$70 bkfst incl.
ℝ
636 Rue d'Aiguillon
G1R 1M5
☎ *522-2173*

Chez Pierre is a bed and breakfast with three rooms. Two of them are situated in the renovated basement, but the third room is upstairs and has all the charm of a faubourg Saint-Jean-Baptiste apartment. However, the bathroom of this last room is also situated in the basement. Pierre, your host, is a painter and his large coloured canvases brighten up the house. He serves a generous breakfast in the morning.

Québec Hilton
$149
≈, ⊘, △, ℝ, ⚒
1100 Boulevard René-Lévesque Est
G1J 1H3
☎ *647-2411*
☎ *800-447-2411*
≈ *647-6488*

Located just outside Vieux-Québec, the Québec Hilton offers rooms with the kind of comfort associated with an international hotel chain. The Place Québec shopping mall, is located in the lobby, which is connected to the new Centre des Congres.

Hôtel du Théâtre Capitole
$180
ℝ, ≡, ⊛
972 Rue St-Jean
G1R 1R5
☎ *694-9930*
☎ *800-363-4040*
≈ *647-2146*

Hôtel du Théâtre Capitole

Adjoining the newly renovated theatre, the Hôtel du Théâtre Capitole is located in surrounding the theatre. While not luxurious, the rooms are amusing, the decor resembling a stage set. At the entrance is the restaurant Il Teatro (see p 233).

winter, pure white snow, Christmas decorations and sparkling lights bathe the city in magic and romance. - *T. Philiptchenko*

A lovely view of the multicoloured roofs in the Basse-Ville sector of Vieux Québec that can be admired from Cap Diamant.
- *S. Schanz*

February is Carnaval de Québec time, when a multitude of activities is held all over the city and its surroundings. Here, a canoe race tackles the icy river.
- *Y. Tessier*

Radisson Gouverneurs Québec
$205
≈, ≡, ⊘, ⅄, △, ℜ
690 Boulevard Rene-Lévesque Est
G1R 5A8
☎ *647-1717ou 800-910-1111*
≠ *647-2146*

The Radisson Gouverneurs Québec is located close to Vieux-Québec. This hotel has over 350 rooms, all nicely decorated. Regular rooms are furnished with slightly rustic but elegant pine furniture. The hotel's heated outdoor pool is open all year.

Tour E: Chemin Sainte-Foy

Sainte-Foy

Université Laval
$20
Université Laval, Pavillon Parent
Office 1604
G1K 7P4
☎ *656-2801*

It is possible to rent a room on the university campus from the beginning of May to mid-August. The Service des Résidences on campus is responsible for renting these rooms, which offer the basic comfort of a single bed and a bureau. The bathrooms are shared by all residents on the floor. This is an inexpensive place to stay and is worth considering. There is also a weekly rate. It is better to reserve in advance. Public transportation serves this area well; it takes about 10min to get downtown.

YWCA
$40
≡, *P*
855 Avenue Holland
G1S 3S5
☎ *683-2155*
≠ *683-5526*

The YWCA residence is found on the border of Sillery and Québec City. For a modest sum you can rent, for either a long or short stay, one of the small rudimentary rooms. There is a cafeteria, laundry room, swimming pool and parking.

Château Bonne-Entente
$56-194
ℜ, ≡, K, tv, ⊛, =, ✪
3400 Chemin Sainte-Foy
G1X 1S6
☎ *653-5221*
☎ *800-463-4390*
≠ *653-3098*

This magnificent old-English-Style property is spread out over 4.5ha and is covered with greenery and flowers. Rooms have been decorated with taste and refinement, and the entire inn has plenty of comfort and charm. You can also participate in a number of indoor and outdoor activities here, or simply enjoy the ducks splashing about in the nearby pond. Château Bonne-Entente offers all the advan

Several Hotels near the Airport

The area around the airport is not particularly pleasant so travellers tend to spend only one night here. Here are some good choices:

Château Repotel
$70 bkfst incl.
≡, ⊛, ♿
6555 Boulevard Wilfrid-Hamel, G2E 5W3
☎872-1111
≈872-5989
Château Repotel is well set up to make your stay pleasant. The rooms are not luxurious but they are peaceful and have large bathrooms.

Confortel Québec
$82 bkfst incl.
≡, ⊛, ♿
6500 Boulevard Wilfrid-Hamel, G2E 2J1
☎877-4777
≈877-0013
As its name indicates, Confortel Québec is a hotel concerned with comfort. Furnished in bland colours and modern furniture, the rooms are austere but spacious.

Confort Inn L'Ancienne-Lorette
$83
≡, ♿
1255 Autoroute Duplessis, G2G 2B4
☎872-5900
≈872-9550
Confort Inn L'Ancienne-Lorette is on the road leading to the airport. Despite the laminated furniture, rooms are attractive.

tages and benefits of a country resort right in the city. Its restaurant, Le Pailleur (see p 234), serves gourmet Québécois cooking. There are also several conference rooms.

Hôtel Gouverneur
$170
ℜ, ≡, *tv*, ⊛, ≈
3030 Boulevard Laurier
G1V 2M5
☎*651-3030 or 888-910-1111*
≠*651-6797*
Hôtel Gouverneur is a top-notch establishment with warm-coloured rooms and maximum comfort. It is judiciously located near the bridges, a few minutes away from the shopping centres and right next to the expressways that lead to the region's various sports centres. It's dining room, restaurant La Verrière, will delight your taste buds as well as your eyes. A large area in the back has been landscaped with lush greenery and a lovely swimming pool.

Tour F: Saint-Roch

Hôtel Royal William
$150
ℜ, ≡
360 Boulevard Charest Est
G1K 3H4
☎*521-4488 or 888-541-0405*
www.royalwilliam.com
During this period of restoration in the Saint-Roch neighbourhood, a large hotel has opened, expressing very well the spirit of revival as well as livening up the surrounding area. Hôtel Royal William is located on Boulevard Charest. Business people are particularly pleased with the practical aspect of the 40-odd rooms. In fact, the rooms are equipped with work tables, telephone outlets and Internet access and are located near everything. The decor is modern and comfortable, like most hotels in this category.

Tour J: Heading North

Sainte-Catherine-de-la-Jacques-Cartier

Chaumière Juchereau-Duchesnay
$75 bkfst incl.
ℜ, ≈
5050 Route Fossambault
G0A 3M0
☎*875-2751 or 800-501-2122*
≠*875-2752*
Not far from Station Forestière de Duchesnay, where you can take part in a variety of outdoor activities, Chaumière Juchereau-Duchesnay offers room and board. Its nine pastel-coloured rooms are all similarly decorated. They are very comfortable despite the fact that they do not have the same antique

elegance as the dining room. This inn, with its trees, swimming pool and terrace, will allow you to relax in peace and quiet.

Parc de la Jacques-Cartier

Parc de la Jacques-Cartier
$17.50
Centre d'Accueil et d'Interpretation, Stoneham, G0A 4P0
☎*848-7272*

In Parc de la Jacques-Cartier you can camp in magnificent surroundings. Along the river, there are numerous campsites, some rustic, others with some facilities. And of course there's no lack of things to do!

Tour K: Côte-de-Beaupré and Île d'Orléans

Beauport

Hôtel Ambassadeur
$79
☉, △, ℜ
321 boul. Ste-Anne, G1E 3L4
☎*666-2828 ou 800-363-4619*
≠*666-2775*

This hotel was built on the outskirts of town in an area where travellers usually only stop for one night. The rooms are large and attractive, and on the ground floor is a good Chinese restaurant.

Journey's End
$90
240 Boulevard Sainte-Anne
G1E 3L7
☎*666-1226*
≠*666-5088*

This member of the Journey's End hotel chain lives up to companu standards. It offers travellers comfortable rooms where they can relax. Journey's End is better known for its low prices than for its variety of services.

Château-Richer

Auberge du Petit Pré
$60 bkfst incl.
sb
7126 Avenue Royale, G0A 1N0
☎*824-3852*
≠*824-3098*

At the Auberge du Petit Pré in an 18th-century house, you will be warmly received and well treated. Their four bedrooms are cosy and tastefully decorated. There's a large picture window which is open when the weather is nice, two lounges, one with a T.V. and the other with a fireplace, as well as two bathrooms with clawfoot tubs. Breakfasts are generous and finely prepared.

Also, if requested in advance, the owner will prepare one of his delicious dinners for you. The splendid aroma of the food fills the house and adds to its overall warmth.

Auberge Baker
$65-$85 bkfst incl.
ℑ, ⊛, ℜ, K
8790 Avenue Royale, G0A 1N0
☎666-5509
≠824-4412

For over 50 years, the Auberge Baker has existed in this hundred-year-old Côte-de-Beaupré house. Its stone walls, low ceilings, wood floors and wide-frame windows enchant visitors. The five bedrooms are on the dimly-lit upper floor but there are also a kitchenette, a bathroom and an adjoining terrace on the same floor. The rooms are meticulously decorated in authentic fashion and furnished with antiques. They serve delicious food.

Sainte-Anne-de-Beaupré

La Bécassine
$75
ℜ
9341 Boulevard Sainte-Anne
G0A 3C0
☎827-4988

La Bécassine is located less than 10min from Mont Sainte-Anne. It is actually a motel since most of the rooms are next to the main building. The rooms are simply but quite pleasantly decorated. There is also a large dining room, and the kitchen's specialty is game.

Beaupré (Mont Sainte-Anne)

Camping Mont Ste-Anne
$20
C.P. 400, Beaupré, G0A 1E0
☎827-4561 or 826-2323

Camping Mont Ste-Anne located at Mont-Sainte-Anne, has 166 campsites in a wooded area traversed by the Rivière Jean-Larose. Essential services are offered, and, because the campground is close to all the park's outdoor activities, the location is great.

Hôtel L'Aventure
$69
ℜ, ≡, tv, =
355 Rue Dupont
G0A 1E0
☎827-5748
≠827-3663

Just before getting to the top of the hill leading to Mont Sainte-Anne, take the first street on the left to reach Hôtel L'Aventure. This hotel is a modern construction offering a young, dynamic atmosphere and moderate comfort. From here there is a view of Mont Sainte-Anne and its ski trails. The very popular restaurant serves a variety of dishes, including fondue and pizza.

Villégiature Mont-Sainte-Anne
$88-200
≡, K, tv, ⊛, ℑ, =
2000 Boulevard Beaupré
G0A 1E0
☎ *827-1871*
☎ *800-463-1568, ext. 155*
Situated at the foot of the mountain, Villégiature Mont-Sainte-Anne is the dream spot for those who prefer to stay put rather than travel from one place to another. There are several apartments of varying sizes that can accommodate from two to eight people. Some rooms have whirlpool baths and a mezzanine. All accommodations are equipped with modern kitchens and functional fireplaces and are very comfortable. Several apartments have views overlooking the trails.

Hôtel Val des Neiges
$90 ½b
≈, ⊙, △, ℜ, ⊛, ℑ
201 Val des Neiges, G0A 1E0
☎ *827-5711 or 888-554-6005*
≈ *827-5997*
Many chalets have recently been built around the base of the Mont Sainte-Anne, in newly developed areas. Among these is the Hôtel Val des Neiges The decor is rustic and the rooms are comfortable. The complex also includes small, well-equipped condos. They also offer cruise packages.

La Camarine
$105
≡, ℜ
10947 Sainte-Anne, G0A   1E0
☎ *827-5703 or 800-567-3939*
≈ *827-5430*
La Camarine faces the Saint Lawrence River. This charming high-quality inn has thirty rooms. The decor successfully combines the rustic feel of the house with the more modern wooden furniture. This is a delightful spot and its restaurant has a very good reputation (see p 238).

Île d'Orléans

On île d'Orléans, there are about 50 bed and breakfasts! A list can be obtained from the tourist office. There are also a few guesthouses with solid reputations and a campground. There are plenty of options therefore for getting the most out of your stay on this enchanting island.

Camping Orléans
$22
≈
357 Chemin Royal, St-François, G0A 3S0
☎ *829-2953*
≈ *829-2563*
Camping Orléans has close to 80 campsites, most of which are shaded and offer a view of the river. Many

services are offered. There is access to the river bank where you can go for a pleasant walk.

Le Vieux-Presbytère
$60-$70 bkfst incl., $110-$145 ½b
pb/sb, ℜ
1247 Avenue Monseigneur-d'Esgly
St-Pierre, G0A 4E0
☎ ***828-9723 or 888-282-9723***
≠ ***828-2189***

The guesthouse Le Vieux-Presbytère is in fact located in an old presbytery just behind the village church. The structure is predominantly made out of wood and stone. Low ceilings with wide beams, wide-frame windows and antiques such as woven bedcovers and braided rugs take you back to the era of New France. The dining room and the lounge are inviting. It is a tranquil spot with rustic charm.

Église Sainte-Famille

Le Canard Huppée
$125 bkfst incl., $175 ½b
≡, ℜ
2198 Chemin Royal, St-Laurent,
G0A 3Z0
☎ ***828-2292 or 800-838-2292***
≠ ***828-0966***

Le Canard Huppée has enjoyed a very good reputation over the last few years. Their eight clean, comfortable, country-style rooms are scattered with wooden ducks. The restaurant is also just as renowned and appealing (see p 239). The service is conscientious, and the surrounding, beautiful.

Auberge Chaumonot
$149 bkfst incl.
$189 1/2b
=, ℜ
425 Chemin Royal
Saint-François, G0A 3S0
☎ ***829-2735***
☎ ***800-520-2735***

This small inn only has eight rooms and is open exclusively in the summer. Located on the south shore of the island, Auberge Chaumonot was built near the banks of the river and is surrounded by charming countryside, far from the village and the road. The country-style rooms are comfortable.

La Goéliche
$174 bkfst incl., $242 ½b
ℜ, ≈, ≡
22 Chemin du Quai, Ste-Pétronille,
G0A 4C0
☎ ***828-2248 or 888-511-2248***
≠ ***828-2745***

La Goéliche has reopened in a new building, after the former inn burned to the ground in 1996. The new establishment is slightly smaller, and does not have the antique charm that made the original such a hit. Nevertheless, the modern setup still has a certain country-style appeal. The 18 rooms are comfortable and offer a lovely view of Québec City. There is a small living room with a fireplace and games. You can also rent a "chalet-condo" for the night, or for longer stays. The restaurant (see p 239) is worth the trip.

Restaurants

F ine dining is without question one of Québec City's best attractions.

Whether you wish to enjoy a gourmet meal, a light healthy snack or simply an espresso, your only difficulty will be choosing among the great selection of romantic restaurants and charming cafés.

As a general rule, restaurants offer, from Monday to Friday, specials that include a full menu at a reasonable price. Served at lunch only, theses *menus du jour* often feature a choice of appetizers and main courses with coffee and dessert. In the evening, the table d'hôte (same formula at a slightly higher cost) are often quite interesting as well.

Prices in this guide apply to **dinner** for one person **excluding** taxes, tip (see

"Taxes and Tipping" p 56) and drinks. The restaurant listing begins with the least expensive.

$	less than $10
$$	$10 to $20
$$$	$20 to $30
$$$$	more than $30

It is always preferable to make reservations, especially if you are several people. This also allows you to make sure the restaurant you have chosen is open that evening. Some restaurants are closed at the beginning of the week in the winter; however, most of them are open every day in high season (summer).

If you want to travel by car to Vieux-Québec, check with the restaurant to see if they offer valet service when you make reservations. This will save you a lot of trouble. If they do not provide this service, the best thing to do is to find for an indoor parking garage. They are usually easy to locate.

Bring Your Own Wine

There are in fact many restaurants here where you can bring your own bottle of wine, a practice that often seems unusual to Europeans. This tradition stems from the fact that in order to serve alcohol, an establishment must pur chase a rather expensive liquor license. Consequently, restaurant owners who wish to offer their clientele a more economical solution prefer a license which allows customers to bring their own wine. In such cases, there is usually a sign in the window.

Here's another unusual tradition: there exists, in addition to the liquor license, a bar license. In other words, restaurants who solely display a liquor license can only sell you beer, wine or other drinks when you order a meal. Some restaurants, however, have both permits and can t sell you alcohol without you having to order a meal.

Ulysses's Favourites

The finest establishments in Québec City and surroundings:
Laurie Raphaël (p 222), La Grande Table (p 217),
La Closerie (p 203) Le Champlain (p 216),
La Camarine (p 238),
La Fenouillère (p 237) and Le Michelangelo (p 236).

For the romantic atmosphere:
Le Saint-Amour (p 213), Le Graffiti (p 226),
La Crémaillère (p 216), Le Michelangelo (p 236) and
Poisson d'Avril (p 221).

For the terrace:
Il Teatro (p 233), À la Bastille Chez Bahüaud (p 214) and
Le Saint-Amour (p 213).

For traditional Québéc cuisine:
Aux Anciens Canadiens (p 215) and
L'Auberge Baker (p 238).

For the view:
L'Astral (p 230), Le Manoir Montmorency (p 237),
La Goéliche (p 239), Café de la Terrasse (p 216)
and Café-Resto du Musée (p 228).

For elegant decor:
Voo Doo Grill (p 229),
Le Marie Clarisse (p 221), Café du Monde (p 220),
La Playa (p 233), Aviatic Club (p 220) Cosmos Café (p 223)
and Le Montego (p 236).

For originality:
Café du Clocher Penché (p 234), Le Bonnet d'Âne (p 231)
Les Salons d'Edgar (p 234), and Dazibo Café (p 230).

For the best *espresso* :
Chez Temporel (p 208) and
Café Krieghoff (p 224).

Cafés

Many Québécois are fans of espresso, which is why cafés and small, friendly restaurants are highly popular. These types of establishments have often been in neighbourhoods for many years. The gleaming coffee machine is often the most popular attraction, but you can also find lovely light dishes such as soups, salads and *croque-monsieur*, as well as croissants and desserts, of course!

On weekends, breakfast is usually served until early afternoon. To find the list of cafés we recommend, look under "Restaurants by Type of Cuisine."

This chapter will recommend the best places to eat. The selection was made with all budgets and tastes in mind. There are two listings: the first is by type of cuisine (see below) and the second is by alphabetical order (see under "Restaurants" in the index at the back of the guide). Our logo indicates "Ulysses's Favourites" and the insets feature outstanding establishments; these pointers should help you make a wise choice. *Bon appétit!*

Restaurants by Type of Cuisine

Belgian
Le Môss 220
Mon Manège à Toi ... 229

Bistro
L'Ardoise 221
Le Bonnet d'Âne 231
Café du Monde 220
Le Chantauteuil 210
Cochon Dingue 218
L'Entrecôte Saint-Jean . 210
Le Figaro 226
Les Frères de la Côte . 211
Le Hobbit 231
Le Péché Véniel 218
Le Saint-James 211
Les Salons d'Edgar ... 234

Cafés
Le Bonnet d'Âne 231
Brûlerie Tatum 208
Café du Clocher
  Penché 234
Café Krieghoff 224
Chez Temporel 208
Cochon Dingue 218
Le Hobbit 231
L'Impasse des Deux
  Anges 234
Java Java 224
Le Péché Véniel 218
Le Petit Coin Latin ... 208

California-Style
Le Montego 236
La Playa 233

Chinese
L'Élysée-Mandarin 213
Le Quartier Chinois ... 225
Les Épices du
  Széchouan 232

Crepes
Casse-Crêpe Breton . . 208
La Crêperie de Sophie 217
Au Petit Coin Breton . . 211

Family-style
Bistro Sous-le-Fort . . . 218
Buffet de l'Antiquaire . 217
Buffet du Passant 235
Café Buade 210
Café de Mon Village . . 238
Chez Victor 231
L'Omelette 211

French
À la Bastille
  Chez Bahüaud . . . 214
L'Astral 230
Auberge du Trésor . . . 214
Au Paris-Brest 230
Au Parmesan 212
Aux Vieux Canons . . . 226
Le Bonaparte 229
Café d'Europe 215
Café de la Paix 213
Café-Restaurant
  du Musée 228
Café Saint-Malo 218
Café Serge Bruyère . . . 212
Initiale 222
Le Canard Huppé 239
La Caravelle 214
Le Champlain 216
Charles Baillargé 215
Chez Livernois 213
Chez Rabelais 221
Ciccio Café 233
Le Continental 215
La Crémaillère 216
Le Gambrinus 216

La Goéliche 239
Le Graffiti 226
Guido Le Gourmet . . . 216
Le Lapin Sauté 220
Le Louis-Hébert 228
Le Moulin
  Saint-Laurent 239
Le Parlementaire 224
Le Patriarche 213
La Ripaille 214
Le Vendôme 222

On the Grill
Aux Vieux Canons . . . 226
L'Entrecôte Saint-Jean . 210
La Maison du Steak . . . 230
La Scalla 228

Huron-Wendat
Nek8arre 237

Indian
Garam Massala . . . .

Innovative Cuisine
À la Bastille Chez
  Bahüaud 214
Initiale 222
La Camarine 238
Le Champlain 216
La Closerie 230
L'Échaudé 222
La Fenouillère 237
La Grande Table 217
Le Laurie Raphaël 222
Le Michelangelo 236
Le Saint-Amour 213
Voo Doo Grill 229

International
Aviatic Club 220
Cosmos Café 223
Le Montego 236
La Playa 233

Irish
Dazibo Café 230

Italian
Au Parmesan 212
Café d'Europe 215
Ciccio Café 233
La Crémaillère 216
La Fougasse 236
Guido Le Gourmet . . . 216
Jaune Tomate 226
Le Michelangelo 236
Le Momento 226
Le Paparazzi 236
La Petite Italie 211
Portofino 212
Le Rivoli 229
Il Teatro 233
Trattoria Sant-Angelo . 220

Japanese
Le Métropolitain 228

North African
Le Carthage 232

Pizza
Frères de la Côte 211
La Scalla 228
Le Maizerets 235
Piazzetta 231
Pizza Mag 218
Pizzédélic 224
Pointe des Amériques . 232

Portuguese
Le Portugais 228

Québécois
L'Auberge Baker 238
Café-Restaurant
 du Musée 228
La Camarine 238
Le Canard Huppé 239
Charles Baillargé 215
Le Galopin 236
La Goéliche 239
Le Graffiti 226
Le Manoir
 Montmorency 237
Le Moulin
 Saint-Laurent 239
Le Pailleur 234
Le Parlementaire 224
La Tanière 236
Le Vieux-Presbytère . . 239

Québécois (traditional)
Aux Anciens
 Canadiens 215
L'Auberge Baker 238

Sandwiches
Bügel 223
Les Finesses de
 Charlot 223
La Lunchonnette 208
Le Petit Baluchon 238
Titanic 210
Wrap 223

Seafood
Chez Rabelais 221
Le Gambrinus 216
Le Louis-Hébert 228
Le Marie Clarisse 221
Le Métropolitain 228
Poisson d'Avril 221

Smoked meat
La Boîte à Smoked
  Meat 223
Le Byrnd 235

Southeastern Asian
Apsara 210
Asia 217
La Campagne 232
Fleur de Lotus 211
Lotus Cartier 228
Ly-Hai 224
Thang Long 231

Spanish
La Caravelle 214

Swiss
Café Suisse 212
La Grolla 233
Le Petit Coin Latin . . . 208

Restaurants with terraces
À la Bastille
  Chez Bahüaud . . . 214
Auberge du Trésor . . . 214
Au Paris-Brest 230
Aux Vieux Canons . . . 226
Le Bonaparte 229
Le Bonnet d'Âne 231
Buffet du passant 235
Bügel 223
Café Krieghoff 224
Café de Mon Village . . 238
Café Suisse 212

Café-Restaurant
  du Musée 228
Chez Rabelais 221
Cochon Dingue 218
Cosmos Café 223
L'Échaudé 222
Le Figaro 226
Les Finesses de Charlot 223
Le Gambrinus 216
Jaune Tomate 226
Le Lapin Sauté 220
Le Laurie Raphaël 222
Le Louis-Hébert 228
La Maison du Steak . . . 230
Le Maizerets 235
Le Mille-Feuilles 233
Mon Manège à Toi . . . 229
Le Marie Clarisse 221
Le Montego 236
Le Moulin
  Saint-Laurent 239
Le Paparazzi 236
La Playa 233
Petit Coin Latin 208
Pizzédélic 224
Pointe des Amériques . 232
Poisson d'Avril 221
Le Rivoli 229
Le Saint-Amour 213
La Scalla 228
Trattoria Sant-Angelo . 220

Vegetarian
Le Commensal 230
Le Mille-Feuilles 233

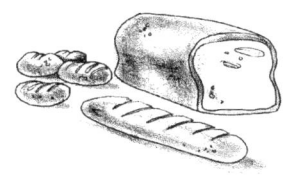

Tour A: Vieux-Québec

Brûlerie Tatum
$
1084 Rue St-Jean
☎ *692-3900*
Brûlerie Tatum is located in a lovely narrow building with a mezzanine and is decorated in reddish hues. This café roasts its own beans in a gleaming coffee machine installed at the entrance. They serve mouth-watering light meals such as *croque-monsieur* and sandwiches, as well as a great selection of coffee and hot chocolate.

Casse-Crêpe Breton
$
1136 Rue St-Jean
Little Casse-Crêpe Breton draws big crowds. Though it has been expanded, patrons still have to line up for a taste of its delicious crepes. Prepared right before your eyes, these are filled with your favourite ingredients by waitresses who manage to keep smiling in the midst of the hubbub. High-backed, upholstered seats help lend the place a warm atmosphere.

Chez Temporel
$
25 Rue Couillard
At Chez Temporel, the food is prepared on the premises. Whether you opt for a rich butter croissant, a *croque-monsieur*, a salad or the special of the day, you can be sure that it will be fresh and tasty. To top it all off, the establishment serves the best espresso in town! The waiters and waitresses sometimes have more work than they can handle, but a little understanding on your part will be rewarded a hundred times over. Tucked away on little Rue Couillard, the two-storey Temporel has been welcoming people of all ages and all stripes for over 20 years now. Open early in the morning to late at night.

Lunchonnette
$
50 Côte de la Fabrique
☎ *692-0813*
Lunchonnette is a sandwich place with a slightly retro decor where you can stop for a light snack. The clientele is made up of people of all ages. The express menu offers breakfast, sandwiches and sorbets.

Petit Coin Latin
$
8½ Rue Sainte-Ursule
☎ *692-2022*
Petit Coin Latin serves homestyle cooking in an ambiance reminiscent of a Paris café. The decor is dominated by parlour chairs and mirrors, creating a relaxed, convivial atmosphere. The menu includes

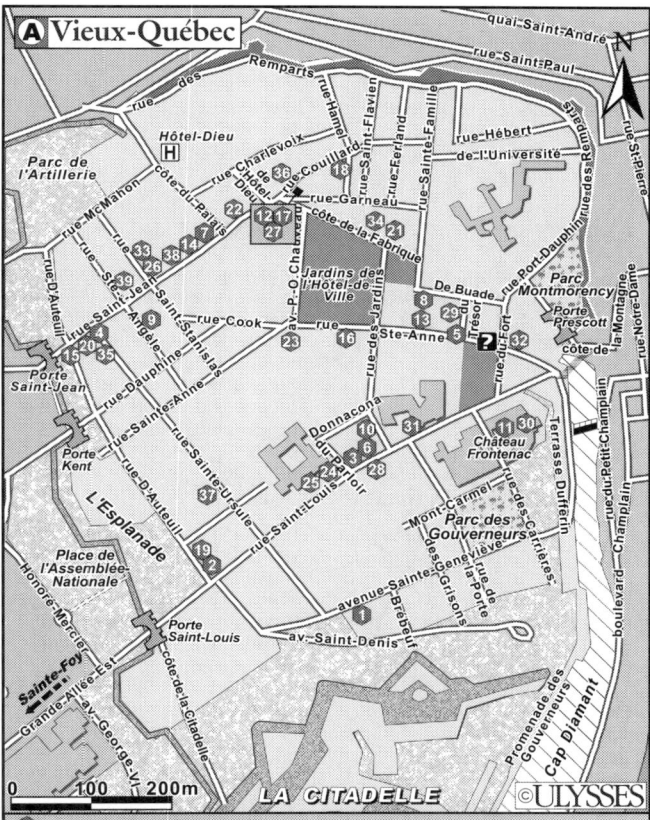

A Vieux-Québec

RESTAURANTS

1. À la Bastille Chez Bahüaud
2. Apsara
3. Au Parmesan
4. Au Petit Coin Breton
5. Auberge du Trésor
6. Aux Anciens Canadiens
7. Brûlerie Tatum
8. Café Buade
9. Café d'Europe
10. Café de la Paix
11. Café de la Terrasse
12. Café Serge Bruyère
13. Café Suisse
14. Casse-Crêpe Breton
15. Chantauteuil
16. Charles Baillairgé
17. Chez Livernois
18. Chez Temporel
19. Élysée-Mandarin
20. Entrecôte Saint-Jean
21. Fleur de Lotus
22. Frères de la Côte
23. Guido Le Gourmet
24. L'Omelette
25. La Caravelle
26. La Crémaillère
27. La Grande Table
28. La Petite Italie
29. La Ripaille
30. Le Champlain
31. Le Continental
32. Le Gambrinus
33. Le Patriarche
34. Lunchonnette
35. Petit Coin Latin
36. Portofino
37. Saint-Amour
38. Saint-James
39. Titanic

croûtons au fromage, quiche and pâté. You can also snack on *raclette* (a type of cheese fondue) served at the table on small burners with potatoes and cold cuts. Delicious! During summer, a lovely outdoor seating area enclosed by stone walls is open out back; to get there from the street, use the carriage entrance.

Titanic
$
21 Rue Sainte-Angèle
☎694-7000
Titanic is a small sandwich shop on a street that runs perpendicularly to Rue St-Jean. The menu is fast food but is still good. Submarines, bagels, salads, soups and desserts are the main items. Free delivery.

Chantauteuil
$-$$
1001 Rue St-Jean
☎692-2030
The Chantauteuil is a quaint resto-bar. The pretty decor is reminiscent of Paris with its lace curtains and attractive paintings hanging on the stone walls. This café has lots of character, service is friendly and communication is easily established between staff and customers. Lunch time always features a delicious *menu du jour*. Light meals such as *croque-monsieur* and sandwiches are served all day.

Entrecôte Saint-Jean
$$
1011 rue Saint-Jean
☎694-0234
The Entrecôte Saint-Jean serves steaks prepared in a variety of ways accompanied by matchstick potatoes. The salad with nuts and the chocolate profiteroles will be a perfect ending to your meal. Great value for your money.

Apsara
$$
71 Rue d'Auteuil
☎694-0232
The Apsara is located near Porte Saint-Louis, Apsara featuring Southeastern Asian cuisine. Full meals are served at both lunch and dinner time and prices are reasonable.

Café Buade
$$
31 Rue de Buade
☎692-3909
Near Rue du Trésor and Terrasse Dufferin, Café Buade has a large dining room with an attractive but modest decor. It is a pleasant establishment with a family atmosphere where you can enjoy a good meal without having to spend a fortune. The house specialty is roast beef.

Fleur de Lotus
$$
38 Côte de la Fabrique
☎*692-4286*
Popular for its Asian music, peaceful atmosphere and courteous service, Fleur de Lotus is also appreciated for its delectably different cuisine which will transport you to the heart of Asia.

Frères de la Côte
$$
1190 Rue St-Jean
☎*692-5445*
Frères de la Côte serves delicious bistro fare, including pasta, grill, and thin-crust pizzas baked in a wood-burning oven and topped with delicious fresh ingredients, as well as unlimited mussels and fries on certain evenings. The atmosphere is lively and laid-back and the place is often packed, which is only fitting here on bustling Rue St-Jean. Guests can take in the action through the restaurant's large windows.

L'Omelette
$$
64 Rue St-Louis
☎*694-9626*
L'Omelette is a very friendly place that serves copious breakfasts early in the morning. Later in the day, choose from a large variety of omelettes, pasta, pizza, hamburgers and submarines. Quality food at a reasonable cost.

Au Petit Coin Breton
$$
1029 Rue St-Jean
☎*694-0758*
The atmosphere, decor and traditional costumes worn by the personnel at Au Petit Coin Breton will surprise you. And the crepes, filled with your very own choice of ingredients, are quite satisfying. The dessert crepes are especially yummy.

La Petite Italie
$$
49 ½ Rue St-Louis
☎*694-0044*
La Petite Italie serves Italian specialties at affordable prices. The menu features pizza and pasta and the decor is pleasant to the eye. This restaurant is right in the heart of a lively tourist area.

Saint-James
$$
1110 Rue St-Jean
☎*692-1030*
The Saint-James bistro is part of Manoir Victoria (see p 184) even though it has its own entrance on Rue St-Jean. The decor is elegant, similar to that of the Manoir. An innovative formula lets you create your own meal combination from a large choice of pasta and sauces. There are also steaks, sandwiches and an interesting table d'hôte.

Café Serge Bruyère
$$-$$$
1200 Rue St-Jean
☎694-0618

An institution in Vieux-Québec, Maison Serge Bruyère is located in Maison Livernois, a large bourgeois residence built in the 19th century. It houses three restaurants, which increase in refinement as you climb the stairs. The last floor is being occupied by La Grande Table (see p 217). On the ground floor, the Café offers a typical menu of salads, sandwiches and Viennese breads and rolls to accompany a beer or an espresso. In the cellar is an Irish pub, Pub St-Patrick, which serves all kinds of beer and occasionally presents Celtic music.

Portofino
$$-$$$
54 Rue Couillard
☎692-8888

Portofino was designed to resemble a typical Italian trattoria. A long bar, blue glasses, mirrors on the wall and soccer banners on the ceiling help create a warm, lively atmosphere. Don't be surprised if the owner greets you with a kiss! To top it all off, there are the mouth-watering Italian aromas. During tourist season, the place is always full. Valet parking.

Au Parmesan
$$-$$$
38 Rue St-Louis
☎692-0341

Upon entering Au Parmesan, one is struck by the extensive collection of pots and bottles exhibited on the cornices along the walls. If you are looking for a quiet spot to have a private conversation, this is not the place. A *chansonnier* playing the accordion contributes to the excitement of the place, and in the summer, it is *la dolce vita* every evening of the week! The clientele is mostly made up of tourists. The specialties are French and Italian; pasta, seafood platters and smoked salmon are among the favourites.

Café Suisse
$$$
32 Rue Sainte-Anne
☎694-1320

All kinds of fondue (Swiss, Chinese, Bourguignonne and even seafood) are on the menu at Café Suisse, along with *raclette*, grilled dishes and light meals. The terrace opens onto the pedestrian street, Rue Sainte-Anne, making your summertime dinner even more pleasant. You can watch painters and caricaturists at work and occasionally listen to street musicians.

Chez Livernois
$$$
1200 Rue St-Jean
☎*694-0618*

Chez Livernois is a bistro located inside Maison Serge-Bruyère. It is named after photographer Jules Livernois, who set up his studio in this imposing 19th-century house in 1889. The excellent cuisine consists mainly of pasta and dishes from the grill, and the atmosphere is a bit more relaxed than at La Grande Table (see p 217).

Café de la Paix
$$$
44 Rue Desjardins
☎*692-1430*

Café de la Paix occupies a narrow space a few steps from the sidewalk on little Rue Desjardins. It has been around for years and enjoys a solid reputation among Québec City residents. The menu features traditional French cuisine such as frog's legs, beef Wellington, rabbit with mustard and grilled salmon.

Élysée-Mandarin
$$$
65 Rue d'Auteuil
☎*692-0909*

Élysée-Mandarin, which also boasts prime locations in Montréal and Paris, serves excellent Szechuan, Cantonese and Mandarin cuisine in a decor featuring a small indoor garden and Chinese sculptures and vases. The food is always succulent and the service extremely courteous. If you are in a group, try the sampler menu: it would be a taste not to sample as many dishes as possible!

Le Saint-Amour
$$$
48 Rue Sainte-Ursule
☎*694-0667*

Chef and co-owner Jean-Luc Boulay creates succulent, innovative cuisine that is a feast for both the eyes and the palate. The desserts concocted in the *chocolaterie*, on the second floor, are absolutely divine. A truly gastronomic experience! To top it all off, the place is beautiful, comfortable and has a warm atmosphere. The solarium, open year-round and decorated with all sorts of flowers and other plants, brightens up the decor. On sunny summer days, the roof is removed, transforming it into a great patio. Valet parking.

Le Patriarche
$$$
17 Rue St-Stanislas
☎*692-5488*

Le Patriarche's decor is charming and unpretentious. The dining room has beautiful stone walls creating quite a relaxed, pleasant atmosphere. The reception is warm and the service very friendly. The inviting menu of French cuisine includes wild game and seafood.

La Ripaille
$$$
closed at Christmas
9 Rue de Buade
☎692-2450

Right near the Château Frontenac and quaint Rue du Trésor, La Ripaille always offers lovely surprises, whether it is the French or the seafood dishes. The atmosphere is warm and inviting.

À la Bastille Chez Bahüaud
$$$
closed Mon in winter, closed Jan
47 avenue Ste-Geneviève
☎692-2544

À la Bastille Chez Bahüaud is located near the Plaines d'Abraham and is surrounded by trees. The wonderfully quiet terrace makes this the ideal spot for an intimate moonlit dinner. Inside, the decor is both elegant and comfortable and includes a billiard table, while the charming downstairs bar has a more intimate atmosphere. Fine French cooking awaits you.

Auberge du Trésor
$$$-$$$$
20 Rue Sainte-Anne
☎694-1876

Established in a house built in 1679 during the French Regime, the Auberge du Trésor's clientele is mostly made up of tourists. The cuisine here is French and the ambiance recalls an Old French manor house. During the summer, the terrace is an ideal spot to enjoy a drink and admire the magnificent view of Château Frontenac and the various activities taking place in Parc de la Place d'Armes. Musicians play here in the evening. Note however that a simple coffee on the terrace may cost more than you expect.

La Caravelle
$$$-$$$$
68 ½ Rue St-Louis
☎694-9022

Located on Rue St-Louis, a popular street for tourists, La Caravelle is busy at all hours of the day and night. A mixed clientele frequents this attractive, luxuriously decorated place. The stone walls, wood panelling, lighting and plants give it a pleasant, inviting atmosphere. The personnel caters to your every need and makes every effort to serve you. In the evening, a *chansonnier* entertains the appreciative audience. Exquisite French cuisine is served here, with a few Spanish additions to the menu.

Charles Baillargé
$$$-$$$$
57 Rue Sainte-Anne
☎*692-2480*

The Charles Baillargé restaurant is located on the main floor of the beautiful Hôtel Clarendon (see p 186). Discriminating diners come here for excellent, traditional French cuisine served in comfortable surroundings.

Le Continental
$$$-$$$$
26 Rue St-Louis
☎*694-9995*

Le Continental, just steps away from Château Frontenac, is one of the oldest restaurants in Québec City. The continental cuisine includes seafood, lamb, duck, among others. Service *au guéridon* (pedestal table) in a large, comfortable dining room.

Aux Anciens Canadiens
$$$-$$$$
34 Rue St-Louis
☎*692-1627*

Located in one of the oldest houses in Québec City, the restaurant Aux Anciens Canadiens serves upscale versions of traditional Québec specialties. Dishes include ham with maple syrup, pork and beans, and blueberry pie.

Café d'Europe
$$$-$$$$
27 Rue Sainte-Angèle
☎*692-3835*

Café d'Europe has a sober, slightly outdated decor. There is limited space, and when the place is busy, the noise level gets pretty high. The service is courteous with a personal touch. Sophisticated French and Italian cuisine is presented in a traditional manner and served in generous portions. The flambée dishes are expertly prepared, and the smooth, flavourful sauces make this an unforgettable culinary experience.

Maison Jacquet

La Crémaillère
closed at noon Sat-Sun
$$$-$$$$
21 Rue St-Stanislas at the corner of Rue St-Jean
☎**692-2216**

Friendly service and exquisite cooking with a European flavour await you at La Crémaillère. A great deal of attention is given here to make your meal memorable. The attractive decor adds to the charm of the place.

Le Gambrinus
$$$-$$$$
15 Rue du Fort
☎**692-5144**

Le Gambrinus is a beautiful restaurant that already has a good reputation with the people of Québec City. The welcoming dining room is adorned with lace curtains reaching midway to the small paned windows. The entire room is decorated with ivy, and elegant ornamental plates hang on the walls. The atmosphere could not be more enjoyable in this warm and appealing room. On summer evenings a singer is a pleasure to listen to, making the ambiance even more inviting. The terrace overlooks Château Frontenac. The cuisine is French with a large selection of fish and seafood.

Guido Le Gourmet
$$$-$$$$
closed Sat and Sun at lunch in winter
73 Rue Sainte-Anne
☎**692-3856**

Guido Le Gourmet will transport you to the world of fine dining. The menu, made up of French and Italian cuisine, includes quail, veal, salmon and other delicacies from both land and sea. Elegant decor. The large, lovely plates on the table are a good indication of good things to come. Brunch on weekends.

Café de la Terrasse
$$$$
1 Rue des Carrières
☎**692-3861**

The Café de la Terrasse, in Château Frontenac, has picture windows looking out onto Terrasse Dufferin. Attractive decor and delicious French cuisine.

Le Champlain
$$$$
1 Rue des Carrières
☎**692-3861**

Le Champlain is Château Frontenac's own restaurant. Needless to say, its decor is extremely luxurious in keeping with the opulence of the rest of the hotel. The outstanding French cuisine also does justice to the Château's reputation. Chef Jean Soular, whose recipes have been published, adds a unique touch to classic dishes. Impeccable service.

La Grande Table
$$$$
1200 Rue St-Jean
☎694-0618
La Grande Table in Maison Serge-Bruyère has a solid reputation that extends far beyond the walls of the old city. First established by the excellent late cook who gave the place its name, this reputation has been maintained from year to year by the skills of various well-known chefs. Since the beginning of the year 2000, Serge Bruyère's former student, Martin Côté, has carried on the tradition after having travelled around the world perfecting his art. He creates magnificent French gastronomic dishes with the most exquisite, creamy sauces you will ever taste. La Grande Table is on the top floor of an historic house situated between Rue Garneau and Rue Couillard. The decor is attractive and paintings by Québec artists hang on the walls. Valet parking.

Tour B: Petit-Champlain to Vieux-Port

Buffet de l'Antiquaire
$
95 Rue St-Paul
☎692-2661
Buffet de l'Antiquaire is a pleasant snack bar that serves homestyle cooking. As indicated by its name, it is located in the heart of the antiquedealers' quarter and is a good place to take a little break while treasure-hunting. It is also one of the first restaurants to open in the morning (6am).

La Crêperie de Sophie
$-$$
48 Rue St-Paul
☎694-9595
The tastes of Brittany are not only found in the food but also on the walls of this establishment where peasant scenes of rural France are hung. This *creperie* is innovative in the preparation of pancakes, but the taste comes second to presentation, which is exemplary.

Asia
$$
89 Rue Sault-au-Matelot
☎692-3799
Asia serves excellent cuisine from Thailand and Vietnam. Vegetarians will also be delighted with the selections of dishes. Their trade

mark is cooking on the grill or in a wok, which results in light, healthy meals.

Cochon Dingue
$$

46 Boulevard Champlain
☎692-2013

Cochon Dingue is a charming café-bistro located between Boulevard Champlain and Rue du Petit-Champlain. Mirrors and a checkerboard floor create a fun, attractive decor. The menu features bistro-style dishes such as *steak-frites* and *moules-frites* combos (steak and fries or mussels with fries). The desserts are heavenly!

Pizza Mag
$$

363 Rue St-Paul, Québec
☎692-1910

For a delicious thick-crusted all-dressed pizza, stop at one of the Pizza Mag counters. The toppings are quite unusual, with choices such as La Biquette (goat cheese) La Crème (leeks) La Parmentière (potatoes dusted with parmesan cheese) La Louloutte (snails) or La Kamouraska (smoked sturgeon). There are also a few tables where you can sit and relax while you eat. Pizza Mag's menu offers four choices for $24, an interesting option considering the fact that prices are higher than traditional pizzerias. Free delivery.

Péché Véniel
$$-$$$

233 Rue St-Paul
☎692-5642

Once inside Péché Véniel you will find a most enjoyable atmosphere. Whether it is for breakfast, lunch or dinner, meals there are always excellent. To name just a few specialties, we suggest the smoked meat sandwich on a baguette, *moules poulettes* (mussels), steak and fries and the popular Lac Saint-Jean *tourtière* (meat pie). A more elaborate table d'hôte is also available and just as tasty.

Café Saint-Malo
$$-$$$

75 Rue St-Paul

Café Saint-Malo is a small restaurant that has been on Rue St-Paul for almost 20 years. The place is decorated with many assorted objects that give it a friendly atmosphere, as do the low ceilings, booths and fireplace. French cuisine specialties can be enjoyed here. The *cassoulet* (bean casserole) and *boudin aux pommes* (blood sausage with apples) are particularly good.

Bistro Sous le Fort
$$-$$$

48 Rue Sous le Fort
☎694-0852

Bistro Sous le Fort has a somewhat stark decor and is frequented mostly by tourists. The restaurant

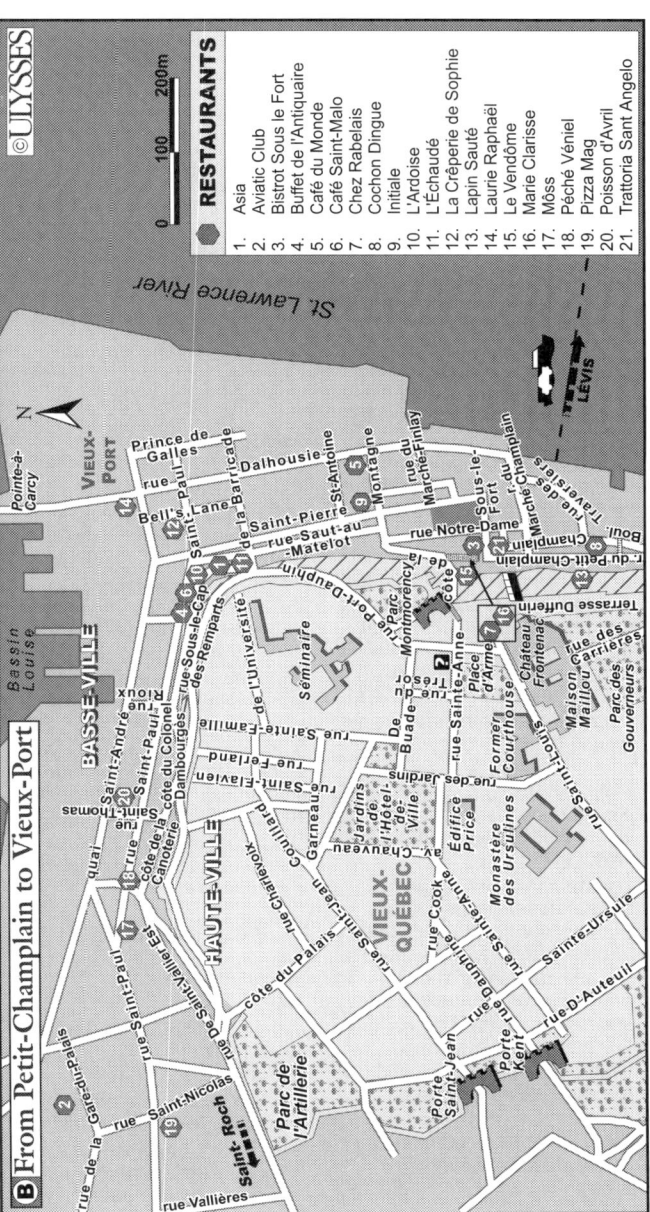

serves delicious, reasonably priced Québécois cuisine.

Trattoria Sant-Angelo
$$-$$$
10 Rue Cul-de-Sac
☎*692-4862*
Discover Italy at Trattoria Sant-Angelo, in the heart of the Petit-Champlain neighbourhood. The decor is a little austere but the wood fire in the centre of the restaurant makes the establishment more cheerful. And on a starlit summer evening, your dining experience will be enhanced if you eat out on the terrace. The clientele is mostly made up of tourists in high season, and is mixed during the rest of the year. As the advertising states, "Pasta-Pizza-Amore," the menu has a great variety of pasta and pizza cooked with love in a wood-burning oven.

Lapin Sauté
$$-$2$$
52 Rue du Petit-Champlain
☎*692-5325*
Located in a 200-year-old house in the Petit-Champlain neighbourhood, Lapin Sauté is furnished in a simple manner. The rough walls are white with a few spots of colour. The terrace is next to the Maison de la Chanson, at the foot of Cap Diamant. You may have guessed that they serve *lapin* (rabbit) prepared in many different ways.

Môss
$$-$$$
255 Rue St-Paul
☎*692-0265*
Môss is a Belgian bistro. Its decor is somewhat cold, with black tables, brick walls, a stainless-steel counter and halogen lights, but its *moules-frites* combo, dishes from the grill and desserts made with Belgian chocolate are delicious.

Aviatic Club
$$-$$$
450 de la Gare-du-Palais
☎*522-3555*
There are two restaurants in the magnificent Gare du Palais: a brand-new one with the evocative name of Charbon, which serves, as you might have guessed, food from the grill, and a second, which has been there for a number of years. The Aviatic Club takes you back in time with its mid-19th-century English decor featuring rattan armchairs, burgundy curtains, palm trees and a cosmopolitan menu.

Café du Monde
$$$
57 Rue Dalhousie
☎*692-4455*
Café du Monde is a large Parisian-style brasserie serving dishes one would expect from such a place, including *magret de canard* (duck filet), *tartare* (raw minced steak with herbs,

etc.), *bavette* (beef steak), *boudin* (blood sausage) and of course, *moules-frites* (mussels and french fries). The lunch menu is interesting with its delicious *profiteroles* (cream puffs) served for dessert. On the weekend there are great brunches as well. The bright decor invites relaxation and discussion: it has black and white tiles on the floor, leather seats, large windows overlooking the port and a long bar adorned with an imposing copper coffee machine. There is a singles bar at the entrance. The waiters, dressed in long aprons, are quite helpful.

L'Ardoise
$$$
71 Rue St-Paul
☎*694-0213*
On a street lined with antique shops and art galleries, the chic little bistro L'Ardoise is the ideal spot to take a break from touring the town. Although the service tends to be pretentious at times, it is a place where you will quickly feel at ease. The mahogany panelling combines harmoniously with the stone walls. Among the dishes prepared are *boudin grillé aux pommes* (grilled blood sausage with apples) *foie de veau à l'anglaise* (English style liver), *entrecôte* (rib steak) and a selection of fish. Breakfast is also served.

Poisson d'Avril
$$$
115 Rue St-André
☎*692-1010*
Poisson d'Avril has moved to the Vieux-Port. Its new home is an old house with stone walls and wooden beams that lend it a great deal of charm. The decor is enhanced by clever lighting and also by the shell-patterned fabric on the chairs. The menu includes well-prepared pasta, grilled and seafood dishes. Try the mussels!

Two good restaurants are perched on picturesque Escalier Casse-Cou, which leads to Rue du Petit-Champlain. On the top floor, **Chez Rabelais** *($$$-$$$$; 2 Rue du Petit-Champlain, ☎694-9460)* serves French cuisine with an emphasis on seafood. A little lower down is **Marie-Clarisse** *($$$$; 12 Rue du Petit-Champlain, ☎692-0857)*, where everything, except for the stone walls, is as blue as the sea – and with good reason: seafood is the house specialty. These divine dishes are served in a lovely dining room that has been very ornately decorated. When the cold weather sets in, a crackling fire warms you up.

Le Vendôme
$$$
36 Côte de la Montagne
☎692-0557

Le Vendôme is located halfway up Côte de la Montagne, and is one of the oldest restaurants in Québec City. It serves classic French dishes like Chateaubriand, *coq au vin* and *duck à l'orange* in an intimate decor.

L'Échaudé
$$$-$$$$
Sat and Sun for lunch
73 Rue Sault-au-Matelot
☎692-1299

L'Échaudé is an appealing restaurant with an Art Deco decor featuring a checkerboard floor and a mirrored wall. Relaxed atmosphere. Sophisticated cuisine prepared daily with fresh ingredients from the market.

Laurie Raphäel
$$$-$$$$
17 Rue Dalhousie
☎692-4555

Chef and co-owner Daniel Vézina was named the best chef in Québec in 1997. The same year, a book of his tempting recipes was published. When creating his mouth-watering dishes, Vézina draws inspiration from culinary traditions from all over the world, preparing giblets, sea food, meat, and other dishes. in innovative ways. It goes without saying, that the food at Laurie Raphaël is delicious! In May 1996 the restaurant moved into newer, more spacious quarters with a semi-circular exterior glass wall. The elegant decor includes creamy white curtains, sand and earth tones and a few decorative, wrought-iron objects.

Initiale
$$$$
54 Rue St-Pierre
☎694-1818

Initiale is located on Rue St-Pierre in an old bank building with a high ceiling and decorative mouldings. Formerly in Sillery, the restaurant's clientele has followed it here because of its fine food prepared by chef Yvan Lebrun. He knows how to create exquisite food where lamb, salmon, *filet mignon*, and kidneys are served alongside *foie gras poêlé* (liver cooked in a pan with carrots and bacon) and, for the adventurous, pigeon! In a classical decor with semi-circular bar and light streaming in through high windows, you will be won over by these delicious dishes. The atmosphere is welcoming, although slightly stiff.

Tour C: Grande Allée

Bügel
$
164 Rue Crémazie Ouest
☎*523-7666*

Craving a bagel? You'll find all different kinds at Bügel, a bagel bakery on pretty little Rue Crémazie. In a warm atmosphere enhanced by the aroma of a wood fire, you can snack on bagels with salami, cream cheese or veggie pâté and stock up on goodies to take back home.

Wrap
$
closed in winter
637 Grande Allée Est

If you are suddenly hungry while strolling along Grande Allée, you can always stop and find something to eat at this small snack-bar which serves sandwich wraps. The counter is open in the summer and serves a variety of different fillings rolled in a plain, tomato or spinach-flavoured flat bread, cousin of the tortilla. Surprisingly, the fillings are made with marinated chicken and jasmine rice. They also serve salads and smoothies, thick drinks made from fresh fruit.

Les Finesses de Charlot
$
1125 Avenue Cartier
☎*524-5636*

Tiny Les Finesses de Charlot has excellent made-to-order submarines of all kinds. For a picnic tuck one or two into a basket and head for the Plains of Abraham (only a 10 min walk away!) If it is raining you can always eat inside the restaurant. In the summer, it is also a milk bar.

La Boîte à Smoked Meat
$-$$
122 Rue Crémazie Ouest
☎*523-8148*

Blue note enthusiasts will find an electric touch in the blue and yellow decor in this smoked-meat restaurant. These colours surely inspire the jazzmen that the owner, a trumpeter himself, invites every Thursday and Friday evening for a musical jam. You can savour a smokedmeat sandwich or a salad between sets. They alone are worth a visit to this forgotten corner of the neighbourhood.

Cosmos Café
$-$$
575 Grande-Allée Est
☎*692-1316*

The Cosmos Café promises a good time in a hip atmosphere, serving burgers, sandwiches and salads with a cosmopolitan flavour. Breakfasts here are quite good.

Le Parlementaire
$-$$
closed Sat, Sun and Mon
at the corner of Dufferin and Grande Allée
☎*643-6640*

Visitors who might want to rub shoulders with members of Québec's National Assembly should have breakfast at Le Parlementaire. The menu features European and Québécois dishes. The restaurant is often packed, particularly at lunch, but the food is good. Open only for breakfast and lunch.

Pizzédélic
$-$$
1145 Avenue Cartier
☎*525-5981*

This is a pizza place with a colourful setting and welcoming personnel. At Pizzédélic you can taste the latest trend in pizza, as they prepare it in hundreds of different ways. You can even choose your own combination of ingredients. The clientele here is young and lively.

Garam Massala
$$
1114 Avenue Cartier
☎*522-4979*

At Garam Massala you can savour curry, tandoori and other spicy dishes from the Indian menu. Though the restaurant has the disadvantage of being located in a basement, its decor is nonetheless attractive. Pleasant Indian music adds to the ambiance.

Java Java
$$
1112 Avenue Cartier
☎*522-5282*

The subtle and original decor at Java Java creates a fun atmosphere. This is an excellent place to savour a light meal when you need a bite or merely wish to watch people walking by.

Ly-Hai
$$
815 Avenue Cartier
☎*522-2031*

Specializing in Vietnamese cooking, this restaurant looks quite plain. However, Ly-Hai offers a very good meal at a good price.

Café Krieghoff
$$
1809 Avenue Cartier
☎*521-3711*

Named after the Dutch-born artist whose former home is located at the end of Avenue Cartier, Café Krieghoff occupies an old house on the same street. It serves tasty light meal (quiche, salads, etc.) and also has a good daily menu. The casual, convivial atmosphere is reminiscent of a Northern European café. During summer, its two outdoor seating areas are often packed.

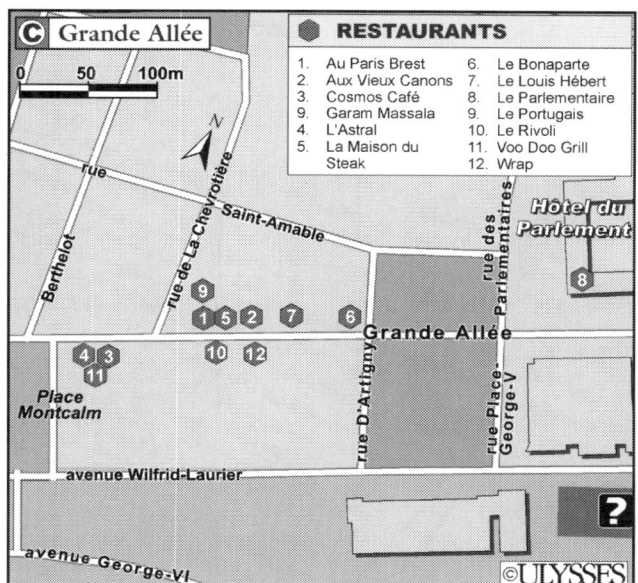

Grande Allée

RESTAURANTS

1. Au Paris Brest
2. Aux Vieux Canons
3. Cosmos Café
9. Garam Massala
4. L'Astral
5. La Maison du Steak
6. Le Bonaparte
7. Le Louis Hébert
8. Le Parlementaire
9. Le Portugais
10. Le Rivoli
11. Voo Doo Grill
12. Wrap

Le Cochon Dingue
$$
46 Boulevard René-Lévesque Ouest
☎*523-2013*

A pretty terrace in the back of this Boulevard René-Lévesque establishment is heated when the temperature is cool.

La Piazzetta
$$
1191 Avenue Cartier
☎*649-8896*
(see p 231)

Quartier Chinois
$$
980 Avenue Cartier corner of René-Lévesque
☎*522-8888*

Quartier Chinois has a very appropriate decor. Lovely folding screens and authentic Chinese curios create a pleasant setting. The Chinese, or more precisely Cantonese and Szechuan, cuisine is delicious. The vegetables are crunchy, the sauces tasty and the meat grilled to perfection. You can even eat at a table placed lower than floor level to give you the illusion of sitting on the ground. This practice is usual to Western people, but is still comfortable.

Le Figaro
$$-$$$
closed Sun in autumn
1019 Avenue Cartier
☎*525-3535*

A pleasant bistro located in a lovely spot on Avenue Cartier, Le Figaro offers delicious bistro-style cuisine. The decor is beautiful and the service courteous. In summer, people sit on the terrace to watch others and to be seen. Brunch is served on the weekends.

Graffiti
$$-$$$
1191 Rue Cartier
☎*529-4949*

The old-fashioned decor of Graffiti, is distinguished by exposed beams and brick walls, creates a warm ambience. Graffiti serves excellent French cuisine.

Jaune Tomate
$$-$$$
120 Boulevard René-Lévesque Ouest
☎*523-8777*

A pretty yellow and red restaurant called Jaune Tomate just opened on Boulevard René-Lévesque near Avenue Cartier. It serves good Italian cuisine in a country-style decor. The eggplant Parmesan, to name but one item on the menu, is excellent. Come here on Saturday and Sunday mornings and try the delicious and inventive brunches. The fruit plate with ricotta cheese and a slice of pound cake, or the eggs benedictine with hollandaise sauce flavoured with a zest of orange or teriyaki will make your weekend mornings a delight.

Momento
$$-$$$
closed Sat and Sun at lunch
1144 Avenue Cartier
☎*647-1313*

Momento is decorated in modern fashion with warm colours and adorned with a fresco taken from a Boticelli painting. As you may have guessed, they serve refined, original Italian cuisine that is sure to offer some pleasant surprises. Basil, oregano, dried tomatoes, capers, olives; the sauces are rich, but not excessively, and quite savoury. The marinated salmon is perfectly prepared and will melt in your mouth.

Aux Vieux Canons
$$-$$$
650 Grande Allée Est
☎*529-9461*

The terrace at Aux Vieux Canons is very lively during the summer season. Try the delicious wine-flavoured French cooking or the succulent, expertly flambéed dishes. The atmosphere is festive thanks to singers, dancers and musicians performing gypsy music.

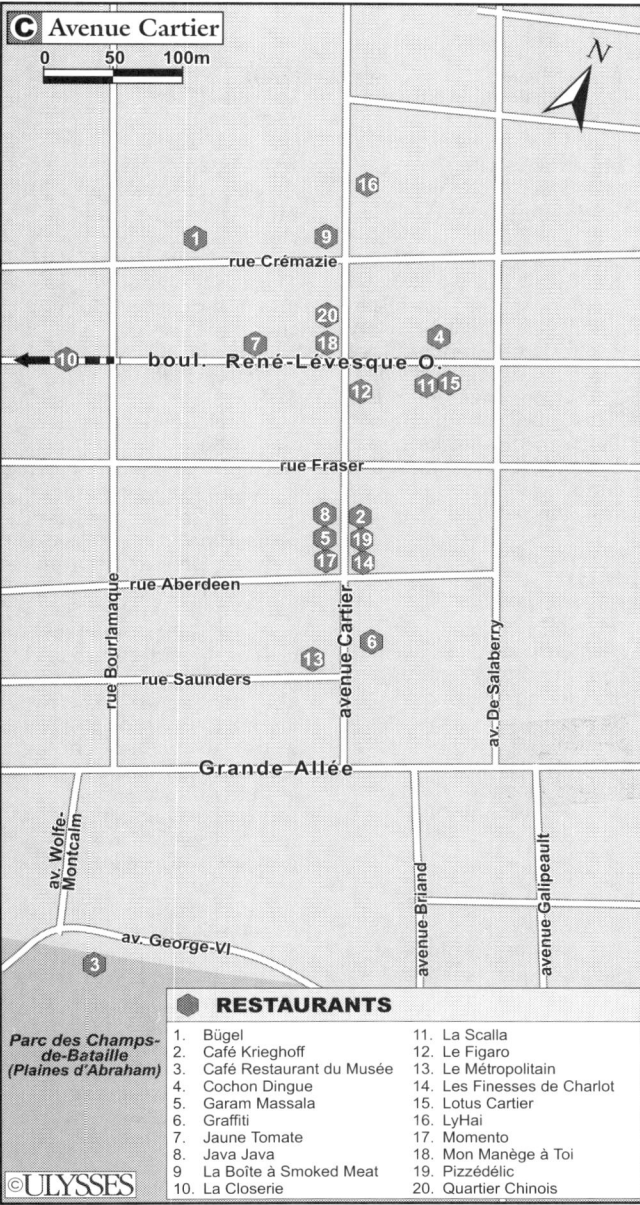

Café-Restaurant du Musée
$$-$$$
same hours as the museum
1 Avenue Wolfe-Montcalm
☎ *644-6780*

Inside the Musée du Québec, you'll find the lovely Café-Restaurant du Musée. Run by a nearby hotel-management school, the restaurant makes it a top priority to offer well-prepared food and outstanding service. Guests can gaze out at the Plains of Abraham and at the river through large windows; during summer, the same view can be enjoyed from the patio.

Le Portugais
$$-$$$
1155 de la Chevrotière
☎ *529-1675*

Located near Grande Allée, Le Portugais is reminiscent of certain parts of Old Europe. The music and decor certainly evoke Lisbon restaurants. Try it and discover Portugal's national and regional specialties.

La Scalla
$$-$$$
31 Boulevard René-Lévesque Ouest
☎ *529-8457*

The cozy atmosphere at La Scalla is quite suitable for intimate conversation. Close to Avenue Cartier, this restaurant offers friendly and courteous service. They serve excellent pizza and dishes grilled on a wood fire.

Le Louis-Hébert
$$-$$$
668 Grande Allée Est
☎ *525-7812*

An elegant restaurant with a plush decor, Le Louis-Hébert serves French cuisine and delectable seafood. There is a plant-filled solarium at the back. Courteous, attentive service.

Le Métropolitain
$$-$$$
1188 Avenue Cartier
☎ *649-1096*

Le Métropolitain is *the* place for sushi in Québec City. These delicious Japanese morsels are a real feast, they are prepared before your very eyes by expert hands behind the glass counter. Other oriental specialties, including fish and seafood dishes, are available here as well. The restaurant used to be located in the basement of another building and had a big sign at the entrance similar to those adorning certain metro stops in Paris. Its new, two-storey quarters are brighter.

Le Lotus Cartier
$$$
29 Boulevard René-Lévesque Ouest
☎ *649-9991*

Here at Le Lotus Cartier, flavourful cuisine from Southeastern Asia is served in a calm, pleasant atmosphere. The soups are particularly delicious.

🍴 Mon Manège à Toi
$$$
closed Sat and Sun at lunch
102 Boulevard Réne Lévesque Ouest, corner Cartier
☎ *649-0478*

Mon Manège à Toi is a Belgian restaurant with exquisite food inspired by Belgian and French cuisine. Service is efficient and friendly and the atmosphere is comfortable. The decor offers an elegant mix of bistro and bourgeois elements. This spot is worth a visit.

Le Rivoli
$$$
closed Sun and Mon Nov to Feb
601 Grande Allée Est
☎ *529-3071*

The Rivoli is an Italian trattoria with lots of charm. It features stone walls and pink woodwork. You can enjoy the sun on the terrace during the summer months as you sample the pizza, which is served in hundreds of different ways, along with veal and pasta.

Le Bonaparte
$$$
680 Grande Allée Est
☎ *647-4747*

Le Bonaparte is an excellent restaurant when it comes to French gourmet cooking. To add to the experience, why not participate in one of the "Murder Mystery" evenings where intrigue and suspense are part of the fun? The terrace overlooks Grande Allée, which is popular among the young fashionable crowd.

🍴 VooDoo Grill
$$$
575 Grande Allée Est
☎ *647-2000*

This old house was once the social club of the Union Nationale, the political party of the unforgettable Maurice Duplessis. Thus the name of the nightclub occupying the building's two upper floors (see p 245) where you can end the evening after a copious meal. Located on the second floor, the restaurant has kept some of the original architectural features and displays a most ingenious decor. A collection of African art work is displayed and features, among others, masks, sculptures and dolls, which makes the decor entrancing. Unfortunately the music is not African, but *djumbé* players come occasionally in during the evening and add a bit of rhythm to the already lively atmosphere. The VooDoo Grill menu has grilled food, of course, meat, fish and fowl as well as dishes cooked in a wok and served on spicy rice or satay with choice of sauce. All are tasty, creatively prepared and beautifully presented. The kitchen is open late.

La Maison du Steak
$$$-$$$$
641 Grande Allée Est
closed on holidays
☎*529-3020*

La Maison du Steak is the most popular steakhouse in town. High quality food is served in a very cheerful atmosphere. In addition to the house specialty, French cuisine is also offered. There is a terrace.

Paris Brest
$$$-$$$$
590 Grande Allée Est, corner De La Cherotière
☎*529-2243*

At the Paris Brest, French cuisine is the specialty. Prepared with care, the food here will satisfy the most demanding gourmets. In summer, the restaurant opens its small terrace which looks onto Grande Allée.

L'Astral
$$$-$$$$
Hotel Loews Le Concorde
1225 Place Montcalm
☎*647-2222*

A rotating restaurant located at the top of one of the city's largest hotels, L'Astral serves excellent French food and provides a stunning view of the river, the Plains of Abraham, the Laurentian mountains and the city. It takes about one hour for the restaurant to make a complete rotation. This is a particularly good place for Sunday brunch.

La Closerie
$$$$
966 Boulevard René-Lévesque Ouest
☎*687-9975*

La Closerie serves fine French cuisine. The chef, who has a well-established reputation, creates meals from fresh, prime quality ingredients. The exterior of this townhouse, located at a distance from tourist attractions, is no indication of what's inside – a gorgeous, intimate decor that guarantees pleasurable moments.

Tour D: Saint-Jean-Baptiste

Dazibo Café
$-$$
closed Mon
526 Rue St-Jean
☎*525-2405*

Dazibo Café is very small but quite pleasant. It is painted in warm colours and offers Irish specialties in a friendly family atmosphere. The most popular item on the menu is *briks*, small rolls of crusty pastry garnished to order.

Le Commensal
$-$$
860 Rue St-Jean
☎*647-3733*

The buffet style of Le Commensal has earned the public's affection over the years. Vegetarian dishes are the specialty here and are sold by weight. Strangely enough though, the plants are all artificial. However, this open space features a modern and tidy decor, which helps make it an enjoyable setting for a meal.

Chez Victor
$$
145 Rue St-Jean
☎**529-7702**
Located in a basement with a retro decor, Chez Victor serves salads and burgers – and not just any old burgers! The menu offers several different kinds (including a delicious veggie burger), all big, juicy and served with fresh toppings. The homemade fries are sublime! Cordial service.

Thang Long
$$
869 Côte d'Abraham
☎**524-0572**
Thang Long, located on Côte d'Abraham, is tiny, but its menu will transport you to Vietnam, Thailand, China and even Japan! The decor of this neighbourhood restaurant is simple and unpretentious; the cuisine is truly up to the mark, and the service, very attentive. Try one of the meal-size soups – comfort food at bargain prices!

Bonnet d'Âne
$$
298 Rue St-Jean
☎**647-3031**
It truly takes the originality of children's art to come up with an idea like Bonnet d'Âne. The theme here is elementary school and the menu is as varied as the subjects that name the dishes. Hamburgers, pizza and light meals are served on big beautiful plates that will delight both young and old. The decor is also part of the game with many evocative objects and lovely wood trim. There is a pretty terrace in the summer.

Le Hobbit
$$
700 Rue St-Jean
☎**647-2677**
Le Hobbit has occupied an old house in the Saint-Jean-Baptiste neighbourhood for years, and its stone walls, checkerboard floor and big windows that look onto bustling Rue St-Jean have not lost their appeal. There are two sections: the first is a café-style room where you can linger over an espresso and have a light meal; the second, a dining room with a delicious menu that changes daily and is never disappointing. Works by local artists are displayed here regularly.

La Piazzetta
$$
707 Rue St-Jean
☎**529-7489**
1191 Rue Cartier
☎**649-8896**
The layout of modern-looking Piazzetta is not really suitable for intimate dining.

The restaurant is generally crowded but lively. An infinite variety of European-style pizzas is served. There are many franchises of this restaurant all over Québec, this one is the original, but located in a house on Rue St-Jean.

Pointe des Amériques
$$
964 Rue St-Jean
☎*694-1199*
Pointe des Amériques is located in the heart of lively Place d'Youville. This large restaurant is charming and attractively decorated, featuring gourmet pizza as its specialty. Let yourself be tempted by the many toppings inspired by cooking from around the world. If you are a small party, you can each choose a different kind of pizza and ask that they give a slice to everyone. You will certainly have a hard time deciding which is your favourite!
The ambiance is delightful.

La Campagne
$$-$$$
bring your own wine
555 Rue St-Jean
☎*525-5247*
On the second floor of a house on Rue St-Jean, behind a large window filled with green plants, is La Campagne. This establishment is well-known for its tasty, well-prepared Vietnamese dishes.

Les Épices du Széchouan
$$-$$$
215 Rue St-Jean
☎*648-6440*
For exotic cuisine with succulent flavours and enticing aromas, try Les Épices du Széchouan, which occupies an old house in the Saint-Jean-Baptiste quarter. Its pretty decor is enhanced by a thousand and one Chinese trinkets. One table with banquette is nestled beneath a corbelled wall. The house is a little far from the street, so be careful not to miss it!

Le Carthage
$$-$$$
399 Rue St-Jean
☎*529-0576*
Le Carthage is a superb restaurant decorated in typical North African style. The ceiling is finely-worked and adorned with gilt. Mahogany-coloured woodwork is found everywhere as well as a good number of Tunisian decorative objects. Here, a wonderful gastronomic experience awaits you. Seated on a cushion on the floor, a stool or simply at a table, you will be delighted by the Tunisian specialties. For example, couscous with vegetables and merguez (spicy sausages) or chicken are among the mouth-watering choices. Belly dancers are also occasionally on hand to liven the celebrations.

La Grolla
$$-$$$
closed Mon
815 Côte d'Abraham
☎ *529-8107*

La Grolla welcomes you with the cozy atmosphere of a Swiss chalet. Wood beams, dried flowers and even the traditional Swiss cuckoo clock are all part of the decor. Next to a lovely wood fire, enjoy the delicious *raclette*, fondue, *röstis* or buckwheat crepes served by waitresses who are experts in the art of putting you at ease. The apple cider is light and delicious, and although this is not specified on the menu, it is non-alcoholic.

La Playa
$$$
780 Rue St-Jean
☎ *522-3989*

La Playa, a small restaurant with a beautiful, cozy decor, offers Californian cuisine and dishes from other sunny spots. Top billing on the menu goes to pasta, which is served with flavourful sauces including one for tandoori chicken. The restaurant also has a table d'hôte featuring delicious meat and fish dishes. During summer, guests can dine on a charming little patio.

Ciccio Café
$$$
875 Rue Claire-Fontaine
☎ *525-6161*

Ciccio Café is located on a quiet street near the Grand Théâtre de Québec. The atmosphere is relaxed and beautiful stone walls enhance the decor. Progressive French cuisine, gourmet pizza and excellent pasta are featured on the menu.

Il Teatro
$$$
972 Rue St-Jean
☎ *694-9996*

Il Teatro, located inside the magnificent Théâtre Capitole, serves excellent Italian cuisine in a lovely dining room with a long bar and big, sparkling windows all around. The courteous service is on a par with the delicious food. During summer, guests can dine in a small outdoor seating area sheltered from the hustle and bustle of Place d'Youville.

Tour E: Chemin Sainte-Foy

Mille-Feuilles
$$
1405 Chemin Ste-Foy
☎ *681-4520*

Mille-Feuilles is a vegetarian restaurant. They offer dishes that are both healthy and delicious, as well as carefully prepared. Located on a section of Chemin Ste-Foy that has a few shops and restaurants, its decor is a bit cold, but the ambiance is relaxed. They also have a little bookstore that sells health books.

Le Pailleur
$$$
3400 Chemin Sainte-Foy
☎*653-5221*

As Château Bonne-Entente's dining room (see p 193), Le Pailleur has just been renovated to offer its guests a higher level of comfort. The decor is attractive and beautiful light streams seep in through large windows on the facade, which overlooks the grounds and the swimming pool. Well-prepared gourmet Québec cuisine, such as of rabbit, duck, deer and salmon is served here. On weekends there is also a large buffet brunch.

Tour F: Saint-Roch

Salons d'Edgar
$
Wed to Sun
263 Rue St-Vallier Est
☎*523-7811*

In the attractive Salons d'Edgar, which also is a bar (see p 248), the food is simple and hearty. European hot-dogs and beef bourguignon, among others, are flavourful and presented with a creative touch, such as a green salad topped with blueberries. The muffled atmosphere creates a slightly dramatic setting just right for relaxing and chatting.

Café du Clocher Penché
$-$$
203 Rue St-Joseph Est
☎*640-0597*

In an old bank building in the Saint-Roch neighbourhood, across from the church with the leaning steeple, Café du Clocher Penché serves great little dishes prepared with a touch of originality. If you go for breakfast on the weekend, try the "voleur de bicyclette" (bicycle thief)! Located on a street corner, it has several windows that make up for the austere high ceilings.

Impasse des Deux Anges
$$
275 Rue St-Vallier Est
☎*647-6452*

Here is proof that coming to a dead end (*impasse*) can be a good thing. Such is the case when you reach Impasse des Deux Anges. This small café-restaurant painted in warm colours always features delicious dishes à la carte or as a table d'hôte. The decor is pleasant and the atmosphere relaxed. You will recognize the place by its intriguing bas-relief on the facade.

Tour G: Limoilou

Le Maizerets
$$
2006 Chemin de la Canardière
☎661-3764
It is said that Le Maizerets serves "the best pizza west of Rome." Well, this is true! For a really delicious pizza with a thin spicy crust cooked in a wood oven, make sure you visit this place. There is also a terrace.

Tour I: Sillery to Cap-Rouge

Sillery

Brynd
$
1360 Rue Maguire
☎527-3844
Brynd is the place to go to for smoked meat and everything to satisfy all tastes and appetites. There are also items on the menu for those who don't wish to try the house specialty. (Quite a shame!) The meat is smoked and sliced in front of your eyes, just like in a real delicatessen.

Buffet du Passant
$
Apr to Oct
1698 Côte de l'Église
☎681-6583
In Sillery, stop at Buffet du Passant, located halfway down the steep Côte de l'Église. You may ask yourself why, since it appears to be a traditional snack bar serving hamburgers and french fries. The secret is that it hides a little-known treasure in the back: from Rue des Voiliers, there is a superb view of the River and both its shores. A few picnic tables have been set up there so that you can eat lunch and enjoy the view.

Pizza Mag
$$
465 Avenue Maguire, Sillery
☎683-1561
see p 218

Le Cochon Dingue
$$
1365 Avenue Maguire
☎683-8111
see p 218

Pont de Québec

La Fougasse
$$
1648 Chemin St-Louis
☎*682-6585*

This small Italian restaurant is established in a house on Chemin St-Louis in Sillery and is worth the detour. In fact, La Fougasse offers an appealing menu of classical Italian cuisine at very reasonable prices. The decor is fashionable with long velvet drapes, and a clientele of regulars hurries to get in for lunch, dinner and brunch on the weekend.

Paparazzi
$$$
1365 Avenue Maguire
☎*683-8111*

Paparazzi serves Italian dishes. The salad with warm goat-cheese, spinach and caramelized walnuts is a true delight, as are other menu items. The decor is modern and pleasant with pretty tables covered in ceramic tiles set up on various levels.

Montego
$$-$$$
1460 Avenue Maguire
☎*688-7991*

The Montego restaurant-club promises a "sunny experience." The warmly decorated interior, large colourful plates and food presentation are a pleasure. And the cooking will delight your tastebuds with sweet, hot and spicy flavours inspired by the cuisine of California and other sunny places.

Sainte-Foy

Galopin
$$$-$$$$
Closed Dec 31 and Jan 1
3135 Chemin St-Louis
☎*652-0991*

The Galopin dining room is in a Sainte-Foy hotel, near the bridges. It is very large and comfortable, and the quality gourmet cuisine is served in a pleasant manner.

Michelangelo
$$$-$$$$
3111 Chemin St-Louis
☎*651-6262*

Michelangelo serves fine Italian cuisine that both smells and tastes wonderful. The classically decorated dining-room, although busy, remains warm and intimate. The courteous and attentive service adds to the pleasure.

La Tanière
$$$$
2115 Rang St-Ange
☎*872-4386*

La Tanière specializes in wild game, as you might have guessed (*tanière* is a den or lair). Although located in Sainte-Foy, this restaurant is slightly off the tour, near the airport. Paradoxically housed in a bungalow, the restaurant features a hunting-style decor, complete with stuffed trophies. Here you can experience tasty and delicious specialties from the Québec forest.

La Fenouillère
$$$$
Closed several days for Christmas
3100 Chemin St-Louis
☎*653-3886*
At La Fenouillère, the menu of refined and creative French cuisine promises a succulent dining experience. This restaurant is also the proud omner of one of the best wine cellars in Québec. The decor is simple and comfortable.

Tour J: Heading North

Wendake

Nek8arre
$$-$$$
9am to 5pm
575 Rue Stanislas-Kosca
☎*842-4308*
≠*842-3473*
In Onhoüa Chetek8e, the Huron-Wendat village (see p 167), there's a pleasant restaurant whose name means "the meal is ready to be served" introduces you to traditional Huron-Wendat cooking. Wonderful dishes such as clay trout, caribou or venison *brochettes* with mushrooms accompanied by wild rice and corn, are some of the items on the menu. The wood tables are engraved with texts explaining the eating habits of Aboriginal cultures. Numerous objects scattered here and there will arouse your curiosity, and luckily, the waitresses act as part-time "ethnologists" and can answer your questions. All this in a pleasant atmosphere. The entry fee to the village will be waived if you're only going to the restaurant.

Tour K: Côte-de-Beaupré and Île d'Orléans

Beauport

Manoir Montmorency
$$$
closed Jan
2490 Avenue Royale
☎*663-3330*
Manoir Montmorency (see p 168) benefits from a superb location above the Montmorency Falls. From the dining room surrounded by bay windows, there's an absolutely magnificent view of the falls, the river and Île d'Orléans. Fine French cuisine, prepared with the best products in the region, is served in pleasant surroundings. A wonderful experience for the view and the food! The entrance fee

to the Parc de la Chute Montmorency (where the restaurant is located) and the parking fees are waived upon presentation of your receipt or by mentioning your reservation.

Manoir Montmorency

Château-Richer

Auberge Baker
$$$-$$$$
8790 Avenue Royale
☎824-4852 or 824-4478
The Auberge Baker (see p 197) has two dining rooms. One has stone walls and a fireplace, while the other features a colder decor. They serve fine traditional Québec cuisine: game, meat and fowl are well-prepared and presented with care.

Beaupré (Mont Sainte-Anne)

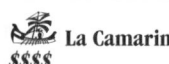 ### La Camarine
$$$$
closed Mon evening during low season
10947 Sainte-Anne
☎827-5703
La Camarine is an excellent restaurant that serves Québec nouvelle cuisine. The dining room is peaceful with a simple decor. The innovative dishes are a feast for the senses. In the basement of the inn is another small restaurant, the Bistro, which offers the same menu and prices as upstairs, but is only open in the winter. Equipped with a fireplace, it is a cozy spot for après-ski. It is open in the evening for drinks.

Île d'Orléans

Le Petit Baluchon
$
June to Sep
1222 Chemin Royal, St-Pierre
☎828-0122
In the heat of the summer, Le Petit Baluchon offers a decent alternative to restaurants. This self-proclaimed "picnic specialist" offers good food to complement your lunch box.

Café de Mon Village
$$
May to mid-Oct
3963 Chemin Royal, Sainte-Famille
☎829-3656
Café de Mon Village offers a good *menu du jour* as well

as bagels, croissants and salads. The decor is simple and the staff friendly. In the summer, the terrace has a magnificent view of the river.

Moulin de Saint-Laurent
$$$-$$$$
May to mid Oct
754 Chemin Royal, Saint-Laurent
☎*829-3888*
The Moulin de Saint-Laurent serves Québécois cuisine and is charmingly decorated with antiques. In the large dining room, which regularly receives groups, the chairs, wooden beams, stone walls and copper utensils hung here and there harmoniously complement this old building. The food is well presented and varied. On sunny days you can sit on the terrace which has a view of the waterfalls beside the mill.

Vieux-Presbytère
Winter, only Thu to Sat
$$$
1247 Avenue Mgr-d'Esgly, Saint-Pierre
☎*828-9723*
(see p 199)
The Vieux-Presbytère specializes in unusual meat such as bison, wapiti and ostrich. This is because the next-door neighbour raises them! You may even be able to see the animals on the farm. The restaurant prepares them as well as other dishes in a most delectable manner. The attractive dining room of this historic building also offers a superb view of the river.

Canard Huppé
$$$-$$$$
2198 Chemin Royal, St-Laurent
☎*828-2292*
The dining room of the Canard Huppé serves fine regional cuisine. Prepared with fresh ingredients that abound in the area, such as duck, trout and maple products, these little dishes will delight the most demanding palate. Although the room is somewhat dark (forest green is being the predominant colour) the country decor is, on the whole, pleasant.

La Goéliche
$$$-$$$$
22 Chemin du Quai, Ste-Pétronille
☎*828-2248*
The dining room at La Goéliche has unfortunately lost its old-time splendour (see p 199). It's still pleasant though, and you can still get one of the most beautiful views of Québec City. They serve fine French cuisine: stuffed quail, nuggets of lamb and saddle of hare.

Entertainment

As well as possessing unquestionable charm, Québec City is a highly entertaining town.

Whether you are in the mood for cultural activities, festivals or simply bars and nightclubs, this unique place will not disappoint you.

In many Québec City shops, restaurants and bars, you will find three newspapers containing information on current cultural activities. ***Québec Scope***, published every two weeks, is a small bilingual magazine that gives a brief overview of Québec City's main cultural events. The weekly ***Voir*** provides a few articles on current events as well as a listing of the main cultural activities. ***Le Clap*** is a magazine published by the movie theatre of the same name (see p 250). It features films reviews and articles on the movie industry. All three publications are free. Ask for them!

Bars and Nightclubs

All year long, the city's bars and nightclubs are filled with people from all walks of life. Whether it is the nightclubs of the young and dynamic Grande Allée, the coolest places on Avenue Cartier or the few "underground" bars in the Saint-Jean-Baptiste and Vieux-Québec areas, there are countless places to choose from. Why not discover them all?

There is no cover charge at most bars and nightclubs in Québec City, except when they are hosting a special event or a show. During winter, most places require customers to check their coats, which costs a dollar or two.

Tour A: Vieux-Québec

L'Arlequin
1070 Rue Saint-Jean
☎654-9464

For the best in underground sounds, live or mixed by a DJ, visit L'Arlequin. Located upstairs in a house on Rue Saint-Jean, its fantastic decor and party atmosphere are sure to get your feet moving.

Le d'Auteuil
35 Rue d'Auteuil
☎694-3383

All different kinds of musicians perform at Le D'Auteuil which occupies an old chapel most of whose architecture remains intact.

Le Chantauteuil
1001 Rue Saint-Jean

Le Chanteuteuil at the foot of the hill on Rue d'Auteuil is a pleasant bistro. People spend hours here chatting away, seated at bench-tables around bottles of wine or beers.

Chez Son Père
24 Rue Saint-Stanislas, corner Saint-Jean
☎692-5308

This bar is one of the rare spots where you can listen to Québécois music. An air of nationalism prevails in this place... The decor is nothing special: a large hall with a small stage. *Chansonniers* regularly perform hit songs by Québécois singers such as Paul Piché, Beau Dommage, Michel Rivard and Robert Charlebois. The atmosphere is often festive and audience members show their enthusiasm by clapping their hands and tapping their feet.

Le D'Orsay
65 Rue de Buade
☎694-1582

Le D'Orsay is a *brasserie* where people congregate to eat and drink. The black lacquered tables and wobbly chairs covered in pastel fabric harmoniously match to embellish the decor. It has a pub atmosphere and a slightly preppy clientele. During the summer, a *chansonnier* usually entertains the crowd on the large back terrace.

L'Ostradamus
29 Rue Couillard

For a laid-back atmosphere, go to L'Ostradamus, a gathering place for non-conformists of all sorts. It is this peculiar ambiance that makes the place interesting. Unusual-sounding music also invites you to just have a good time!

Emprise
Hôtel Clarendon
57 Rue Sainte-Anne;
☎692-2480

The oldest hotel in the city houses the Emprise (see p 186). This elegant bar is recommended to jazz fans. There is a long L-shaped shaped bar and, in the centre of the room, a magnificent black grand piano. While relaxing comfortably in an armchair, you can listen to one of the informal shows that are frequently presented here. There is no cover charge.

La Fourmi Atomik
33 Rue d'Auteuil
☎694-1473

Hidden away beneath Le d'Auteuil, La Fourmi Atomik is *the* underground bar in Québec City. There is a different musical theme every night from black beat, punk rock, alternative and 80s techno to the latest releases. During summer, the patio is always packed.

Le Kashmir
1018 Rue Saint-Jean
☎694-1648

Upstairs in a Rue Saint-Jean building is Le Kashmir, a rock and roll bar which often features live entertainment. The dance floor and the shows generally draw a large crowd.

Petit Paris
48 Côte de la Fabrique
☎694-0383

During summer, the sounds of people having a good time emanate from the open windows of the Petit Paris where *chansonniers* perform for an appreciative crowd.

Saint-Alexandre
1087 Rue Saint-Jean
☎694-0015

Le Saint-Alexandre is a typical English pub. The Scottish-green colour and stone walls blend perfectly with the mahogany wood panelling and furniture. At the back of the room is a beautiful black grand piano: unfortunately, it is seldom used. Here, great care is given to detail and authenticity. The impressive line-up of imported beers behind the bar is eye-catching and will give you a taste of the exotic. In fact, 200 varieties of beer are served, including about 20 on tap, their handles decorating the long bar. Good light meals are also served.

Sainte-Angèle
26 Rue Sainte-Angèle
☎692-2171

Tucked away in the basement of a building on Rue Saint-Angèle, the Sainte-Angèle looks like an English pub. It's decor is a bit worn, but the place is still comfortable. Though space is cramped, that does not stop local residents of all different ages from packing in here. Regulars sit at the bar and chat with the bartender. Good selection of reasonably priced scotches and cocktails.

Les Yeux Bleus
1117 1/2 Rue Saint-Jean
☎694-9118

The *chansonniers* of Les Yeux Bleus take turns performing and give the bar a festive air. This place is not chic or exceptional, but fun nevertheless. This is the kind of place where friends meet for one, two, three or many drinks! The clientele, aged 25 to 35, is very lively. There is also a terrace.

Tour B: Petit-Champlain to Vieux-Port

L'Innox
37 Rue Saint-André
☎692-2877

A bistro-style brewery and the last bastion of the brewing tradition, L'Inox also has an *économusée* (see p 116). The decor is original and the stainless steel central bar quite eye-catching. The clientele is young and varied. As well as serving beer, they have hot-dogs to satisfy growling stomachs. There are many different activities throughout the year so you should inquire; for example, it might be fun to attend a session of *peinture en direct* where artists paint and then auction pictures, or take part in the launching of a CD.

Pape-Georges
8 Rue Cul-de-Sac
☎692-1320

Pape George is a pleasant wine bar. Beneath the vaults of an old house in Petit Champlain, guests can sample a wide variety of wines while nibbling on snacks like cheese and *charcuteries*. The atmosphere is warm, especially when there's a *chansonnier* to heat things up.

Taverne Belley
249 Rue Saint-Paul
☎692-4595

The Taverne Belley in front of the Marché du Vieux-Port, has a few typical tavern features such as a pool table and small, round, metal tables. The decor of its two rooms is both warm and fun with colourful paintings hanging across exposed brick walls. A tiny fireplace warms the air nicely during winter.

Pub Thomas Dunn
369 Rue Saint-Paul
☎692-4693
Pub Thomas Dunn takes is named after the Honourable Thomas Dunn, a provincial civil servant and politician for many years. At this typical English pub situated opposite the Gare du Palais, you will find one of the best selections of beer in Québec City. The neat and tidy decor of mahogany and Scottish-green go beautifully together. The clientele is very mixed from university graduates to workers of all kinds. The atmosphere is friendly and relaxed.

Le Troubadour
29 Rue Saint-Paul
☎694-9176
Located near Place Royale, Le Troubadour is nestled beneath a vaulted ceiling. The place is made entirely of stone. Combined with the long white candles stuck in bottles on the wooden tables, it makes you feel as if you've stepped back in time to the Middle Ages. During winter, a crackling fire helps banish the cold.

Tour C: Grande Allée

Ballroom
690 Grande Allée Est
The Ballroom is where pool fans congregate. Although large in size, this billiard hall still has a certain charm. Because of the decor and the music, this place is inviting, contrary to most billiard halls that usually look rather cold. The clientele is early 30s and quite dynamic. Shows are occasionally presented here.

Le Dagobert
600 Grande Allée Est
☎522-0393
Better known as the Dag, Le Dagobert is one of the largest clubs in town. According to the regulars, it is the best nightclub for flirting... Taking up three floors of an old house, the Dag is actually very chic-looking just like its clientele. The dance floor is quite large and a horseshoe-shaped mezzanine is ideal for those who prefer to watch rather than join the dancing crowd. Hanging above the crowd, a giant screen shows the latest rock videos. In the summer, the terrace is always packed. There are also shows upstairs.

Maurice
575 Grande Allée Est
☎640-0711
The Maurice nightclub resembles no other in town. The decor is so original that it is difficult to describe. There is red all over the place, and the avant-garde furniture is amazing. The large dance floor in the centre is lined with small bars. Here the doormen

cleverly handpick the customers who are always hip, beautiful and aged between 20 and 35. The atmosphere is quite unique. There is a cover charge. On the top floor, the cigar room called **Charlotte** has a similar style decor. This is a room with sofas that serves its purpose well while a little later on you can jive on a dance floor where they sometimes present live shows. Sunday is Latino day.

Jules et Jim
1060 Avenue Cartier
☎*524-9570*

Little Jules et Jim has graced Avenue Cartier for several years now. It has a smooth atmosphere with banquettes and low tables reminiscent of Paris in the 1920s.

Le Merlin
1175 Avenue Cartier
☎*529-9567*

Le Merlin on lively Avenue Cartier is frequented by a thirtysomething crowd who come here to dance. In the basement, **Le Turf** *(1179 Avenue Cartier, ☎522-9955)*, an English pub, serves imported beer to fashionable regulars. It is also possible to eat at Le Merlin.

Pub Sherlock Holmes
1170 Rue d'Artigny
☎*529-8271*

Aside from its name, there is very little evidence that Pub Sherlock Holmes is an English pub. The decor is unassuming and the music rather commercial without being dance music. The student customers take their minds off schoolbooks by playing pool and darts; the atmosphere therefore is quite relaxed and easygoing.

Vogue
1170 Rue d'Artigny
☎*529-9973*

The Vogue is very popular, as its name indicates, with the 20 to 35 crowd. Attractively decorated and spread out on two floors, this club attracts the beautiful people. To the beat of the infectious dance music the frenzied crowd has a great time on the small dance floor. A modest terrace overlooks the Parc de la Francophonie and Grande Allée.

Tour D: Saint-Jean-Baptiste

L'Étrange
275 Rue Saint-Jean
☎*522-6504*
www.etrange.qu.ca

L'Étrange has been located upstairs in a house in the Saint-Jean-Baptiste neighbourhood for many years. Its specials and giant screen continue to attract the young and not-so-young. L'Étrange recently added another feather to its cap by providing its customers with two computers connected to the Internet.

Fou Bar
519 Rue Saint-Jean
The Fou Bar is an appealing place with a regular clientele who come here to drink, chat with friends or check out the current works of art on display.

Sacrilège
447 Rue Saint-Jean
☎*649-1985*
Sacrilège is a bar in the Saint-Jean-Baptiste neighbourhood with a lovely back terrace where you can just relax and get away from the hustle and bustle of the city.

Tour E: Chemin Sainte-Foy

Sainte-Foy

Le Cactus
814 Rue Myrand
☎*527-9111*
A little bit of Mexico in Québec City? Yes, it's possible! Located near the university, Le Cactus welcomes students who come for a drink and the spicy specialtes. There is a terrace.

Mundial
965 Route de l'Église
☎*652-1170*
Mundial has adopted a formula that's sure to please everyone. The ground floor has a small bar, ideal for quiet chats or for enjoying one of the shows that are regularly presented here. Upstairs is reserved for those who have put on their dancing shoes. There is a lively ambiance on the dance floor where the latest hits can be heard. The clientele is rather young.

La Grimace
2376 Rue Galvani
☎*527-3359*
Located in Sainte-Foy, away from the tourist circuit, La Grimance attracts a clientele of regulars who enjoy evenings spent with a chansonnier who hums well-known tunes from the Québec repertoire.

Tour F: Saint-Roch

Les Folies de Paris
Le Cabaret de Québec
252 Rue St-Joseph Est
☎*523-4777 or 888-775-9977*
This is a nightclub that offers dinner-shows to people who want to be impressed. The kitchen is on the way to creating an enviable reputation for itself in this city.

La Barberie
310 Rue St-Roch
☎ *522-4373*
www.labarberie.com

Set up in a slightly deserted neighbourhood, La Barberie was supposed to brew beer at first. Now open to the public in this local, it has been revamped and painted with warm colours for the occasion. The different beers offered at the counter, as well as those you can taste in various bars around the capital and surrounding area are, for the most part, delicious. Their ales are fermented in oak barrels.

Salons d'Edgar
263 Rue Saint-Vallier Est
☎ *523-7811*

Can't decide whether to eat something, have a drink with friends or play pool? Then go to Salons d'Edgar where all of these possibilities are offered. The beautiful decor, complete with screens and large white draperies, will give you the slight feeling of being on stage. In a long narrow room at the back you'll find high ceilings, armchairs, pool tables, table hockey and, as would any self-respecting lounge, a fireplace. The music is well chosen with often live entertainment.

Le Scanner
291 Rue Saint-Vallier Est
☎ *523-1916*
www.total.net/~scanner1

Are you overcome by a desire to surf? No need to panic, Québec City has its fair share of Internet bars and cafés. Evocatively named, Le Scanner has two computers to help you out and a bar on two floors. Aside from the computers, there are table games such as pool and soccer as well as parlour games. And when Le Scanner presents a musical evening, it would be hard to imagine staying glued to the computer screen.

Tour G: Limoilou

Bal du Lézard
1049 3e Avenue
☎ *529-3829*

The Bal du Lézard is a small bar in the Limoilou neighbourhood with underground music and decor. In the summer, the Bal opens out onto a terrace with wooden floors overlooking the street. Shows are regularly presented here.

Gay and Lesbian Clubs

L'Amour Sorcier
789 Côte Sainte-Geneviève
☎*523-3395*
L'Amour Sorcier is a small bar in the Saint-Jean-Baptiste quarter. The atmosphere really heats up here sometimes. During summer, it features a pretty patio.

Ballon Rouge
811 Rue Saint-Jean
☎*647-9227*
The nightclub Ballon Rouge has an exclusively male clientele. Each of its several rooms have their own particular ambience.

Le Drague
804 Rue St-Joachim
☎*649-7212*
This large gay nightclub has been completely renovated and today displays one of the most beautiful decors in Québec City. There is a spacious dance floor in the basement, and on Sunday evenings, drag queen shows are presented that create a wild atmosphere.

Cultural Events

The intensity of Québec City's cultural life varies from season to season but reaches its peak during the summer. However, you can have the pleasure of discovering different facets of Québec culture all year long through the many shows, concerts and exhibitions that are presented. There are films from all over the world, concerts from here and abroad, exhibition of all kinds and festivals for the public at large. To choose from the many possibilities, consult the region's daily newspapers, magazines mentioned at the beginning of this chapter or the **Télégraphe de Québec Web site** *(www.telegraph.com)*.

Ticket prices vary from one place to another. Many venues also offer student discounts.

Outdoor Activities

In the summer many shows are presented in the city parks, whether it is the gardens of the Hôtel-de-Ville, the Parc de la Francophonie (behind the Parlement, see p 125) or Place d'Youville. They are all very lively especially during the Festival d'Été International de Québec (Québec City International Summer Festival, see p 252). **L'Agora du Vieux-Port** *(84 Rue Dalhousie,* ☎*692-4672)* near the river and the **Pavillon de Musique Edwin-Bélanger** *(*☎*648-4071)*, set up in the centre of the Plaines of Abraham, also add to the excitement.

Musique

The **Orchestre symphonique de Québec**, the oldest in Canada, often performs at the Grand Théâtre de Québec *(269 Blvd. René-Lévesque E., ☎643-8131)*.

Theatres

Le Périscope
2 Rue Crémazie Est
☎*529-2183*
This theatre presents experimental plays.

Théâtre de la Bordée
1143 Rue St-Jean
☎*694-9631*
Small and intimate, this theatre is very charming.

Théâtre du Trident
Grand Théâtre de Québec
269, boul. René-Lévesque O.
☎*643-8131*

Concert Halls

**Auditorium Joseph-Laverge
Bibliothèque Gabrielle-Roy**
350 Rue Saint-Joseph Est
☎*529-0924*
All kinds of shows are presented in this small theatre.

Grand Théâtre de Québec
269 Boul. René-Lévesque Est
☎*643-8131*

Maison de la Chanson
68-78 Rue Du Petit-Champlain
☎*692-4744*
Excellent concerts are held in this intimate hall.

Palais Montcalm
995 Place d'Youville
☎*691-2399*, *tickets* ☎*670-9011*
Concerts as well as thematic exhibitions are presented here.

Salle de l'Institut
42 Rue Saint-Stanislas
☎*691-6981*, *tickets* ☎*691-7411*

Le Capitole de Québec et le Cabaret du Capitole
972 Rue Saint-Jean
☎*694-4444*
First inaugurated in 1903, this theatre was restored in 1992. It is now one of the most beautiful theatres in Québec City.

Salle Albert-Rousseau
Cégep de Ste-Foy
2410 ch. Ste-Foy, Ste-Foy
☎*659-6710*
Various shows are featured here.

Movie Theatres

**Le Clap
Centre Innovation**
2360 Chemin Sainte-Foy, Sainte-Foy
☎*650-2527*
Le Clap shows first-run and repertory films. A program is available (see p 241).

Cinéma Imax
5401 Boulevard Des Galeries, Galeries de la Capitale
☎ **627-8222**

Cinéma Imax is a great Canadian technological invention: larger-than-life movies are presented on a giant screen.

Cinéma des Galeries de la Capitale
5401 boul. des Galeries
☎ **628-2455**

Place Charest
500 rue du Pont
☎ **529-9745**

Spectator Sports

The Montréal Canadien's farm team, the **Citadelles**, shares the Colisée de Québec *(250 Boulevard Wilfrid-Hamel, ☎691-7211)* with the **Remparts** of the Major Junior League and always attracts hockey fans.

Right next door is the **Hippodrome du Québec** *(ExpoCité, 250 Boulevard Wilfrid-Hamel, ☎524-5283)* where fans can watch horse races.

The municipal stadium in Parc Victoria is the home of the **Capitales** baseball team.

Festivals and Cultural Events

February

Carnaval de Québec *(☎626-3716 or 888-737-3789)*, Québec City's winter carnival, takes place annually during the first two weeks of February. It is an opportunity for visitors and residents of Québec City to celebrate the beauty of winter. It is also a good way to add a little life to a cold winter that often seems to never end. Various activities are organized. Some of the most popular include nighttime parades, canoe races over the partially frozen St. Lawrence River as well as the international ice and snow sculpture contests on the Plains of Abraham and in front of the carved ice castle at Place du Parlement. This can be a bitterly cold period of the year, so dressing very warmly is essential.

During Carnaval (see above), the city hosts a number of sporting events, including the **Tournoi International de Hockey Pee-wee de Québec** (☎524-3311).

June

The **Concours Hippique de Québec** (☎647-2727) (equestrian show-jumping) at the end of June is the preliminary for this sport's Coupe du Monde (World Cup). It takes place in the magnificent Parc des Champs-de-Bataille.

July and August

At the end of June, the **Coupe du Monde de Vélo de Montagne** (World Cup Mountain Bike Race) (☎827-1122) is held at Mont-Saint-Anne. Here you can watch top men and women professional racers compete.

Estival Juniart (☎691-6284) is the time to discover up-and-coming youths performing at shows and concerts in Vieux-Québec. This event takes place at the end of July.

The **Festival d'Été de Québec** (mid-Jul; ☎1-888-992-5200) is generally held for 10 days in early July when music, songs, dancing and other kinds of entertainment from all over the world liven up Québec City. The festival has everything it takes to be the city's most important cultural event. The outdoor shows are particularly popular. For most theatres' indoor shows, you must buy tickets. However, those presented outdoors are free.

In early August, Québec City celebrates the beginnings of colonization with the **Fêtes de la Nouvelle-France** (☎694-3311). People dress in period costume, a marketplace is re-created on Place Royale and many festive activities mark the occasion which lasts for a few days.

Wednesday and Saturday evenings at the end of July and beginning of August, the Parc de la Chute-Montmorency comes to life with the **Grand Feux Loto-Québec** (☎523-3389 ou 800-923-3389). The fireworks sparkle above the falls in a spectacular show, while on the river, a multitude of boats admire the display of colours.

Place du Parlement houses the **Plein Art** (late Jul; every day 10am to 11pm; ☎694-0260) exhibit from late July to early August. All kinds of arts and crafts are displayed and sold.

People from the Québec City region have been enjoying themselves at **Expo-Québec** *(Parc d'ExpoCité, ☎691-7110)* every August for 50 years now. This huge fair, complete with an amuseument park, is held in front of the coliseum for about 10 days at the end of the month.

September

For movie buffs, the start of fall (end of August, early September) marks the beginning of the **Festival International du Film de Québec** *(☎694-9920)*. This festival presents the best films from here and abroad.

October

In October, Québec City bars and theatres host musical entertainment and evenings of tales and legends during the **Festival International des Art Traditionnels** *(☎647-1598)*. Some institutions such as the Musée de la Civilisation and the Bibliothèque Gabrielle-Roy also present traditional crafts as part of the festival.

The **Festival de l'Oie des Neiges de Saint-Joachim** *(Cap Tourmente, ☎827-4808 or 827-3402)* is the perfect opportunity to observe an impressive congregation of thousands of snow geese. They stop here in Cap Tourmente (see p 65) marshes and fields before setting off on their long voyage south.

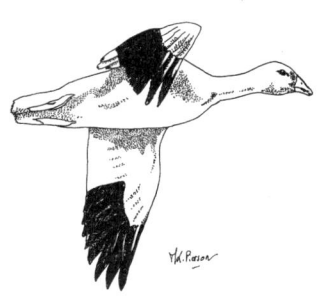

Shopping

Whether you are looking for Québec-made or imported goods, you will find everything your heart desires in Québec City's shops.

There are many shopping centres in the Québec City region. Here are a few: **Galeries de la Capitale** on Boulevard des Galeries; **Place Québec** on Avenue Dufferin (Tour D); **Promenades Sainte-Anne** at 10909 Boulevard Sainte-Anne (Tour K) that includes a few factory outlets. There are also four shopping centres on Boulevard Laurier in Sainte-Foy, namely **Place Laurier**, **Place Ste-Foy**, **Place de la Cité** and **Place Belle-Cour**.

Avenue Maguire is Sillery's most pleasant shopping street. You may make some interesting discoveries here.

In Sainte-Foy, the Laudance area has been set up like a small European town. Brick dwellings with stores on the ground floor, an urban park and a finely designed marketplace are grouped together along **Rue Campanile**. Adorned with a clock tower, the covered market is a long and narrow passageway with stalls on both sides.

Here are a few shops where some wonderful treasures await you.

Antiques

If you are an antique lover, you should not miss attractive Rue Saint-Paul. In fact, the street is known for its many antique and secondhand shops that offer great discoveries.

Then, there is Machins Chouettes *(835 Rue Turnbull, ☎525-9898)* whose wonderful name (thingamabobs) is a perfect description, and **Les Choux Gras** *(1240 Boulevard Charest Ouest, ☎522-2221)* which features a large display of antiques.

Art Galleries

As a city admired by artists, Québec City offers numerous art galleries exhibiting works from many periods and schools. There are also half a dozen galleries scattered around Île d'Orléans and several in the village of Saint-Jean. Here are some Québec City addresses:

Beauchamp & Beauchamp
10 Rue Sault-au-Matelot
☎*694-2244*

Galerie Estampe Plus
49 Rue Saint-Pierre
☎*694-1303*

Galerie d'Art Linda Verge
1049 Avenue des Érables
☎*525-8393*

Galerie d'Art Madeleine Lacerte
1 Côte Dinan
☎*692-1566*

Galerie d'Art Royale
53 Rue Saint-Pierre
☎*692-2244*

Le Chien D'Or
8 Rue du Fort
☎*694-9949*

Le Portal
53 rue du Petit-Champlain, 1er étage
☎*692-0354*

Bookstores

Québec City has many bookstores to offer, but the ones listed here sell English books or books on specific topics such as art. The Saint-Jean-Baptiste neighbourhood abounds in used bookshops, although the books are mainly in French. At the following addresses you will also receive good tips.

Librairie du Musée du Québec
Parc des Champs-de-Bataille
☎*643-0529*
Beautiful books on art.

La Maison Anglaise
Place de la Cité, Sainte-Foy
☎*654-9523*
The best selection of English books in Québec City.

CDs and Cassettes

Here are two good places to buy discs and tapes. They both sell all kinds of music styles and will advise you on the latest releases.

Sillons Le Disquaire
1149 Avenue Cartier
☎*524-8352*

Archambault
1095 Rue Saint-Jean, Vieux-Québec
☎*694-2088*

Clothing

Ladieswear

Atelier La Pomme, **Les Vêteries**, see above.

La Cache
1150 Rue Saint-Jean
☎*692-0398*
La Cache is a Canadian chain of quality clothing. The clothes are made from beautiful rich-coloured fabrics with unusual designs inspired by the nature and culture of India where they are handmade. There are also attractive objects for the house as well as bed coverings made of the same attractive fabrics.

Chez Boomer
970 Avenue Cartier
☎*523-7047*
Chez Boomer is filled with young-looking, comfortable and well-made clothes as well as accessories.

L'Exile
714 Rue Saint-Jean
☎*524-4752*
L'Exile is a charming shop selling carefully selected quality clothing, and fine jewellery.

O'Clan
52 Boulevard Champlain
☎*692-1214*
If you enter O'Clan by Boulevard Champlain, you will find well-made clothes in the latest fashions. Men's clothing is upstairs.

Simons
20 Côte de la Fabrique
☎*692-3630*
Place Sainte-Foy
Galeries de la Capitale
Simons stores have existed since 1840 and are a part of Québec City tradition. In Québec City homes during the holidays, the Christmas trees are often piled high with Simons' characteristic green boxes. All three stores provide everything to dress men, women and children from head to toe and in several different styles. Clothing accessories and bed linens are also sold.

L'Echo-Logik
829 Côte d'Abraham
☎ *648-8288*
L'Écho-Logik is the first store in Québec City to sell clothing made of 100% hemp. There are also hand-crafted leather goods.

La Chienne à Jacques
831 Côte d'Abraham
Right next door, La Chienne à Jacques is a second-hand clothes shop worthy of its name *("chienne à Jacques refers to someone who wears old clothing")* and full of treasures!

In a small area of Boulevard René-Lévesque, between Rue Turnbull and Rue Salaberry, there are several **Québec designer** boutiques selling exclusive creations for women.

In town, along Rue Saint-Jean the large popular chains selling fashionable clothing such as Bedo, Gap, Jacob, Le Château, Roots and San Francisco are found.

Men's Clothing

Chez Boomer, see above.

Louis Laflamme
1192 Rue Saint-Jean
☎ *692-3774*
Louis Laflamme features chic clothing for men on two floors.

O'Clan
67 1/2 Rue du Petit-Champlain
☎ *692-1214*
If you enter O'Clan by the Rue Petit-Champlain entrance, you will find great-looking, well-made clothes for men. Women's clothes are downstairs.

Simons, see above.

In town, the large popular chain stores selling fashionable clothing such as America, Bedo, Gap, Le Château and Roots are located on Rue Saint-Jean.

Furriers

Poste de Traite
76 Rue Saint-Louis
☎ *692-2955*
With its white walls and floor, Poste de Traite does not look much like the trading post that its name suggests. However in the store you will find furs tanned and cut to dress you from head to toe.

Laliberté JB
595 Charest Est
☎ *525-4841*
In the Mail Centre-Ville, a department storenamed Laliberté JB sells a variety of fur coats as well as coats for every season.

Shoes and Hats

In town, large Canadian shoe-store chains such as Aldo, Pegabo and Nero Bianco are found along Rue Saint-Jean.

For all kinds of hats visit the following shops: **Atelier Rachelle Beaulieu** *(583 Rue Saint-Jean, ☎529-9249)* and **Bibi et Compagnie** *(40 Rue Garneau, ☎694-0045).*

Jewellery

Après-Demain
813 Avenue Cartier
☎640-3345
597 Rue Saint-Jean
Après Demain has two very charming little shops where all kinds of jewellery and handicrafts from around the world are sold at reasonable prices.

Lazuli, see "Crafts Shops and Artisans' Studios."

Origines
54 Côte de la Fabrique
☎694-9257
The small shop Origines mainly sells jewellery. The pieces may be simple or elaborate, but they are all very original and elegant.

Louis Perrier *(48 Rue du Petit-Champlain, ☎692-4633)* or **Pierre Vivès** *(23 1/2 Rue du Petit-Champlain, ☎692-5566).*

Craft Shops and Artisans' Studios

Abaca
38 Rue Garneau
☎694-9761
Hidden away on little Rue Garneau, Abaca abounds with beautiful objects from Africa and Asia.

Aux Multiples Collections
69 Rue Sainte-Anne
☎692-4298
43 Rue de Buade
Aux Multiples Collections specializes in Inuit art. Handsome serpentine sculptures depicting daily life in the Far North as well as other handmade objects fill these two attractive shops.

Atelier La Pomme
47 Rue Sous-le-Fort
☎692-2875
Atelier La Pomme is where leather goods and clothes are made, and is one of Petit-Champlain's oldest workshops. The various different kinds and colours of leather accentuate the originality and quality of the clothing. Some of the items you will find here: coats, skirts, hats and even mittens.

Boutique du Musée de la Civilisation
85 Rue Dalhousie
☎ *643-2158*
This small shop within the Musée de la Civilisation sells beautiful handcrafted objects from around the world. There are truly great finds to be made here and at a wide range of prices.

Cinq Nations
20 Rue Cul-de-Sac
25 1/2 Rue du Petit-Champlain
Cinq Nations, an Aboriginal art gallery, you can admire and buy crafts made by First Nations peoples. There is also some superb jewellery.

Corporation des artisans de l'île
☎ *828-9824*
On île d'Orléans you will find a few crafts and antique shops as well as woodworking studios. Behind Église de Saint-Pierre, you can also find the Corporation des artisans de l'île.

Still in Saint-Pierre, the **Boutique Hang'Art** *(751 Chemin Royal, ☎ 828-2519)* is also an *Économusée* of rugs presenting an assortment of woven coverings. In Saint-Jean, in the old presbytery in front of the church facing the river, **Les Échoueries** *(2001 Chemin Royal)* displays a great many objects made by skilled craftspeople.

Forge à Pique-Assaut
2200 Chemin Royal, Saint-Laurent
☎ *828-9300*
On Île d'Orléans, the Forge à Pique-Assaut is a tiny *économusée* that introduces visitors to the art of the blacksmith and presents various wrought iron objects such as chandeliers, furniture and curios. There are also other kinds of handicrafts.

Galerie-Boutique Métiers d'Art
29 Rue Notre-Dame
☎ *694-0267*
Galerie-Boutique Métiers d'Art brings together a whole range of articles made by Québec craftspeople. Located in a beautiful building on Place Royale, the gallery overflows with a variety of wonderful items that include clothing, ceramics and jewellery.

La Corriveau
24 Côte de la Fabrique
☎ *694-0062*
La Corriveau is a large crafts shop. With three floors to peruse, you will find anything and everything you might want as a souvenir of Québec City.

Craft Shops and Artisans' Studios 261

Lazuli
774 Rue Saint-Jean
☎525-6528
Lazuli, an attractive shop, sells crafts from around the world. Silver, wood and ceramic objects of exceptional quality are finely made for those who can appreciate them.

Les Trois Colombes
46 Rue Saint-Louis
☎694-1114
Les Trois Colombes on Rue Saint-Louis sells crafts as well as quality clothing. Among the items are beautiful handmade wool coats.

L'Oiseau du Paradis
80 Rue du Petit-Champlain
☎692-2679
A pretty Petit-Champlain shop, L'Oiseau du Paradis sells all kinds of paper goods as well as handmade paper from Québec workshops.

Pot-en-ciel
27 Rue du Petit-Champlain
☎692-1743
Behind its large windows, Pot-en-ciel exhibits all sorts of curios of a rainbow of colours, especially ceramics.

Sachem
17 Rue Desjardins
☎692-3056
Sachem is situated in the Antoine-Vanfelson historic house (see p 89). Its two rooms are filled with Aboriginal art objects and crafts. They also sell greeting cards, postcards and attractive T-shirts.

La Soierie Huo
91 Rue du Petit-Champlain
☎692-5920
At La Soierie Huo you can purchase lovely silk scarves with designs that are as varied as they are colourful. You may also get the chance to see Dominique Huot as she creates them, paintbrush in hand.

Transparence
1193 Rue St-Jean
☎692-3477
Transparence is a well-named small store selling glass objects, mostly made by craftspeople. Admire these beautiful objects which reflect the coloured light of the various tints of glass.

Verrerie La Mailloche
58 Rue Sous-le-Fort
Verrerie La Mailloche (see p 107) sells blown-glass objects made in the workshop such as bottles, vases and dishes of all shapes and colours.

Verrerie Réjean Burns
159 Rue Saint-Paul
☎694-0013
Verrerie Réjean Burns sells superb stained-glass creations. The lamps and stained-glass windows are worth seeing.

Vêteries
31 1/2 Rue Du Petit-Champlain
☎*694-1215*
At Vêteries you will find hand-woven clothing from a regional weaving studio. The clothes are classical in their colours and cut, but are quite original.

Decorative Objects

L'Art de Vivre
1178 Avenue Cartier
☎*640-3303*
In an old-fashioned decor, L'Art de Vivre sells small things that are sure to embellish your home.

La Cache, see above under Women's Clothing.

La Dentellière
56 Boulevard Champlain
☎*692-2807*
La Dentellière sells lace, lace and more lace! For romantics only.

Quartier Général
1180 Avenue Cartier
☎*529-6083*
For original decorative objects, visit Quartier Général. You can also find the **Paris Cartier** clothing store for women there.

Simons, see above listed under "Ladieswear."

Zone
999 Avenue Cartier
☎*522-7373*
Behind its large windows, Zone, similar to its Montréal shops, overflows with objects for the house. You will find all sorts of items like funny lemon squeezers, casserole dishes or picnic baskets that will make your life easier or simply more pleasant.

Food

Chez Nourcy
131 Avenue Cartier
☎*523-4772*
Chez Nourcy is a gourmet food store that has been around for a long time. Their two locations are in Sillery and in Québec City. The bread, cakes, cheese, sorbets and so on are positively mouth-watering. There are also Lebanese dishes and a selection of salads.

Le CRAC and the **Carotte Joyeuse** *(690 Rue Saint-Jean,* ☎*647-6881)* are two adjoining shops where you will find a whole range of health food including organically grown fruit and vegetables.

Délicatesse Tonkinoise
732 Rue Saint-Jean
☎*523-6211*
The small Délicatesse Tonkinoise sells products from Asia to use when cooking exotic dishes as well as delicious dishes for take-out.

Épicerie Européenne
560 Rue Saint-Jean
☎ 529-4847
Épicerie Européenne sells European gourmet products, particularly from Italy where the shopowners came from. In French or Italian, they will kindly offer you judicious advice. If you like blue cheese, you must taste their Stilton with port.

Épicerie Méditerranéenne
64 Boulevard René-Lévesque
☎ 529-9235
Épicerie Méditerranéenne is a chic specialty grocery store adorned with granite, a tiled floor and glass counters. With recipes from Mediterranean countries, all sorts of tempting dishes are offered. Products from this store can also be found in a large store in the Saint-Roch neighbourhood (85 Rue Saint-Vallier Est) where bread is baked daily on the premises.

J.-A. Moisan
699 Rue Saint-Jean
☎ 522-8368
What a pleasure it is to shop at J.-A. Moisan (see p 266). This old grocery store carries all kinds of fresh products such as fruit, vegetables, seafood, spices, bread and delicious cheeses. This gourmet shop also has a few tables to enjoy a snack and a counter where delicious sushi is prepared before your eyes.

For fresh fruit and vegetables in the summer, go to the **Marché du Vieux-Port** in Québec City (see p 118) or **Marché de la Place** in Sainte-Foy (Rue de la Place, near Route de l'Église and Boulevard Hochelage). Every day farmers from the region bring their flavourful fresh products here for sale. On Sunday in Sainte-Foy, the market also becomes a flea market that's sure to please anyone looking for a bargain.

Pâtes à Tout
42 Boulevard René-Lévesque
☎ 529-8999
For fresh pasta and tasty sauces, Pâtes à Tout is the one to go to. They also sell take-out meals and homemade bread.

Poissonnerie Jean-Pierre
951 Avenue Cartier
☎ 525-5067
Poissonnerie Jean-Pierre used to belong to a seasoned connoisseur from Îles-de-la-Madeleine. Today it is still filled with all kinds of the fresh fish and seafood.

Take advantage of your visit to Île d'Orléans to sample all of its goodies. There's market gardeners selling at road-side stands in the summer, sugar shacks in the spring as well as small shops scattered here and there. For example: **Chocolaterie de l'Île d'Orléans** *(196 Chemin Royal, Ste-Pétronille, ☎828-2252)* makes great little homemade sweets; **Ferme Mona** *(723 Chemin Royal, St-Pierre)* concocts delicious liqueurs and crème de cassis (blackcurrent liqueur); and **La Boulange** *(2001 Chemin Royal, ☎829-3162)*, located in the Saint-Jean presbytery, prepares wonderful bread.

Miscellaneous

Animalerie Boutique Tropicale
1028 Avenue Cartier
☎*522-6744*

If you're travelling with Buddy the dog or Fluffy the cat, you will certainly appreciate the following address: Animalerie Boutique Tropicale.

Excalibur
1055 Rue Saint-Jean
☎*692-5959*

Obviously, it is rare today that you would need to shop for a sword or a coat of mail. However, if you are a Medieval history buff or just curious, you will enjoy visiting Excalibur.

L'Attitude
71 Rue Crémazie Ouest
☎*522-0106*

If being on vacation is not enough to relieve your stress, drop by the shop inside L'Attitude relaxation and massotherapy centre. Here you will find many things to help you relax, including essential oils, candles, discs, tapes and books. You can also take this opportunity to enjoy a relaxing therapeutic massage.

Musée de l'Abeille (bee museum)
8862 Boulevard Sainte-Anne
☎*824-4411*

An *économusée* at the Château-Richer, the Musée de l'Abeille (bee museum) offers an interesting look into the world of these tireless workers. Adjoining the museum is a small shop selling a host of objects related to bees such as beauty products made from honey, honey wine and educational material bearing the effigy of this yellow and black insect. Of course, there are also many different kinds of honey that you can taste and buy in various quantities.

Newspapers and Tobacco

To find all kinds of cigars, cigarettes and cigarillos, visit the store at the corner of Rue Crémazie and Avenue Cartier, **Tabac Tremblay** *(955 Avenue Cartier, ☎529-3910)*, or opposite the Cathedral, **J.E. Giguère** *(59 Rue de Buade, ☎692-2296)*. You will also find local newspapers there.

For magazines and newspapers from around the world, drop by either **Maison de la Presse Internationale** *(1050 Rue Saint-Jean)* or **Au Coin du Monde** *(1150 Avenue Cartier)*.

Outdoor Clothing and Equipment

L'Aventurier
710 Rue Bouvier
☎**624-9088**
L'Aventurier is a little far from the Haute-Ville, but here you will find outdoor specialists to help you - especially if you are interested in water sports. Kayaks, tents, clothing and hiking boots and other equipment are sold here.

Azimut
1194 Avenue Cartier
☎**648-9500**
Azimut sells quality tents, sleeping bags, backpacks, hiking boots... everything for Québec's great outdoors.

Course à Pied
25A Rue Marie-de-L'Incarnation
☎**688-7788**
Course à pied is the shoe store to visit if you want to move in comfort no matter what your activity or sport. Clothing and accessories are also sold.

DLX/Deluxe
2480 Chemin Ste-Foy
Ste-Foy
☎**653-0783**
This is where to buy or rent equipment such as a snowboard, a skate board, a BMX. There are also well-known brands of clothing and shoes. This is the place for fans of extreme sports in Québec City!

Latulippe
637 Rue Saint-Vallier Ouest
☎**529-0024**
Latulippe is a store visited by workers whoneed to be well-equipped as well as outdoor enthusiasts. All sorts of articles are sold at reasonable prices.

Tourisme Jeunesse
94 Boulevard René-Lévesque Ouest
☎522-2552
Newly installed at the corner of Avenue Cartier in an attractive setting, Tourisme Jeunesse lives up to its name. It sells everything from airline tickets to backpacks to guide books for young and not-so-young adventurers who want to explore the world.

Stationery

Papeterie du Faubourg
545 Rue Saint-Jean
☎525-5377
The Papeterie du Faubourg sells paper, greeting cards and has a photocopy and fax service.

Les Petits Papiers
1170 Avenue Cartier
☎524-3860
Les Petits Papiers has greeting cards, writing paper, notebooks, wrapping paper, among other items.

Sweets

When the weather is warm, Québécois are very fond of ice cream, frozen yogurt and sorbet. You only have to stroll along Avenue Cartier and spot the many milk bars to know that this is true. This short thoroughfare has at least half a dozen places that sell these tempting treats.

Arnold
1190-A Avenue Cartier
☎522-6053
On Avenue Cartier, Arnold announces its "chocolats cochons" (chocolate pigs) on a sign featuring a pig. Not only will the chocolates but also the ice cream (the fresh-strawberries flavour is irresistible) will make you want to eat more and more, just like a pig!

Érico
634 Rue Saint-Jean
☎524-2122
Rue Saint-Jean harbours a treasure trove for chocolate enthusiasts. Érico is a small business that makes these delights from the best products available, including cocoa, vanilla, caramel, hazelnuts, and much more. In the summer, Érico also sells rich homemade ice cream and sorbet. Even if you don't have a sweet tooth, take the time to stop by because its window design is always creative and amusing: it is made entirely of chocolate!

Au Palais d'Or
60 Rue Garneau
☎692-2488
The pastry shop Au Palais d'Or sells rich pastries made with real butter and cream. Absolutely delicious.

Le Panetier
764 Rue Saint-Jean
☎ *522-3022*
Le Panetier makes great bread, delicious cakes and real croissants cooked to perfection.

Tutto Gelato
837 Rue St-Jean
closed in winter
On Rue Saint-Jean, the small Tutto Gelato counter serves ice cream prepared from traditional Italian recipes. The result is absolutely divine! This is a must if you are an ice cream lover.

Glossary

GREETINGS

Hi (casual)	*Salut*
How are you?	*Comment ça va?*
I'm fine	*Ça va bien*
Hello (during the day)	*Bonjour*
Good evening/night	*Bonsoir*
Goodbye, See you later	*Bonjour, Au revoir, à la prochaine*
Yes	*Oui*
No	*Non*
Maybe	*Peut-être*
Please	*S'il vous plaît*
Thank you	*Merci*
You're welcome	*De rien, Bienvenue*
Excuse me	*Excusez-moi*
I am a tourist.	*Je suis touriste*
I am American (m/f)	*Je suis Américain(e)*
I am Canadian (m/f)	*Je suis Canadien(ne)*
I am British	*Je suis Britannique*
I am German (m/f)	*Je suis Allemand(e)*
I am Italian (male/female)	*Je suis Italien(ne)*
I am Belgian	*Je suis Belge*
I am Swiss	*Je suis Suisse*
I am sorry, I don't speak French	*Je suis désolé(e), je ne parle pas français*
Do you speak English?	*Parlez-vous anglais ?*
Slower, please.	*Plus lentement, s'il vous plaît.*
What is your name?	*Quel est votre nom?*
My name is...	*Je m'appelle...*
spouse (m/f)	*époux(se)*
brother, sister	*frère, soeur*
friend (m/f)	*ami(e)*
son, boy	*garçon*
daughter, girl	*fille*
father	*père*
mother	*mère*
single (m/f)	*celibataire*
married (m/f)	*marié(e)*
divorced (m/f)	*divorcé(e)*
widower/widow	*veuf(ve)*

DIRECTIONS

Is there a tourism office near here?	*Est-ce qu'il y a un bureau de tourisme près d'ici?*
There is no...	*Il n'y a pas de...,*
Where is...?	*Où est le/la ... ?*
straight ahead	*tout droit*
to the right	*à droite*
to the left	*à gauche*
beside	*à côté de*

near	près de
here	ici
there, over there	là, là-bas
into, inside	à l'intérieur
outside	à l'extérieur
far from	loin de
between	entre
in front of	devant
behind	derrière

GETTING AROUND

airport	aéroport
on time	à l'heure
late	en retard
cancelled	annulé
plane	l'avion
car	la voiture
train	le train
boat	le bateau
bicycle	la bicyclette, le vélo
bus	l'autobus
train station	la gare
bus stop	un arrêt d'autobus
The bus stop, please	l'arrêt, s'il vous plaît
street	rue
avenue	avenue
road	route, chemin
highway	autoroute
rural route	rang
path, trail	sentier
corner	coin
neighbourhood	quartier
square	place
tourist office	bureau de tourisme
bridge	pont
building	immeuble
safe	sécuritaire
fast	rapide
baggage	bagages
schedule	horaire
one way ticket	aller simple
return ticket	aller retour
arrival	arrivée
return	retour
departure	départ
north	nord
south	sud
east	est
west	ouest

CARS
for rent	*à louer*
a stop	*un arrêt*
highway	*autoroute*
danger, be careful	*attention*
no passing	*défense de doubler*
no parking	*stationnement interdit*
no exit	*impasse*
stop! (an order)	*arrêtez!*
parking	*stationnement*
pedestrians	*piétons*
gas	*essence*
slow down	*ralentir*
traffic light	*feu de circulation*
service station	*station-service*
speed limit	*limite de vitesse*

MONEY
bank	*banque*
credit union	*caisse populaire*
exchange	*change*
money	*argent*
I don't have any money	*je n'ai pas d'argent*
credit card	*carte de crédit*
traveller's cheques	*chèques de voyage*
The bill please	*l'addition, s'il vous plaît*
receipt	*reçu*

ACCOMMODATION
inn	*auberge*
youth hostel	*auberge de jeunesse*
bed and breakfast	*gîte*
hot water	*eau chaude*
air conditioning	*climatisation*
accommodation	*logement, hébergement*
elevator	*ascenseur*
bathroom	*toilettes, salle de bain*
bed	*lit*
breakfast	*déjeuner*
manager, owner	*gérant, propriétaire*
bedroom	*chambre*
pool	*piscine*
floor (first, second...)	*étage*
main floor	*rez-de-chaussée*
high season	*haute saison*
off season	*basse saison*
fan	*ventilateur*

SHOPPING
open	*ouvert(e)*
closed	*fermé(e)*
How much is this?	*C'est combien?*
I would like...	*Je voudrais...*

I need...	J'ai besoin de...
a store	un magasin
a department store	un magasin à rayons
the market	le marché
salesperson (m/f)	vendeur(se)
the customer (m/f)	le / la client(e)
to buy	acheter
to sell	vendre
t-shirt	un t-shirt
skirt	une jupe
shirt	une chemise
jeans	un jeans
pants	des pantalons
jacket	un blouson
blouse	une blouse
shoes	des souliers
sandals	des sandales
hat	un chapeau
eyeglasses	des lunettes
handbag	un sac
gifts	cadeaux
local crafts	artisanat local
sun protection products	crèmes solaires
cosmetics and perfumes	cosmétiques et parfums
camera	appareil photo
photographic film	pellicule
records, cassettes	disques, cassettes
newspapers	journaux
magazines	revues, magazines
batteries	piles
watches	montres
jewellery	bijouterie
gold	or
silver	argent
precious stones	pierres précieuses
fabric	tissu
wool	laine
cotton	coton
leather	cuir

MISCELLANEOUS

new	nouveau
old	vieux
expensive	cher, dispendieux
inexpensive	pas cher
pretty	joli
beautiful	beau
ugly	laid(e)
big, tall (person)	grand(e)
small, short (person)	petit(e)
short (length)	court(e)
low	bas(se)
wide	large

narrow	*étroit(e)*
dark	*foncé*
light (colour)	*clair*
fat (person)	*gros(se)*
slim, skinny (person)	*mince*
a little	*peu*
a lot	*beaucoup*
something	*quelque chose*
nothing	*rien*
good	*bon*
bad	*mauvais*
more	*plus*
less	*moins*
do not touch	*ne pas toucher*
quickly	*vite*
slowly	*lentement*
big	*grand*
small	*petit*
hot	*chaud*
cold	*froid*
I am ill	*je suis malade*
pharmacy, drugstore	*pharmacie*
I am hungry	*j'ai faim*
I am thirsty	*j'ai soif*
What is this?	*Qu'est-ce que c'est?*
Where?	*Où?*
fixed price menu	*table d'hôte*
order courses separately	*à la carte*

WEATHER

rain	*pluie*
clouds	*nuages*
sun	*soleil*
It is hot out	*Il fait chaud*
It is cold out	*Il fait froid*

TIME

When?	*Quand?*
What time is it?	*Quelle heure est-il?*
minute	*minute*
hour	*heure*
day	*jour*
week	*semaine*
month	*mois*
year	*année*
yesterday	*hier*
today	*aujourd'hui*
tommorrow	*demain*
morning	*le matin*
afternoon	*l'après-midi*
evening	*le soir*
night	*la nuit*
now	*maintenant*

never	*jamais*
Sunday	*dimanche*
Monday	*lundi*
Tuesday	*mardi*
Wednesday	*mercredi*
Thursday	*jeudi*
Friday	*vendredi*
Saturday	*samedi*
January	*janvier*
February	*février*
March	*mars*
April	*avril*
May	*mai*
June	*juin*
July	*juillet*
August	*août*
September	*septembre*
October	*octobre*
November	*novembre*
December	*décembre*

COMMUNICATION

post office	*bureau de poste*
air mail	*par avion*
stamps	*timbres*
envelope	*enveloppe*
telephone book	*bottin téléphonique*
long distance call	*appel outre-mer*
collect call	*appel collecte*
fax	*télécopieur, fax*
rate	*tarif*
dial the regional code	*composer le code régional*
wait for the tone	*attendre la tonalité*

ACTIVITIES

recreational swimming	*la baignade*
beach	*plage*
scuba diving	*la plongée sous-marine*
snorkelling	*la plongée-tuba*
fishing	*la pêche*
recreational sailing	*navigation de plaisance*
windsurfing	*la planche à voile*
bicycling	*faire du vélo*
mountain bike	*vélo tout-terrain (VTT)*
horseback riding	*équitation*
hiking	*la randonnée pédestre*
to walk around	*se promener*
museum or gallery	*musée*
cultural centre	*centre culturel*
cinema	*cinéma*

274 Glossary

TOURING

river	*fleuve, rivière*
waterfalls	*chutes*
garden	*jardin*
wildlife reserve	*réserve faunique*
south/north shore	*côte sud/nord*
town or city hall	*hôtel de ville*
court house	*palais de justice*
church	*église*
house	*maison*
manor	*manoir*
bridge	*pont*
workshop	*atelier*
historic site	*lieu historique*
train station	*gare*
convent	*couvent*
door, archway, gate	*porte*
customs house	*douane*
market	*marché*
canal	*canal*
seaway	*voie maritime*
museum	*musée*
cemetery	*cimetière*
hospital	*hôpital*
high school	*école secondaire*
lighthouse	*phare*

NUMBERS

1	*un*		22	*vingt-deux*
2	*deux*		23	*vingt-trois*
3	*trois*		24	*vingt-quatre*
4	*quatre*		25	*vingt-cinq*
5	*cinq*		26	*vingt-six*
6	*six*		27	*vingt-sept*
7	*sept*		28	*vingt-huit*
8	*huit*		29	*vingt-neuf*
9	*neuf*		30	*trente*
10	*dix*		40	*quarante*
11	*onze*		50	*cinquante*
12	*douze*		60	*soixante*
13	*treize*		70	*soixante-dix*
14	*quatorze*		80	*quatre-vingt*
15	*quinze*		90	*quatre-vingt-dix*
16	*seize*		100	*cent*
17	*dix-sept*		200	*deux cents*
18	*dix-huit*		500	*cinq cents*
19	*dix-neuf*		1,000	*mille*
20	*vingt*		10,000	*dix mille*
21	*vingt-et-un*		1,000,000	*un million*

Index

Accidents 40
Accommodations
  Appartements du
    Cap-Blanc 188
  Au Jardin du Gouverneur 182
  Auberge Baker 197
  Auberge Chaumonot . . . 199
  Auberge de la Paix 182
  Auberge du Petit Pré . . . 196
  Auberge du Quartier . . . 190
  Auberge du Trésor 185
  Auberge Saint-Louis . . . 182
  Auberge Saint-Pierre . . . 189
  Auberge Sainte-Antoine 189
  Café Krieghoff 190
  Camping Mont Ste-Anne 197
  Centre International de
    Séjour (Hostelling
    International) 182
  Château Bellevue 186
  Château Bonne-Entente 193
  Château de Léry 185
  Château de Pierre 186
  Château Frontenac 187
  Chateau Grande Allée . . 191
  Chaumière Juchereau-
    Duchesnay 195
  Chez Pierre 192
  Clarendon 186
  Hayden's Wexford
    House 188
  Hôtel Ambassadeur 196
  Hôtel Belley 187
  Hôtel Cap-Diamant 185
  Hôtel Château Laurier . . 191
  Hôtel Dominion 1912 . . 189
  Hôtel du Théâtre
    Capitole 192
  Hôtel du Vieux-Québec 186
  Hôtel Gouverneur 195
  Hôtel Loews Le
    Concorde 191
  Hôtel L'Aventure 197
  Hôtel Royal William . . . 195
  Hôtel Val des Neiges . . . 198
  Journey's End 196
  La Bécassine 197
  La Camarine 198
  La Goéliche 199
  La Maison d'Elizabeth et
    Emma 190
  Le Canard Huppée 199
  Le Clos Saint-Louis . . . 185
  Le Vieux-Presbytère . . . 199
  Maison Acadienne 184
  Maison du Fort 184
  Manoir Lafayette 190
  Manoir LaSalle 182
  Manoir Victoria 184
  Marquise de Bassano . . 184
  Priori 188
  Québec Hilton 192
  Radisson Gouverneurs
    Québec 193
  Tour A: Vieux-Québec . 182
  Tour B: Petit-Champlain
    to Vieux-Port 187
  Tour C: Grande Allée and
    Avenue Cartier 190
  Tour D: Saint-Jean-
    Baptiste 192
  Tour E: Chemin
    Sainte-Foy 193
  Tour F: Saint-Roch 195
  Tour J: Heading North . 195
  tour K: Côte-de-Beaupré
    and Île d'Orléans 196
  Ulysses's Favourites . . . 181
  Université Laval 193
  Villégiature Mont-
    Sainte-Anne 198
  YWCA 193
Advice for Smokers 59
Airports 38
  Jean-Lesage Airport
    (Québec City) 38
Alcohol 58
Ancien Palais de Justice
  (Vieux-Québec) 85
Ancienne Prison de Québec
  (Vieux-Québec) 99
Anglican Cathedral of the Holy
  Trinity (Vieux-Québec) . . 88
Anglo Canadian Paper Mills
  (Limoilou) 151
Annexe du Musée de la
  Civilisation
  (Vieux Québec) 108

Index

Aquarium du Québec
  (Sillery) 162
Architecture 28
Art Galleries 256
Artillery Park National Historic
  Site (Vieux-Québec) ... 100
Atelier Verrerie La Mailloche
  (Petit-Champlain) 107
Bagatelle (Sillery) 160
Banks 48
Bars and Nightclubs
  Bal du Lézard 248
  Ballon Rouge 249
  Ballroom 245
  Charlotte 246
  Chez Son Père 242
  Emprise 243
  Fou Bar 247
  Jules et Jim 246
  La Barberie 248
  La Fourmi Atomik 243
  La Grimace 247
  Le Cactus 247
  Le Chanteuteuil 242
  Le Dagobert 245
  Le Drague 249
  Le d'Auteuil 242
  Le D'Orsay 242
  Le Kashmir 243
  Le Merlin 246
  Le Scanner 248
  Le Troubadour 245
  Le Turf 246
  Les Folies de Paris 247
  Les Yeux Bleus 244
  L'Amour Sorcier 249
  L'Arlequin 242
  L'Étrange 246
  L'Innox 244
  L'Ostradamus 243
  Maurice 245
  Mundial 247
  Pape-Georges 244
  Petit Paris 243
  Pub Sherlock Holmes ... 246
  Pub Thomas Dunn 245
  Sacrilège 247
  Saint-Alexandre 243
  Sainte-Angèle 244
  Salons d'Edgar 248
  Taverne Belley 244
  Vogue 246

Basilique Sainte-Anne-de-
  Beaupré (Ste-Anne-de-
  Beaupré) 170
Bassin Louise (Vieux-Port) 116
Batterie Royale (Petit-
  Champlain) 109
Beauport 168
Beer 58
Bibliothèque Gabrielle-Roy
  (Saint-Roch) 146
Bicycling 66
Bird-Watching 70
Bois-de-Coulonge (Sillery) 159
Bookstores 256
Bureau de Poste
  (Vieux-Québec) 95
Business Hours 51
Cafés 204
Camping
  Parc de la
    Jacques-Cartier 196
Cap-Rouge 162
Capitole
  (Saint-Jean-Baptiste) ... 132
Car 39
Car Rentals 40
Cartier-Brébeuf National
  Historic Site (Limoilou) . 152
Cathédrale Catholique
  Notre-Dame (Vieux-
  Québec) 90
Cavalier du Moulin
  (Vieux-Québec) 81
CDs and Cassettes 257
Centre d'Interprétation
  Archéologique
  (Vieux-Port) 120
Centre d'Interprétation de la
  Côte de Beaupré (Côte-de-
  Beaupré) 170
Centre d'Interprétation de la
  Vie Urbaine de Québec . 90
Centre d'Interprétation des
  Champs-de-Bataille
  (Grande Allée) 130
Centre de Développement
  Urbain de Québec
  (Saint-Roch) 145
Centre des Congrès de Québec
  (Saint-Jean-Baptiste) ... 134
Centre d'Interprétation de
  Place-Royale (Petit-
  Champlain) 113

Centre d'Interpretation du Trait-Carré (Charlesbourg) 165
Centre Muséographique de l'Université Laval (Ste-Foy) 141
Chalmers-Wesley United Church (Vieux-Québec) . 80
Chapel of St. Peter (Limoilou) 152
Chapelle Commémorative (Ste-Anne-de-Beaupré) . 171
Chapelle des Franciscaines de Marie (Grande Allée) .. 127
Chapelle du Bon-Pasteur (Grande Allée) 126
Chapelle du Couvent des Soeurs de la Charité (St-Jean-Baptiste) 134
Charlesbourg 163
Château Frontenac (Vieux-Québec) 83
Children 60
Church and Cemetery of Saint Matthew (St-Jean-Baptiste) 135
Cimetière de Sillery (Sillery) 160
Citadelle (Vieux-Québec) . 102
Climate 52
Clothing 257
Club de la Garnison (Vieux-Québec) 80
Colisée de Québec (Limoilou) 153
Complexe G (Grande Allée) 125
Conservatoire d'Art Dramatique (Vieux Québec) 100
Consulates 32
Couvent des Sœurs de Saint-Joseph-de-Saint-Vallier (Ste-Foy) 138
Craft Shops and Artisans' Studios 259
Credit Cards 48
Cross-country Skiing 72
Cruises 68
Cultural Events
 concert Halls 250
 movie Theatres 250
 outdoor Activities 249
 theatres 250
Culture 26

Currency 50
Cyclorama de Jérusalem (Ste-Anne-de-Beaupré) . 172
Decorative Objects 262
Direction Générale des Archives Nationales du Québec (Ste-Foy) 141
Disabled People 59
Domaine Cataraqui (Sillery) 161
Domaine Maizerets (Limoilou) 151
Domaine Porteous (Sainte-Pétronille) 174
École des Arts Visuel de l'Université Laval (Saint-Roch) 145
École technique (Saint-Sauveur) 158
Économusée de la Bière (Vieux-Port) 116
Economy 24
Édifice de la Douane (Vieux-Port) 116
Édifice Louis-Saint-Laurent (Vieux-Québec) 96
Édifice Marie-Guyart (Grande Allée) 126
Édifice Price (Vieux-Québec) 89
Église des Jésuites (Vieux-Québec) 101
Église du Très-Saint-Sacrement 140
Église Notre-Dame-de-Grâce (Saint-Sauveur) 156
Église Notre-Dame-de-Jacques-Cartier (Saint-Roch) 146
Église Notre-Dame-de-Lorette (Wendake) 166
Église Notre-Dame-des-Victoires (Petit-Champlain) 110
Église Saint-Charles-Borromée (Charlesbourg) 164
Église Saint-Charles-de-Limoilou (Limoilou) 151
Église Saint-Cœur de Marie (Grande Allée) 127
Église Saint-Jean-Baptiste (St-Jean-Baptiste) 136
Église Saint-Michel (Sillery) 160
Église Saint-Pierre (île d'Orléans) 178
Église Saint-Roch (Saint-Roch) 147

278 Index

Église Saint-Sauveur
  (Saint-Sauveur) 156
Église Sainte-Famille (Sainte-
  Famille) 177
Embassies 32
Emergencies 40
Emplacement de la Terre de
  Jean Bourdon (Ste-Foy) . 140
Entrance Formalities 31
Entrepôt Thibaudeau
  (Petit-Champlain) 114
Entrepôt Thibaudeau
  (Vieux Québec) 114
Escalier Casse-Cou
  (Petit-Champlain) 106
Ex Machina (Vieux-Port) . . 116
Explore - Son et Lumière
  (Vieux-Port) 116
Exploring
  Tour A: Vieux-Québec . . 78
  Tour B: From Petit-
    Champlain to
    Vieux-Port 104
  Tour C: Grande Allée . . 120
  Tour D: Saint-Jean-
    Baptiste 132
  Tour E: chemin
    Sainte-Foy 136
  Tour F: Saint-Roch 142
  Tour G: Limoilou 148
  Tour H: Saint-Sauveur . . 154
  Tour I: from Sillery to
    Cap-Rouge 158
  Tour J: Heading North . 163
  Tour K: Côte-de-Beaupré
    and Île d'Orléans 167
ExpoCité (Limoilou) 153
Extended Visits 32
Festivals and Cultural Events
  Carnaval de Québec . . . 251
  Concours Hippique de
    Québec 252
  Coupe du Monde de Vélo
    de Montagne 252
  Estival Juniart 252
  Expo-Québec 253
  Festival de l'Oie des Neiges
    de Saint-Joachim 253
  Festival d'Été de Québec 252
  Festival International des
    Art Traditionnels 253
  Festival International du
    Film de Québec 253
  Fêtes de la
    Nouvelle-France 252
  Plein Art 252
  Tournoi International
    de Hockey Pee-wee de
    Québec 252
Feux Sacrés (Vieux-Québec) 92
Finding Your Way Around . 39
Food 262
Former Franciscan Monastery
  (Ste-Foy) 138
Fresque des Québécois
  (Petit-Champlain) 112
Funiculaire
  (Petit-Champlain) 104
Galerie d'art du Trait-Carré
  (Charlesbourg) 165
Gare du Palais (Vieux-Port) 118
Gay 59
Gay and Lesbian Clubs
  Ballon Rouge 249
  Le Drague 249
  L'Amour Sorcier 249
Gay Life 59
Getting There 37
Golf 71
Grand Théâtre
  (Grande Allée) 127
Guided tours 46
Health 51
Hiking 66
Hippodrome de Québec
  (Limoilou) 153
History 14
Holidays 51
Hôpital Général
  (Saint-Sauveur) 157
Hôtel Clarendon (Vieux-
  Québec) 89
Hôtel de Ville
  (Vieux-Québec) 89
Hôtel du Parlement
  (Grande Allée) 122
Hôtel du Parlement
  (Vieux-Québec) 102
Hôtel Jean-Baptiste-Chevalier
  (Petit-Champlain) 108
Ice Skating 71
Île d'Orléans 172
Îlot Fleuri (Saint-Roch) . . . 144
Imperial Bank of Commerce
  (Vieux-Port) 117
In-Line Skating 69

Institut Canadien
  (Vieux-Québec) 99
Insurance 50
Internet 37
Jardin de Saint-Roch
  (Saint-Roch) 145
Jardin des Gouverneurs
  (Vieux-Québec) 82
Jardin Jeanne-d'Arc
  (Grande Allée) 126
Jardin Roger-Van den Hende
  (Ste-Foy) 141
Jardin Zoologique du Québec
  (Charlesbourg) 165
Jean-Lesage Airport
  (Québec City) 38
Jogging
  Québec City 69
Kiosque Edwin-Bélanger
  (Grande Allée) 131
L'Îlot Saint-Nicolas
  (Vieux-Port) 119
La Fabrique (Saint-Roch) .. 145
La Scala Santa (Ste-Anne-
  de-Beaupré) 171
Laundromats 62
Lesbian Life 59
Lieu Historique National des
  Fortifications de Québec . 80
Maison Antoine-Vanfelson
  (Vieux-Québec) 89
Maison Aroüanne
  (Wendake) 166
Maison Barbel
  (Petit-Champlain) ... 111
Maison Bruneau-Rageot-
  Drapeau (Petit-
  Champlain) 112
Maison Chevalier
  (Petit-Champlain) ... 108
Maison Cirice-Têtu
  (Vieux-Québec) 81
Maison de l'Armateur Chevalier
  (Petit-Champlain) ... 108
Maison de la Découverte
  (Grande Allée) 125
Maison Demers
  (Petit-Champlain) ... 107
Maison des Dames Protestantes
  (Grande Allée) 128
Maison des Jésuites de Sillery
  (Sillery) 161
Maison Dolbec
  (Petit-Champlain) ... 108
Maison Drouin
  (Sainte-Famille) 177
Maison du Manufacturier
  de Chaussures W. A. Marsh
  (Grande Allée) 126
Maison du Tourisme
  (Vieux-Québec) 84
Maison Dumont
  (Petit-Champlain) ... 112
Maison Éphraïm-Bédard
  (Charlesbourg) 164
Maison Estèbe
  (Petit-Champlain) ... 114
Maison François-Xavier-
  Garneau (Vieux-Québec) 98
Maison Frérot
  (Petit-Champlain) ... 108
Maison Garneau-Meredith
  (Grande Allée) 126
Maison Gendreau
  (Saint-Laurent) 175
Maison Hamel-Bruneau
  (Sillery) 162
Maison Henry-Stuart
  (Grande Allée) 128
Maison Horatio-Walker
  (Sainte-Pétronille) .. 174
Maison Jacquet
  (Vieux-Québec) 86
Maison Kent
  (Vieux Québec) 85
Maison Krieghoff
  (Grande Allée) 129
Maison Louis-Jolliet
  (Petit-Champlain) ... 107
Maison Maillou
  (Vieux-Québec) 85
Maison McGreevy
  (Vieux-Québec) 102
Maison Paradis
  (Petit-Champlain) ... 112
Maison Pierre-Lefevbre
  (Charlesbourg) 165
Maison Pollack
  (Grande Allée) 128
Maisons Ouvrières de Saint-
  Roch (Saint-Roch) ... 146
Manège Militaire
  (Grande Allée) 124
Manoir Gourdeau
  (Sainte-Pétronille) .. 174

Manoir Mauvide-Genest
 (Saint-Jean) 175
Manoir Montmorency
 (Beauport) 168
Marché du Vieux-Port
 (Vieux-Port) 118
Méduse (Saint-Roch) 144
Methodist Church
 (Vieux-Québec) 99
Miscellaneous 60, 264
Monastère des Dominicains
 (Grande Allée) 129
Monastère des Ursulines
 (Vieux-Québec) 86
Money 48
Montcalm's Maison
 (Vieux-Québec) 97
Monument to General Wolfe
 (Grande Allée) 129
Moulin de l'Hôpital Général
 (Saint-Sauveur) 158
Moulin des Jésuites
 (Charlesbourg) 165
Moulin Gosselin
 (Saint-Laurent) 175
Musée de Cire
 (Vieux-Québec) 85
Musée de Géologie du Pavillon
 Adrien-Pouliot (Ste-Foy) . 141
Musée de l'Amérique Française
 (Vieux-Québec) 94
Musée de l'Hôtel-Dieu
 (Vieux-Québec) 98
Musée de la Citadelle
 (Vieux-Québec) 103
Musée de la Civilisation
 (Vieux-Port) 115
Musée de Québec
 (Grande Allée) 129
Musée de Sainte Anne
 (Ste-Anne-de-Beaupré) . 172
Musée des Augustines
 (Saint-Sauveur) 157
Musée des Augustines de
 l'Hôtel-Dieu
 (Vieux-Québec) 99
Musée des Soeurs du Bon-
 Pasteur (Vieux-Québec) . 97
Musée des Ursulines
 (Vieux-Québec) 88
Musée du Fort
 (Vieux-Québec) 85

Musée d'Art Inuit Brousseau
 (Vieux-Québec) 86
Newspapers and Tobacco . 265
Observatoire de la Pointe-à-
 Puiseaux (Sillery) 160
Old Université Laval
 (Vieux-Québec) 97
Onhoüa Chetek8e
 (Wendake) 167
Orchestre symphonique
 de Québec 250
Outdoor Activities
 Bicycling 66
 Cross-country Skiing 72
 Cruises 68
 Fruit-picking 69
 Golf 71
 Hiking 66
 In-Line Skating 69
 Jogging 69
 Rafting 70
Outdoor Clothing and
 Equipment 265
Palais Archiépiscopal
 (Vieux-Québec) 96
Parc and Monument des
 Braves (Ste-Foy) 139
Parc de l'Amérique Française
 (Grande Allée) 127
Parc de la chute Montmorency
 (Beauport) 169
Parc de la Falaise et de la
 Chute Kabir Kouba
 (Wendake) 167
Parc de la Francophonie
 (Grande Allée) 125
Parc des Champs-de-Bataille
 (Grande Allée) 130
Parc Maritime de Saint-Laurent
 (Saint-Laurent) 175
Parc Montcalm
 (Grande Allée) 126
Parc Montmorency
 (Vieux-Québec) 96
Parc Victoria
 (Saint-Sauveur) 156
Parks
 Jacques-Cartier 64
Parks Canada Exhibition Hall
 (Vieux-Québec) 96
Passports 31
Pavillon Louis-Jacques-Casault
 (Ste-Foy) 140

Pets 60
Place d'Armes
  (Vieux-Québec) 84
Place d'Youville (Saint-Jean-
  Baptiste) 134
Place de la FAO
  (Vieux-Port) 117
Place de Paris (Petit-
  Champlain) 114
Place George V
  (Grande Allée) 124
Place Hôtel-de-Ville
  (Vieux-Quebec) 89
Place Jacques-Cartier
  (Saint-Roch) 146
Pointe-à-Carcy (Vieux-Port) 116
Politics 21
Pont de Québec (Sillery) . . 160
Porte Kent (Vieux-Québec) 102
Porte Prescott (Petit-
  Champlain) 106
Porte Saint-Jean
  (Vieux-Québec) 101
Porte Saint-Louis
  (Vieux-Québec) 78
Portrait 13
Poudrière de l'Esplanade
  (Vieux-Québec) 80
Promenade des Gouverneurs
  (Grande Allée) 131
Promenade Desjardins
  (St-Jean-Baptiste) 135
Promenades du Vieux-Québec
  (Vieux-Québec) 94
Quebec Cuisine 57
Québec Expérience
  (Vieux-Québec) 95
Quebec Literary and Historical
  Society (Vieux-Québec) . 99
Relais (Lac-Beauport) 73
Religion 62
Restaurants
  À la Bastille Chez
    Bahüaud 214
  Apsara 210
  Asia 217
  Au Parmesan 212
  Au Petit Coin Breton ... 211
  Auberge Baker 238
  Auberge du Trésor ... 214
  Aux Anciens Canadiens . 215
  Aux Vieux Canons 226
  Aviatic Club 220

Bistro Sous le Fort 218
Bonnet d'Âne 231
Brûlerie Tatum 208
Buffet de l'Antiquaire .. 217
Buffet du Passant 235
Bügel 223
Byrnd 235
Café Buade 210
Café de la Paix 213
Café de la Terrasse ... 216
Café de Mon Village ... 238
Café du Clocher Penché 234
Café du Monde 220
Café d'Europe 215
Café Krieghoff 224
Café Saint-Malo 218
Café Serge Bruyère ... 212
Café Suisse 212
Café-Restaurant du
  Musée 228
Canard Huppé 239
Casse-Crêpe Breton ... 208
Chantauteuil 210
Charles Baillargé 215
Chez Livernois 213
Chez Rabelais 221
Chez Temporel 208
Chez Victor 231
Ciccio Café 233
Cochon Dingue 218
Cosmos Café 223
Dazibo Café 230
Élysée-Mandarin 213
Entrecôte Saint-Jean ... 210
Fleur de Lotus 211
Frères de la Côte 211
Galopin 236
Garam Massala 224
Graffiti 226
Guido Le Gourmet ... 216
Il Teatro 233
Initiale 222
Jaune Tomate 226
Java Java 224
La Boîte à Smoked Meat 223
La Camarine 238
La Campagne 232
La Caravelle 214
La Closerie 230
La Crémaillère 216
La Crêperie de Sophie .. 217
La Fenouillère 237
La Fougasse 236

La Goéliche	239	Paris Brest	230
La Grande Table	217	Péché Véniel	218
La Grolla	233	Petit Coin Latin	208
La Maison du Steak	230	Piazzetta	231
La Petite Italie	211	Pizza Mag	218, 235
La Playa	233	Pizzédélic	224
La Ripaille	214	Pointe des Amériques	232
La Scalla	228	Poisson d'Avril	221
La Tanière	236	Portofino	212
Laurie Raphäel	222	Quartier Chinois	225
Le Bonaparte	229	Saint-James	211
Le Carthage	232	Salons d'Edgar	234
Le Champlain	216	Thang Long	231
Le Cochon Dingue	225, 235	Titanic	210
Le Commensal	230	Tour A: Vieux-Quebec	208
Le Continental	215	Tour B: Petit-Champlain to Vieux-Port	217
Le Figaro	226	Tour C: Grande Allée	223
Le Gambrinus	216	Tour D: Saint-Jean-Baptiste	230
Le Hobbit	231	Tour E: Chemin Sainte-Foy	233
Le Lotus Cartier	228	Tour F: Saint-Roch	234
Le Louis-Hébert	228	Tour G: Limoilou	235
Le Maizerets	235	Tour I: Sillery to Cap-Rouge	235
Le Métropolitain	228	Tour J: Heading North	237
Le Momento	226	Tour K: Côte-de-Beaupré and Île d'Orléans	237
Le Pailleur	234	Trattoria Sant-Angelo	220
Le Parlementaire	224	Vieux-Presbytère	239
Le Patriarche	213	VooDoo Grill	229
Le Petit Baluchon	238	Wrap	223
Le Portugais	228	Restaurants by Type of Cuisine	204
Le Rivoli	229	Rivière Saint-Charles (Limoilou)	150
Le Saint-Amour	213	Rue du Petit-Champlain (Vieux Québec)	106
Le Vendôme	222	Rue du Trésor (Vieux-Québec)	95
Les Épices du Széchouan	232	Saint-François (Île d'Orléans)	176
Les Finesses de Charlot	223	Saint-Jean (Île d'Orléans)	175
Lunchonnette	208	Saint-Laurent (Île d'Orléans)	174
Ly-Hai	224	Saint-Pierre (Île d'Orléans)	178
L'Ardoise	221	Sainte-Anne- de-Beaupré	170
L'Astral	230	Sainte-Famille (Île d'Orléans)	176
L'Échaudé	222	Sainte-Pétronille (Île d'Orléans)	173
L'Impasse des Deux Anges	234	Sanctuaire Notre-Dame-du-Sacré-Coeur (Vieux-Québec)	81
L'Omelette	211		
Manoir Montmorency	237		
Marie Clarisse	221		
Michelangelo	236		
Mille-Feuilles	233		
Mon Manège à Toi	229		
Montego	236		
Môss	220		
Moulin de Saint-Laurent	239		
Nek8arre	237		
Paparazzi	236		

Security 54
Séminaire de Québec
 (Vieux-Québec) 92
Senior Citizens 59
Shopping 255, 256
Site Archéologique des Voûtes
 du Palais (Vieux-Port) . . 120
Site du Palais de l'Intendant
 (Vieux-Port) 120
Site Historique de Cap-Rouge
 (Cap-Rouge) 163
Spencer Grange Villa
 (Sillery) 160
St. Andrew's Presbyterian
 Church (Vieux-Québec) . 99
Station Touristique Stoneham
 (Stoneham) 73
Stationery 266
Sweets 266
Tax Refunds 56
Taxes 56
Taxes and Tipping 56
Telecommunications 54
Terrasse Dufferin
 (Vieux-Québec) 82
Terrasse Stadacona
 (Grande Allée) 125
Time Difference 51
Tipping 56
Tobogganing 73
Tourigny et Marois
 (Saint-Roch) 145
Tourist Information 35
Tours Martello no.1 and no. 2
 (Grande Allée) 131
Traveller's Cheques 48
Université Laval Campus
 (Ste-Foy) 140
Vieux-Port 116
Villa Sans-Bruit (Ste-Foy) . 139
Villa Westfield (Ste-Foy) . . 138
Wendake 166
Wine 58

Travel Notes

Surf our site to travel better, enjoy more

www.ulyssesguides.com

For enlightened travel

Travel Notes

Order Form

Ulysses Travel Guides

☐	Atlantic Canada	$24.95 CAN $17.95 US	☐ Louisiana	$29.95 CAN $21.95 US
☐	Bahamas	$24.95 CAN $17.95 US	☐ Martinique	$24.95 CAN $17.95 US
☐	Beaches of Maine	$12.95 CAN $9.95 US	☐ Montréal	$19.95 CAN $14.95 US
☐	Bed & Breakfasts in Québec	$14.95 CAN $10.95 US	☐ New Orleans	$17.95 CAN $12.95 US
☐	Belize	$16.95 CAN $12.95 US	☐ New York City	$19.95 CAN $14.95 US
☐	Calgary	$17.95 CAN $12.95 US	☐ Nicaragua	$24.95 CAN $16.95 US
☐	Canada	$29.95 CAN $21.95 US	☐ Ontario	$27.95 CAN $19.95US
☐	Chicago	$19.95 CAN $14.95 US	☐ Ottawa	$17.95 CAN $12.95 US
☐	Chile	$27.95 CAN $17.95 US	☐ Panamá	$24.95 CAN $17.95 US
☐	Colombia	$29.95 CAN $21.95 US	☐ Peru	$27.95 CAN $19.95 US
☐	Costa Rica	$27.95 CAN $19.95 US	☐ Portugal	$24.95 CAN $16.95 US
☐	Cuba	$24.95 CAN $17.95 US	☐ Provence - Côte d'Azur	$29.95 CAN $21.95US
☐	Dominican Republic	$24.95 CAN $17.95 US	☐ Puerto Rico	$24.95 CAN $17.95 US
☐	Ecuador and Galapagos Islands	$24.95 CAN $17.95 US	☐ Québec	$29.95 CAN $21.95 US
☐	El Salvador	$22.95 CAN $14.95 US	☐ Québec and Ontario with Via	$9.95 CAN $7.95 US
☐	Guadeloupe	$24.95 CAN $17.95 US	☐ Seattle	$17.95 CAN $12.95 US
☐	Guatemala	$24.95 CAN $17.95 US	☐ Toronto	$18.95 CAN $13.95 US
☐	Honduras	$24.95 CAN $17.95 US	☐ Vancouver	$17.95 CAN $12.95 US
☐	Las Vegas	$17.95 $12.95	☐ Washington D.C.	$18.95 CAN $13.95 US
☐	Lisbon	$18.95 CAN $13.95 US	☐ Western Canada	$29.95 CAN $21.95 US

Ulysses Due South

☐	Acapulco	$14.95 CAN $9.95 US	Puerto Escondido	$12.95 US
☐	Belize	$16.95 CAN $12.95 US	☐ Los Cabos and La Paz	$14.95 CAN $7.99 US
☐	Cartagena (Colombia)	$12.95 CAN $9.95 US	☐ Puerto Plata - Sosua	$14.95 CAN $9.95 US
☐	Cancun Cozumel	$17.95 CAN $12.95 US	☐ Puerto Vallarta	$14.95 CAN $9.95 US
☐	Huatulco - Oaxaca	$17.95 CAN	☐ St. Martin and St. Barts	$16.95 CAN $12.95 US

Ulysses Travel Journals

☐ Ulysses Travel Journal $9.95 CAN
(Blue, Red, Green, Yellow, Sextant)
$7.95 US

☐ Ulysses Travel Journal $14.95 CAN
(80 Days) $9.95 US

Ulysses Green Escapes

☐ Cycling in France . . $22.95 CAN
$16.95 US
☐ Cycling in Ontario $22.95 CAN
$16.95 US

☐ Hiking in the . . . . . $19.95 CAN
Northeastern U.S. $13.95 US
☐ Hiking in Québec . . $19.95 CAN
$13.95 US

Ulysses Conversation Guides

☐ French for Better . . $9.95 CAN
Travel $6.50 US

☐ Spanish for Better . $9.95 CAN
Travel in Latin America $6.50 US

Title	Qty	Price	Total

Name:

Subtotal

Shipping

Address:

Subtotal

GST in Canada 7%

Total

Tel: Fax:

E-mail:

Payment: ☐ Cheque ☐ Visa ☐ MasterCard

Card number_____ Expiry date_____

Signature_____

ULYSSES TRAVEL GUIDES
4176 St-Denis,
Montréal, Québec, H2W 2M5
(514) 843-9447 fax (514) 843-9448
Toll free: 1-877-542-7247
www.ulyssesguides.com
info@ulysses.ca